ZERO HUNGER

ZERO

Aaron Ansell

POLITICAL CULTURE AND
ANTIPOVERTY POLICY IN
NORTHEAST BRAZIL

HUNGER

THE UNIVERSITY OF NORTH CAROLINA PRESS
Chapel Hill

Publication of this work was assisted by a generous gift from Florence and James Peacock and by the Authors Fund of the University of North Carolina Press.

Designed and set in Charis and Calluna Sans types
by Rebecca Evans
Manufactured in the United States of America

The paper in this book meets the guidelines for
permanence and durability of the Committee on
Production Guidelines for Book Longevity of the
Council on Library Resources.

The University of North Carolina Press has been a
member of the Green Press Initiative since 2003.

Library of Congress Cataloging-in-Publication Data
Ansell, Aaron Michael.
Zero hunger : political culture and antipoverty policy
in Northeast Brazil / Aaron Ansell.
pages cm
Includes bibliographical references and index.
ISBN 978-1-4696-1397-0 (pbk : alk. paper)
ISBN 978-1-4696-1398-7 (ebook)
1. Poverty—Government policy—Brazil. 2. Economic
assistance, Domestic—Political aspects—Brazil.
3. Brazil—Politics and government—2003– 4. Brazil—
Economic conditions—21st century. 5. Brazil—Social
conditions—21st century. I. Title.
HC190.P63A57 2014
362.5'2610981—dc23
2013044477

18 17 16 15 14   5 4 3 2 1

This book was digitally printed.

TO MY PARENTS,

BATYA AND HERBERT ANSELL

Contents

Tables and Figures

Acknowledgments

The research for this book began in 2001 at the Workers' Party (Partido dos Trabalhadores, or PT) headquarters in Rio de Janeiro. General Secretary Ernani Coelho and other party members spent weeks educating me in Brazilian politics and history, and inspired me with their passion for justice. Like them, I wondered how the PT's rise to power would change the nation, and this question motivated the two years of fieldwork that went into this project. Yet this book does not pretend to be a comprehensive account of Brazil under Workers' Party rule, or even a full reckoning of the antipoverty policy Zero Hunger. It is an interpretation of the interaction between a historically impoverished segment of the nation and an activist state that sought to transform both the material and cultural reality of that population.

Funding from the Center for Latin American Studies and the Department of Anthropology at the University of Chicago supported my early exploratory trips to Brazil. For my main field stint in Piauí State, I relied on generous grants from the Fulbright-Hays and Wenner Gren Foundations. Financial support from the U.S. Department of Education's Foreign Language and Area Studies Fellowship allowed me to work on this book following my return from Brazil. Monmouth University also provided me with funds to support the write-up.

Hundreds of people have helped to bring this project to fruition. My mentors at the University of Chicago patiently read and critiqued numerous chapter drafts and made themselves available for long consultations. I am particularly indebted to Dain Borges, Manuela Carneiro da Cunha, Claudio Lomnitz, Tanya Luhrmann, Moishe Postone, Michael Silverstein, Susan Stokes, and the late Michel-Rolph Trouillot. Many other colleagues have also commented on sections of this work, challenging and deepening my vision of Brazil and its rural communities. Among them are Chris Ball, Gregory Beckett, Russell Bither-Terry, Brian Brazeal, John Collins,

Jan Hoffman French, João Gonçalves, Sidney Greenfield, Courtney Handman, Elina Hartikainen, Bill Mitchell, Gregory Morton, James Slotta, Lisa Vetere, and Jorge Mattar Villela. Abigail Rosenthal read and commented on work I wrote while in the field. Sean Mitchell modeled observant and ethically centered ethnography during our initial forays to Rio, commented on several chapters, and has trenchantly argued with me on matters of patronage ever since. At the University of North Carolina Press, my editor Elaine Maisner and her colleagues showed me how to increase this book's accessibility to various audiences and gently shepherded me through the publishing process. My anonymous reviewers provided detailed and extensive comments on two drafts of this book. I am very grateful.

In Piauí, I learned that the success of ethnographic fieldwork depends on the patience, integrity, and generosity of one's consultants. In my case, it also depended on the transparency and commitment to academic inquiry of dozens of workers throughout the state government of Piauí. These people gave me full and ready access to Zero Hunger documents, allowed me to attend plenary meetings, and entertained many hours of conversation on policy and patronage. In Piauí's Zero Hunger Coordenadoria, I received the enthusiastic cooperation of Norma Sueli M. C. Alberto, Isabel Herika Matia Gomes, Maria Genilda Marques Cardoso, Simplício Mário de Oliveira, José Pessoa Neto, Amália Rodrigues de Almeida, Rosângela Maria Sobrinho Sousa, Rosemberg Batista de Araújo, and many others. I owe special thanks to Jascira da Silva Lima for our warm friendship, and for her willingness to reflect critically and acutely on the program she worked so hard to implement. I am also grateful to the administrators of the Zero Hunger and Bolsa Família programs in Brasília who afforded me interviews: Adriana Aranha, José Graziano da Silva, Chico Menezes, and others.

Investigating local politics can be an awkward and invasive enterprise. Passarinho's residents did far more to make my time in Brazil happy and productive than I could rightfully expect. They welcomed me into their homes and families and consented to speak to me about aspects of their lives that were sometimes unpleasant. To them, I apologize for my pseudonymous reference to their municipality and trust that they will forgive me for using only their first names to thank them: Adailza, Batista, Cândido, Didí, Edgar, Edson, Fátima, Gilberto, José de Valdo, MaeDelena, Maurício, Olegário, Paulo Sérgio, Roselina, Roselma, Serafim, and Zé Carlos. I especially acknowledge Jorginho and his family, who inspired me to think about the egalitarian postures that made their way into Brazilian patronage relations. As my field assistant, and a man living in poverty, Jorginho might have deferred to my power and patronage. Instead, he joked and quarreled with me, asserted his research competence despite his fourth grade education, and told me when it was time for me to get out of bed and help him lay roofing on his house. I am forever grateful for his intelligence, honesty, and friendship.

Many people have helped to make me an anthropologist. Michael Meeker introduced me to the discipline and guided me through my first writings. My sister, Lisa Ansell, taught me to appreciate the music of other languages and the sensibilities they encoded. Phil Ansell, my brother, read and gave keen feedback on several chapters and has been a superb interlocutor throughout my career. My father-in-law, Edwin Barry, read and edited a complete draft of the book and helped me to make it more appealing to nonspecialists. My mother, Batya, cultivated my empathy and helped me to find the words to express it—a key skill for an ethnographer. Sabrina Barry's love and insight have influenced me in ways I can't begin to understand. She is the person to whom all my writing is ultimately addressed—and my wife.

My father, Herbert Ansell, helped working people of all backgrounds find justice in California's courts. I am grateful for the legal reasoning he taught me, and for his beloved memory, which graces all of my endeavors.

ZERO HUNGER

Intimate Hierarchy and Its Enemies

One evening in June 2003, Henrique, a Brazilian politician running for mayor of a small, impoverished northeastern town, attended a charity auction in a village along with several hundred people. He had made a fortune from the market and butcher shop he owned in a nearby city, and he was ready to put his money to work for his campaign, bidding on prize after prize (plates of cooked food, liquor, and soft drinks), all to be eaten right then and there, just outside the village chapel. As he won the bids, Henrique set them on a table and yelled, "Grab it, my people." Dozens from the crowd slowly closed in to partake. The host villagers were glad to see Henrique square off against rival candidates, because bidders with big egos spelled big bucks, and regardless of who won, all that cash would underwrite the refurbishing of the village chapel. Henrique, the richest man in town, was coasting with little competition until a small group of men from town started to bid against him. They were political adversaries, but not politicians—just ordinary "weaklings" (*os fracos*) who had pooled their money to compete with him. Even with their money pooled, they were no match for Henrique's wallet, but they put Henrique into double-bind: if he simply outbid the group of commoners, he would appear a bully, rather than a generous man-of-the-people. But if he let them win, their success might appear a symbolic victory for the opposing political faction. A look of pain crossed Henrique's face as he indicated his withdrawal. But no sooner had he made his decision than a small group of commoners sprang up to bid against the first team. Henrique smiled from the sidelines as one among them cried, "Now, it's our time!" The price rose only a bit before this second team had won the bid. Later, I watched from afar as one of these young men chatted quietly with Henrique in the shadows of the chapel. As the two parted, the young man said, "We are here for you, Henrique. Whatever you need, we are here."

Fundraising auctions like this one are quite common in the impoverished rural interior of Piauí State, but they are not of great economic importance to village organizations, nor do they make or break any local election for would-be mayors like Henrique. Nonetheless, this brief spectacle distilled the ambiguity built into a regional political culture founded on class inequality and personalized reciprocities. Henrique's grandeur and generosity at the auction that night helped him to cultivate an image as a "friend to his friends," a man of honor and means, but also a man whose public face was fragile and in constant need of community support. In the semiarid backlands (*sertão*) of northeast Brazil, a region home to some 30 million people, this double-sided dynamic defines electoral politics. In fact, for many in the region the formal institutions of representative democracy appear as artificial impositions from faraway men in suits, as legal formalities superimposed onto humanity's prime material: reciprocity. "Life is an exchange" (*a vida é uma troca*) as the saying goes. Electors vote for politicians *in exchange* for private resources such as cash, farm inputs, transportation to a city, medical care, and so on. What it means to exchange something, however, is by no means simple in northeast Brazil; different objects and services create different kinds of debt and open up distinct possibilities for political action. Yet there is a tendency among scholars and activists alike to reduce these varieties of exchange to "vote buying" or to condemn them all as exploitative. There is some truth to that allegation, but that is not how the people of the sertão think or feel about these hierarchical exchanges—at least it wasn't in 2004 when I first took up residence in this small municipality in Piauí State.

The auction events that I saw that night point to two key features of the "lopsided friendships" that are so salient to political life in this region of Brazil (Wolf 1966: 16). The first is that commoners (cultivators and townspeople) approach their allied politicians with a dignified demeanor, not a servile or self-effacing one. Such was the attitude of the young man who stood speaking to Henrique next to the chapel—his head up, his shoulders squarely facing front, his eyes locked on Henrique's, and his own voice filling the conversational space as much as the wealthier politician's. I've seen the parties to these interactions engage each other this way before disappearing into a private home, where I assume they negotiated the terms of a private exchange. This assertion of dignity is the necessary precursor to a second, also overlooked feature of the politician-elector encounter. When each person makes his or her need transparent to the other, the encounter between them becomes one of mutual vulnerability.

The politician reveals that he lacks votes in the elector's village and that he cannot sustain his good name unless flattering stories of his gifts, skills, and virtues resound from the municipality's porches, street corners, and general stores. For their part, the commoners' vulnerability goes beyond the mere fact of their poverty; it shows itself in the way they tell their allied politician about the deficiencies of their crops and livestock, sharing information that they would never reveal to a neighbor for fear of inspiring malicious (and spiritually dangerous) gossip. Facing one another in these confessional moments, politicians and electors forge intimate ties that can endure for decades, weathering the changing fates of both parties and making each a part of the other's support system.

This book is an ethnographic study of the frank and vulnerable encounters between politicians and subsistence cultivators. At the same time, this is also a study of the Brazilian state's effort to dismantle these hierarchical exchanges in the name of social justice and democracy. In 2003, left-wing state officials charged with implementing federal antipoverty policy determined that these relationships were an impediment to the impartial, fair-minded distribution of state resources, and a pervasive source of poor people's disempowerment.

The Workers' Party Government and Its Condemnation of "Patronage"

The government that came to power in Brazil in 2003 was, in some sense, revolutionary. President Luiz Inácio Lula da Silva of the Workers' Party (Partido dos Trabalhadores—PT) had unsuccessfully run as a socialist candidate in every election since Brazil's military dictatorship (1964–85) had ended.[1] His victory in 2002 led to a surge of hope throughout the country, but it was an unfocused hope. Lula's many supporters differed in their understanding of what was wrong with the nation and what had to be done to fix it. Lula's first flagship social policy, the "Zero Hunger Program" (Programa Fome Zero), was a multifaceted agglomeration of cash grants, nutritional policies, development projects, and various other measures that mobilized an array of governmental and nongovernmental actors in the fight against extreme poverty. Launched with fanfare (both domestic and international), Zero Hunger seemed to flop rather quickly, leading Lula to engage in some administrative reshuffling, policy rebranding, and a redoubling of his commitment to cash grants that resulted in the now celebrated Bolsa Família ("Family Stipend") program. It was through the day-to-day implementation of these policies (especially Zero Hunger) that an array of governmental and nongovernmental actors—who I claim were all, in some sense, "state officials"—worked to discredit hierarchical exchange relationships. My analysis of these processes is based on events that unfolded in one of Zero Hunger's pilot municipalities, a place I call "Passarinho" (in Piauí State), where I lived for two years.

I offer this account as a cautionary note to progressive Brazilian officials—those who used the state to bring about greater economic equity and political empowerment. Generally speaking, their understanding of rural political transactions did not align with that of Passarinho's inhabitants. State officials tended to ignore the distinction between intimate political exchange and plain vote-buying that guided the ethical reflections of local people. To the officials, both modes of transaction exemplified the Northeast's most notorious problem: patron-client relationships, also known as "patronage" or *clientelismo*. Zero Hunger policy documents and early scholarly articles evaluating the program reveal the antagonism toward municipal clientelismo harbored by the left-wing intellectuals who designed Lula's social policies. Here are some examples:[2]

> The challenge (of Zero Hunger) is to break with the logic, and to overcome the identifications . . . with the fragmenting power of clientelismo. (Yasbek 2004: 112)

> Practically the totality of the [prior] social policies directed at the poor have conformed to the logic of political clientelismo . . . that play[s] the role of conservative ideological cement, pinning enormous contingents of the population under the weight of political alienation . . . and perpetuates a false inclusion. (Pontes 2003: 3)

> The Zero Hunger program touched a taboo, provoking an equally strong hostility because it undermines the very foundation of the political control exercised by local oligarchies in the poorest areas of the interior. (Branford and Kucinski 2003: 15)

Such euphoric affirmations of Zero Hunger's antipathy toward municipal clientelismo reverberated throughout the informal talk of the state officials charged with implementing Zero Hunger's many component initiatives.

Social scientists traditionally used the terms "clientelism"/"clientelismo," "patronage," and "patron-client reciprocity" to refer to "a more or less personalized relationship between actors [i.e., patrons and clients], or sets of actors, commanding unequal wealth, status or influence, based

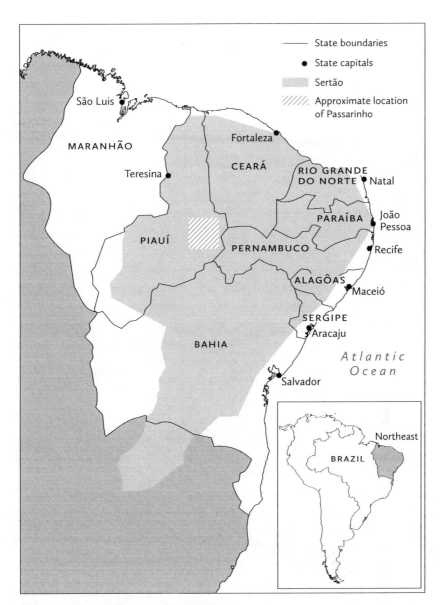

FIGURE 1 The Northeast and the sertão with the approximate location of Passarinho.

on conditional loyalties and involving mutually beneficial transactions" (Lemarchand and Legg 1972: 150). These terms (which all mean basically the same thing) originally carried no pejorative connotation. Indeed, an early generation of anthropologists intuited that poor people experience these patronage exchanges as the lifeblood of "problem solving networks" (Auyero 2001). Yet over the last thirty years, many scholars and activists have come to condemn patronage exchanges, claiming that "they seem to undermine group solidarity (i.e., class, strata) among clients" (Roniger 1990: 4). In fact, no other concept has been more frequently invoked to explain the deficits of democracy and social justice in Latin America, and in Brazil specifically (e.g., Roett 1999; Weyland 1996, Mainwaring 1999; Roniger 1990; Nylen 2003; Holston 2008). The PT government's ideological outlook drew from this intellectual tradition.

At a more pragmatic level, the PT's opposition to patronage reflected its need for votes, both those of the general electorate (to gain office) and those of legislators (to pass laws in Congress). This is particularly true for northeast Brazil, a haven of political conservatism. Many within the PT blamed the PT's electoral difficulties in the Northeast on the political culture of patronage that allegedly locked voters into private deals and kept them ignorant or uninterested in the progressive policies that PT politicians championed. Because political "clients" often cast their votes for state or federal candidates recommended by their trusted municipal "patrons," PT officials elected to executive office have terrible trouble passing legislation that benefits the poor. Thus, Zero Hunger's assault on municipal patronage was, in part, an effort to carve out a foothold for the PT in these small towns and thereby undermine the electoral base of conservative politicians at the state and federal levels.

The Lula administration's choice to merge its antipoverty initiative with a social engineering project must also be interpreted in light of the broader geopolitical context of the early twenty-first century. Lula was one of the first of a spate of left-leaning presidents to be elected in South America, including Hugo Chávez in Venezuela, Evo Morales in Bolivia, Néstor Kirchner in Argentina, Tabaré Vázquez in Uruguay, Michelle Bachelet in Chile, and others who were critical of free-market policies that had reorganized their national economies during the 1980s and 1990s. Given his background as the leader of a party that once described itself as "socialist," the U.S. government (led by the right-wing Bush administration) and much of the global financial class stood by nervously, waiting to see how radical this President Lula would turn out to be. Some PT affiliates feared that President Bush would try to engineer another military coup (such as the one that overthrew the left-leaning president João Goulart in 1964). Indeed, the Bush administration had supported a coup against Chavez in 2002. But the more pressing concern was that global financiers would simply withdraw investment from Brazil at the first sign of a "socialist turn" (e.g., if President Lula stopped payment on Brazil's foreign debt to the International Monetary Fund [IMF]). Such a withdrawal of foreign investment threatened all of the left-leaning presidents who came to power across Latin America between 2000 and 2005. If their policies threatened powerful interests, financial crisis (and perhaps trade embargos and military coups) lay around the corner.

All of these Latin American presidents sought to redefine the very meaning of the political "Left" at this moment in world history. Venezuela's Chávez and Bolivia's Morales became the most stridently anticapitalist presidents. For instance, Chávez, whose long reign became increasingly authoritarian, renationalized part of Venezuela's energy industry and accused the United States of "domination, exploitation, and pillage of the peoples of the world" (address to U.N. General Assembly, September 20, 2006). By contrast, President Lula charted a more moderate course, leading Kirchner, Bachelet, and Vázquez to define "the Left" not through an agenda of loan default, economic protectionism, or the nationalization of industry but with social policies that targeted extreme poverty and promoted the democratic participation and the empowerment of previously disenfranchised groups. He maintained cordial ties with the Bush administration and repaid Brazil's debt to the IMF. Nonetheless, Lula was inspired by the "warm stream of Marxism," which sought to rescue all society from the cruelest effects of unchecked market competition and build solidarity among the working classes (Bloch 1986; also see Lowy 1996: 16). There was also a liberal element of Lula and the PT's ideology, one that emphasized personal freedom and responsibility, social mobility through virtuous labor, and the improvement of family consumption. Social inclusion, rather than class-based revolution, was the mantra of the PT administration. In fact, the government's slogan under Lula was "Brazil, a Country for Everyone" (*Brasil, um País para Todos*). As a political concept, social inclusion meant the right kind of participation in the institutions of representative democracy. In the eyes of this administration, patronage silenced the voices of the poor.

As an account of political culture per se, this book is part of a growing body of literature that rethinks scholarly condemnations of patronage as undemocratic (Auyero 2001; Palmeira 1996; Marques 1999; Villela 2005). I agree with the late Guillermo O'Donnell (1996: 166) that we go too far when we claim that patronage and personalism are "incompatible with the unhindered exercise of suffrage." The very term "patronage" has become such a lightning rod for so many social ills that I adopt a less judgmental, more descriptive language for political exchange. I offer the term "intimate hierarchy" because it better captures the emotional and symbolic posture of local political alliances mediated by exchange, a posture of moral equality within the context of material hierarchy. My ethnography of Passarinho distinguishes various forms of local exchange by attending to the language through which Passarinho's inhabitants describe acts of giving, receiving, and repaying gifts. Understanding these various exchange modalities provides the key to what Javier Auyero (2001: 26) called the "personalized political mediation" of the state, as well as the moral economy of hunger and evil in village life.

As an account of a political culture under siege, this book explores the way state officials tried to stamp out vertical exchanges and engender horizontal alliances. I look at how urban state officials understood rural patronage (and its relation to hunger), the reasons that patronage appeared so malevolent at this moment of Brazilian history, and the actual techniques by which officials attempted to dismantle patronage. I point to three such techniques: "induced nostalgia," "programmatic pilgrimage," and the "marginalizing the mayor." I show how these techniques manifested the tension between the beneficiaries' ideas of political participation and those of the progressive state officials (and the Left in general). At times, these techniques seemed to offer beneficiaries a new language for critiquing the local workings of power; at other times, they sowed confusion among them and even impeded the economic success of the state's antipoverty policies.

Resituating the Concept of Patronage

In addition to the story I tell about the Lula government and the Zero Hunger program, I argue in this book a broader conceptual point pertaining to the nature of patronage as a concept. Rather than using patronage as a scholarly concept that describes exchange relations in places like rural Piauí, I argue that patronage (clientelismo, etc.) should be recast as a folk concept within the contemporary culture of the modern political Left. The premises underlying the notion of patronage, regardless of how universally true they are, act as a lens through which political actors interpret and judge the personal exchanges that they witness . . . and into which they are sometimes personally drawn. To some extent one can see the project of the Lula administration as an effort to spread "patronage" (as a critical category) from the esoteric circles of the intellectual Left to the popular classes.

To steer scholarship away from an analytic use of "patronage," let me point to two premises that are often overgeneralized in academic literature. The first is the idea that such exchanges reinforce the hierarchical relation between the parties involved, that is, that they play out as coercive or demeaning encounters between the poor and the local elite. This presumption (rarely stated overtly) derives from a functionalist interpretation of patron-client relations. For example, Nancy Scheper-Hughes (1992: 126) writes of "clientelism" in Brazil's sugarcane zone that "the 'good boss' in a 'bad faith' economy rescues not only the exploited worker but also the colonizing social system itself." Prioritizing this "system-rescuing" quality, scholars are led to condemn patronage as a kind of "false consciousness" cooked up by elites who want to keep their boots on the necks of the poor. Accordingly, the poor absorb the hegemonic "desires and beliefs [that] could be shown to further not their own interests but those of the dominant" (Stokes 1995: 117). If one begins with the assumption that patronage ideology (reciprocity, loyalty, etc.) functions to dominate the poor, then it's tempting to attribute a mean-spiritedness to actual patronage interactions, seeing them as "coerced exchanges" rather than as expressions of poor people's agency (Holston 2008: 248). In general, the functionalist argument is a dead-end, not because it is necessarily wrong, but because it is impossible to disprove. Any part of a social machine can be blamed for somehow contributing to the functionality of the machine. (This is the same logic that leads some orthodox Marxists to reject liberal democracy on the grounds that it legitimates, and therefore perpetuates, capitalist inequality.) But critiques of functionalism aside, it is important to distinguish between patronage's overall effects on a social system and the up-close dynamics of actual patronage transactions. Those intimate transactions could actually push against the very hierarchy they are blamed for reinforcing.

I confess that the impulse to view patronage interactions as coercive is especially tempting in the case of Brazil, given the prominence of slavery and strong patriarchal authority in the nation's colonial and imperial past. In the early twentieth century, Brazilian anthropology coalesced around the figure of Gilberto Freyre (1986 [1933]), the Boasian scholar of national culture who explained the country's underdevelopment, and especially the backwardness of the Northeast, through an account of the asymmetric intimacies—sexual perversions included—between Portuguese plantation owners and their African slaves. His contemporary, Sérgio Buarque de Holanda (1982 [1926]), also considered slavery one of the roots of the Brazilian psychosocial infatuation with nobility and aristocracy, much to the detriment of the competing liberal ideals that entered Brazil during the nineteenth century. More recently, anthropologist Roberto DaMatta (1991 [1979]) has argued that Brazilian national culture is split between the hierarchical code of the "house" and the egalitarian code of the "street." DaMatta claims that these two ethics interpenetrate in daily life in ways that usually favor the code of the house. For instance, when a stranger on the street insults a man, the man responds by asserting his private connection to powerful persons with the aggressive, rhetorical question: "Do you know who you're talking to?" Thus, when the going gets tough, the surface of egalitarian cordiality collapses, revealing the nation's deep hierarchical core. In writing against this enormous scholarly tradition, my goal is not to disprove the ongoing importance of Brazil's history of violent hierarchy but to qualify arguments that equate that history with the contemporary dynamics of patronage. I do this by pointing to the egalitarian undercurrents of intimate hierarchy, and by framing these undercurrents as part of a regional culture in which dignity has been a key feature of personhood.

A contradiction lies at the center of intimate hierarchical exchanges: To present one's self as worthy of the other's gifts, a person must assert a dignified self-reliance, but in soliciting aid he or she must also reveal that self-reliance to be faulty (see McLean 2007: 60). This is true for the patron as well as the client, even if the needs of the patron are less dire. The very act of asking a politician for farm inputs (fencing wire, seed, etc.) or asking a common person for votes implies that one lacks the ability to provision one's own household appropriately or win an election with one's existing base of support. These vulnerabilities could, if exposed, cause either party to lose prestige. This is why the second moment of the negotiation revolves around the reciprocal suspension of dignity, one that allows for the implicit consecration of an embarrassing secret. Here I am inspired by Michael Herzfeld's (2005 [1997]: 28) landmark treatise on "cultural intimacy," in which he argues that shared embarrassment binds citizens together in a self-deprecating "fellowship of the flawed," and thus serves as a powerful mode of connecting people from different class backgrounds.

Because their self-deprecation undermines the prestige of both parties alike, an undercurrent of equality (and commiseration) takes root in an otherwise unequal relationship.

David Graeber's recent work on debt points to another dimension of egalitarianism in patronage relations. According to Graeber (2011: 108), any true exchange relation presumes some form of equality; each party owes an equal value to the other, as they are "at least potential equals" (120). By contrast, in a fully hierarchical relationship there can be no exchange. Phrased more poetically, "Kings, like gods, can't really enter into relations of exchange with their subjects, since no parity is possible" (83). Reminiscent of DaMatta's analysis of Brazilian street encounters, Graeber notes that "certain principles [hierarchy, equality, and communism] appear to have an inherent tendency to slip into" each other (115). He specifically cites patronage as exemplary of "a slapdash mix of all three principles . . . [even if] . . . those observing them tend to cast them in the language of exchange and debt" (119). Graeber's point is that if there is genuine debt between the two parties, then the relationship is egalitarian. Perhaps the point might better be framed in its performative reversal: it is the act of engaging in debt-generating exchange that pushes people toward an equal footing.[3] Mutual revelations of vulnerability inaugurate this equal footing by rendering both parties to the transaction bare to one another, stripping them of pretense so that they can begin negotiation. Despite my own debt to Graeber, I continue to refer to these intimate exchanges as "hierarchical" in order to emphasize the persistent asymmetry of class and wealth between Passarinho's cultivators and its politicians. Thus, my term "intimate hierarchy" points to a tension between an egalitarian mode of interaction and class stratification.

Scholars prone to viewing patronage as a hindrance to democracy also tend to make a dubious sociological assumption that we might call the "mutual incompatibility premise." S. N. Eisenstadt and Luis Roniger (1984: 48–49) voice this premise plainly: "Patronage seem(s) to undermine the horizontal group organization and solidarity of clients and patrons alike— but especially of the clients." This idea of an incompatibility between horizontal solidarity and vertical exchange relations underlies analyses of patronage around the world, including in India (Wit 1989), Taiwan (Wang 1994), southern Italy (Putnam 1993), and so on. Regarding Brazil, Philippe Schmitter (1971) writes that the nation's political culture is crippled by the tendency of individuals "to seek out . . . autonomous particularistic relationships . . . with local elites" to gain resources (379–80), instead of attaining "awareness of distinctive corporate [i.e., collective] interests and values that might have caused them to mobilize organizationally" (374). Similarly, Kurt Weyland (1996: 54) blames the weak organization of Brazil's social movements for the failure of the Brazilian state to provide better redistributive policies (health care, equitable taxation, and social insurance). Their organization is weak because "clients are exposed to divide-and-conquer tactics . . . [and] by hindering collective action among clients . . . personalism keeps organizational scope low." More recently, James Holston's (2008: 254, 237) analysis of recent (1970s to the present) "insurgent citizenship" in urban São Paulo contrasts a new "egalitarian agency" with an older "entirely clientelistic articulation between the poor peripheries and the apparatus of government," even though Holston notes the coexistence of these two logics.

Strangely, this mutual incompatibility premise is somewhat new to the literature. The first anthropologists to "discover" patronage among Latin American peasants considered vertical and horizontal relations to be two complementary defensive strategies that people used to ward off hunger and gain prestige. Sidney Mintz and Eric Wolf (1950) showed that the fictive kin system (the *compadrazgo*) combined a vertical relation between godparents and godchildren with a horizontal relation between godparents and biological parents (also see Strickon and Greenfield 1972: 3). Building on their work, George Foster (1963: 1285) argued that peasants, in order to get by, combined "colleague contracts" with one another and "patron-client contracts" with local elites. They exchanged the same type of goods (food, labor, etc.) with their peers, while their patrons "received presents of pottery, fish, eggs and chicken, and in return offered medical help, tools and a variety of technical and personal services."

Scholarly recognition of the complementarity of vertical and horizontal exchange mostly disappeared from the literature until Auyero's (2001) landmark study of Argentine shantytowns showed that patronage could be a sociological extension of poor people's problem-solving networks. Rather than seeing clientelism as a pyramid built up from dyadic (two-person) exchange relations, Auyero imagines its networks as "a series of wheels of irregular shape pivoting around the different brokers" (91). The wheel is a metaphor for a loose, egalitarian support network that is held together by its orbit around persons who possess greater access to resources. The power broker's vertical relations to multiple persons in that network actually facilitate egalitarian ties among them. The whole system looks like a nested structure of wheels within wheels, that is, the shantytown's patron-brokers are themselves part of larger egalitarian networks or "wheels" revolving around higher-level gatekeepers of Peronist Party resources. The fact that people within a support network may exchange their votes for direct goods does not preclude them from collective electoral action. For example, in the shantytowns of Rio de Janeiro, the members of neighborhood associations aggregate their votes and offer them en masse to whatever politician delivers them electricity, roads, or plumbing (Gay 1998). Observing as much, Robert Gay notes that "contemporary patronage exhibits both hierarchical . . . *and* elements of collective organization and identity" (ibid.: 14; also see Fox 1994). This book contributes to a growing literature that is more open to the possible synergy between clientelism and democratic modes of political participation (Burgwal 1995; Escobar 1994; Auyero, Lapegna, and Poma 2009; Goldfrank 2011; Tarlau 2013).

More specifically, this book investigates the tension between liberal democracy's proponents who seek to expunge popular culture of its hierarchical components, and populations who try to reconcile hierarchy and egalitarianism. This manifests, for instance, in debates about the democratic status of Candomblé, the Afro-Brazilian religion whose practitioners are "centrally concerned with balancing and recognizing Candomblé's illiberal modes . . . of sociality . . . and the state's liberal project" (Hartikainen 2013: 390). Candomblé practitioners seek to temper egalitarianism with a "traditional" respect for wise elders, but they face opposition from state actors and activists who define democracy in a way that precludes religiously sanctioned hierarchy. Similarly, Brazilian country music manifests a "country critique" of democracy's intended eradication of all hierarchy. Alexander Dent's (2009) ethnography of the *caipira* ("hick") genre shows that performers long for a time when people could balance the hierarchical and egalitarian dimensions of their social relations. If Brazil's cultural democratization includes the ideological spread of the incompatibility premise, those who adhere to certain modes of hierarchy resist that spread, either by keeping democracy at arm's length or by trying to refine its terms.

Even in the urban epicenter of "insurgent" democracy, the grassroots participants of egalitarian social movements do not fully subscribe to the incompatibility premise. Holston's (2008: 249) analysis of urban São Paulo's social movements in late twentieth-century Brazil suggests that clientelism and democratic citizenship are contradictory but that they nonetheless coexist "in the same social space of the city." He argues that the residents of autoconstructed peripheries rejected traditionally clientelist institutions (such as political parties and labor unions) when these failed to meet their specific needs. They started signing petitions, caravanning to the mayor's office, and claiming their rights as "unconditional citizens, taxpayer citizens, and consumer citizens" (246). These practices "appealed to residents of the peripheries . . . because they offered a strategy of . . . negating humiliation through the dignity of participating in the public sphere as bearers of rights" (241). Yet it's unclear whether the rank-and-file urban activists actually hoped that these new forms of mobilization would replace what Holston calls the "coerced exchange of resources for political support"—that is, clientelism (248). Indeed, the daily humiliations of the poor that he describes seem to derive from the city's anonymous rather than its personal hierarchies. Poor workers' relegation to service elevators and general middle-class talk of poor people's bad smells degrade people by reducing them to stigmatized social categories (275–78; also see Caldeira 2001). Such categorical degradation, what Holston calls "differentiated citizenship" (7), should not be confused with clientelism, because clientelist intimacies offer the poor a mode of recuperating the very dignity that differentiated citizenship strips from them. While Brazil's intellectual Left may interpret demonstrations of "insurgent citizenship" as a popular rejection of clientelism, urban residents themselves may appreciate the fact that petitions and such "did not wholly replace other forms of state/society exchange" (248). Indeed, Holston shows that these residents blend hierarchical and egalitarian principles in arguments about rights, as in, "People have rights because they paid for them" (257). Such statements may appear contradictory, but only from the perspective of liberal democratic thought is a social "right" inalienable, rather than contingent on exchange.

This book calls into question the bipolar conceptual grid ("hierarchical patronage" versus "egalitarian democracy") that often organized the thinking of frontline Zero Hunger officials (Vidart 2011: 121; and see Laclau 2005). I suspend my own identification with the liberal democratic project in order to ask how Zero Hunger officials spread certain assumptions about patronage to rural people embedded in relations of intimate hierarchy. For instance, I am critical of state officials' efforts to promote traditional forms of collective labor (*mutirão*) in villages, narrating such labor routines as though they would undo the traumas that had befallen the cultivator population. They imagined that the right kind of labor would allow poor people to work through their shared loss, transmuting it from mute obedience to authority into healthy democratic indignation (the proper emotional posture of insurgent democracy). These efforts tap into aspects of "peasant culture" that indeed conflict with free-market capitalism, but they also typify a general dangerous trend among development agencies throughout the world (Mosse 1999; Agrawal 2005). Global development discourse increasingly valorizes "indigenous" or "traditional" modes of cooperation, claiming that development projects that utilize such labor forms empower "target populations" and preserve their culture. This implies that such people labor for love, not personal interest, and that their loving labor obviates the state's ongoing responsibility to redistribute resources to them (Kearney 1996). I counter this with a description of village life that reveals dimensions of egalitarian community that are based on low-grade rivalry among village households and fear of the evil power that follows hunger. Moreover, I argue that efforts to induce nostalgia and collective labor in village communities backfired in interesting ways that are worth hashing out, even though the administration quickly saw its mistakes and shifted toward policies that focused on augmenting the buying power of poor, rural families—especially women.[4]

The Outline of the Book

I begin with a chapter that situates Lula's election and the Zero Hunger Program within three frameworks: (1) Brazil's fraught history of democracy, (2) the particular history and social structure of Passarinho municipality, and (3) some reflections on my own role in the events I describe.[5] Chapter 1 illuminates the importance of the Zero Hunger Program (and later the Bolsa Família program) as an experiment in "left-wing neoliberalism" (a phrase that some would see as a contradiction-in-terms). Readers interested in Zero Hunger as an expression of the PT's long struggle for power will find discussions in this chapter more useful than those that follow, as will readers interested in the overall configuration of the Zero Hunger program as a "national food security policy."

Chapters 2 and 3 together comprise something of a classical community study, one focused on interhousehold relationships among impoverished villagers and vertical relationships between village families and municipal patrons. I show how interhousehold sociability in Passarinho's villages (chapter 2) is sustained through practices of "respectful distance" that allow rural people to cope with the evil spiritual power that emanates from envious neighbors, especially from those who are chronically hungry. By contrast, reciprocal exchange with municipal elites (chapter 3) is lived through the mutual revelation of each party's tragically imperfect embodiment of dignified personhood. Yet the egalitarian relationships among village families actually help poor people to forge long-term, intimate hierarchical relationships with the political elites, relations that contrast with the short-term exchanges (vote-buying) that more solitary (i.e., abandoned) villagers are resigned to have with politicians.

Chapter 4 turns to Zero Hunger's frontline officials in Piauí State, the "street-level bureaucrats" who shaped the actual contours of state policy at the very site where it contacted the beneficiaries (Lipsky 1980). I explore the officials' attitudes toward their own participation in urban social movements, toward the Lula government that employed them, and toward the program's rural beneficiaries. Most of the officials had grown up as the children of rural migrants in squatter settlements on the outskirts of Piauí's capital city, Teresina. Inspired by both liberation theology and more secular urban movements, they were prone to view the rural world as a place of patronage-based social domination. Narrating their programmatic journeys into the countryside as a return to their own roots, they came to see themselves as "prodigal liberators" of the rural beneficiaries who allegedly lived under the boot of venal patrons. I explore how their condemnation of rural political culture was tinged with nostalgia for their ancestral heartland, giving rise to a sentimental posture that shaped their interactions with rural families.

The next three chapters explore the techniques that officials used to reorient the beneficiaries' sentimental and practical attachments to patronage relations. These were not explicit, and they were certainly not official. They came together below the threshold of the state officials' awareness; each emerged as an effect of a thousand tiny behaviors, mostly improvised, intuitive, symbolic, and ritualistic. These techniques were logically coherent; though in all cases, it was a logic that I reconstructed and that the officials sometimes (though not always) confirmed in our joint reflections. Each of these chapters presents one of three such techniques by discussing it in relation to a particular project in the multifaceted Zero Hunger program (and, in one case, Bolsa Família). I hope this presentational strategy will give the reader a feel for what Lula's early social policies were like, what agencies were involved in implementing them, and how they benefited poor rural Brazilians. But I should be clear that these symbolic techniques for dismantling patronage were not tied to specific component projects; rather, they cut across all (or at least many) of Zero Hunger's numerous initiatives, interweaving with their specific policy structures.

Let me be more specific. In chapter 5, I examine a technique I call "induced nostalgia," which refers to practices by which state officials linked romantic notions of collective labor to idealized visions of the rural past, while portraying vertical intimacies as a fall from a pristine golden age. I show how this technique played out in the context of a community-driven development project that depended on coordinated management of livestock and the officials' fixation on romantic models of traditional labor, which caused problems for villagers whose memory of their past conflicted with the state officials' narrative.

In chapter 6, I explore another of Zero Hunger's component projects, an Afro-Brazilian development project that sought to organize and assist dark-skinned villagers on the basis of their shared racial subordination (addressing them as the descendants of fugitive slaves, *quilombolas*). I argue that state officials turned training-session excursions into "programmatic pilgrimages" in order to resocialize community leaders toward a black (*negro*) identity and instill in them a more indignant attitude toward figures of authority.

Chapter 7 provides a close ethnographic account of the municipal political tensions surrounding Zero Hunger's cash grant policy, Food Card (Cartão Alimentação), and its transition to the now-famous Bolsa Família (Family Stipend) program.[6] In designing the grant's beneficiary selection process, state officials bypassed the mayor's office and humiliated his person through a series of public spectacles. I discuss the consequences of the mayor's marginalization both for local participation in the Zero Hunger management committees set up to select the program's beneficiaries, and for Passarinho's municipal elections in which the Workers' Party (PT) competed for office.

This ethnography is intended to be the start of more work on the democratizing efforts that get entangled with various social policies implemented in Brazil, Latin America, and elsewhere. It both attests to the structural inequality that circumscribes political exchange in places like rural northeast Brazil and offers a sympathetic account of the political arrangements that derive from these inequalities. By balancing a discussion of Zero Hunger's failures and successes in transforming local exchange practices and political consciousness, I try to open up new perspectives on the question of democracy itself. In my concluding remarks, I reflect on the ethics of dismantling patronage in the name of democracy, taking into consideration the critical standpoint that intimate hierarchy affords to those people who experience normative (liberal-market) democracy as indifferent to their suffering.

CHAPTER ONE

Convulsions of Democracy

FROM NATIONAL POLITICS TO LOCAL HUNGER

On the morning of October 27, 2002, hundreds of thousands of people poured into the streets of Rio de Janeiro in tearful celebration of what some called a democratic revolution. A child migrant turned metal-worker—turned union organizer, turned political prisoner, turned party leader—had just completed his final transformation into President-Elect Luiz Inácio Lula da Silva. My friends from the headquarters of the Work-ers' Party (Partido dos Trabalhadores—PT) embraced in the rapture of victory. While they were normally divided into factions that held widely ranging views on capitalism, state policy, and identity politics, on this day they could look to the future together. Like kings, they strode along the boardwalk of Ipanema in groups of twos and threes, miles from their homes on the lowland outskirts of the city. Or maybe they went to the larger, adjacent beach of Copacabana, where there is always a little more trouble to get into. I'm not exactly sure how it all looked. I couldn't be with them that morning because my mother had called two nights be-fore to summon me home to my father's bedside in Los Angeles. But my friends from the PT wrote to me about the euphoria they felt, which they treasured all the more because they knew that the following day their party would have to make good. The PT had been the opposition party for twenty years. Now it would have to enact solutions to Brazil's countless problems. The first name that Lula gave to his plan was "Zero Hunger," and the first place where Zero Hunger would happen was Piauí, a destitute state in the semiarid (sertão) region of the Northeast. I followed Zero Hun-ger into Piauí, thinking that if I could understand the program's dynamics in its small pilot town (Passarinho), I might offer a glimpse into the work-ings of a modern left-wing state.

The structure of President Lula's antipoverty policies and the culture of the state agents who implemented them must be considered in light of the euphoria of Lula's long-awaited victory, which was part of a cycle of revolutionary excitement and disappointment that had exhausted and confused the Brazilian Left for over a century. This cycle demonstrates a long-standing feature of Brazilian politics, the ambivalent posture that politicians, the elite, and the middle classes have assumed with regard to the ideals of freedom and equality. The Lula administration could not escape this tradition of ambivalence and compromise, yet it also sketched a model of democracy that married poverty amelioration to the promotion of egalitarian participation in the political sphere. This was the impulse behind the Zero Hunger program, and it manifested not only in its formal policy structure, but also in the informal and often implicit efforts by state agents to undermine the relations of patronage ("intimate hierarchy") that ordered the lives of beneficiaries. Piloted in the small municipality I call Passarinho, Zero Hunger changed the lives of corn and bean cultivators who had already been struggling to understand democracy and development on their own terms. As for me, I was uncertain as to whether I would throw my hat in with the Zero Hunger officials whose critiques of rural patronage seemed at times so astute, and at other times, somewhat oblivious.

In this chapter, I lay out three levels of ethnographic material central to this book. The first level pertains to Brazil's fraught history with liberal democracy, a history that led the Left to attribute a democratizing function to Zero Hunger. The second level prioritizes the context of Passarinho, a place where deep inequality and egalitarian aspirations intertwined to shape a key setting where Lula's policies were implemented. The final level is a reflection on my own entry into Piauí, on my role in the implementation of Zero Hunger (and later Bolsa Família), and on the ethical dilemmas I faced during my two years in the field.

Patronage, Democracy, and the Emergence of the PT Administration

Democracy has led a troubled life in Brazil, a place where liberal philosophical tenets—universal rights, equality before the law, free trade, habeas corpus, economic rationality, and individualism—were never fully institutionalized.[1] One can always argue that even when these liberal virtues are upheld in full, they mainly serve to justify a society's hidden forms of coercion and exploitation. Perhaps. But, in Brazil, liberalism never even expressed the *outward appearance* of social relations. Liberalism's presence in Brazil has always seemed to be, as Roberto Schwarz (1992: 23) puts it, a "misplaced idea" or what Sérgio Buarque de Holanda (1982 [1926]:

119) earlier called a "lamentable misunderstanding." After all, Brazil maintained a parliamentary monarchy even after its independence from Portugal in 1822, and it remained a slave-driven economy until 1888. Thus, liberal ideas, which entered Brazil in the nineteenth century, were put to use in the service of the powerful.

During much of the nineteenth century, only the most radical statesmen called for full democracy and the abolition of African slavery (Viotti da Costa 1985: 53–78). Instead, the merchant class touted ideals of free trade to protest the commercial constraints imposed by the Crown, and the regional agricultural bosses used similar rhetoric in their struggle against the centralized government in Rio because they wanted to preserve absolute power in their localities. Moderate liberals held parliamentary majorities several times before the end of the Second Empire (1840–89), but they rarely implemented policies that benefited the poor. When they did legislate against slavery (which ended only in 1888), it was with the intent of supporting the free-labor coffee sector in the Southeast over the less efficient, slave-driven sugar industry in the Northeast (ibid.: 82). In parliament, members of both the Liberal and Conservative Parties (and the two were often hard to distinguish ideologically) worried that without slavery, the rural poor would not go to work on the plantations. The Land Law of 1850, supported by many Liberals, made squatting on common (royal) lands illegal and granted private titles only to large estates. This forced the rural poor to reside on large estates and to pay for that privilege with their labor, crop yields, and other tokens of loyalty (ibid.).

The end of the Empire (1889) and the beginning of republican government represented a liberal victory but not the empowerment of the popular classes. The First Republic (1889–1930) brought a limited democracy, with suffrage restricted to literate, propertied men and a legal system that codified their privilege over the masses (Holston 2008: 100–104). The winners were the regional elites, who gained more independence from the central government, and thus more oligarchic control within their regions, what would later be called "states" (Roett 1999: 28–29). At the subregional (municipal) level, however, big landowners saw their wealth decline and with it their absolute control over dependent laborers who resided on their lands. Their authority was further challenged by the advent of the vote (even with its limited suffrage).[2] According to the famous thesis of Victor Nunes Leal, these factors converged to form a compromise: The economically weakened local landowner—often called the "colonel" (*coronel*)—corralled the votes of the rural poor, not only for himself but for the reigning governor, and, in exchange, the governor and his associates allowed the coronel to distribute state-level resources as he saw fit, awarding them to the loyal and subservient poor, whose "weakness, desolation, and disillusionment" allowed the local coronel to "delude himself with a semblance of power and prestige, obtained at the price of [his] political submission [to the state government]" (Leal 1977 [1948]: 24–25).

Reflecting on this history, literary critic Roberto Schwarz (1992) observes that Brazilian ideological life was shaped not so much by slavery as by the more ambiguous relationship between the powerful propertied classes and the legally free masses who needed their help to survive. The caricature of the free worker was that of the *agregado*, the propertyless man or woman who needed to attach (*agregar*) to the extended family of a propertied seignior. Less clear than contractual slavery, this informal hierarchy required ideological elaboration, giving rise to a general culture of "favour." Schwarz writes that, "under a thousand forms and names, favour formed and flavoured the whole of national life . . . present everywhere. . . . As the professional depended on favour to exercise his profession, so the small proprietor depended on it for the security of his property, and the public servant for his position. Favour was our quasi-universal social mediation. . . . Slavery gives the lie to liberal ideas; but favour, more insidiously uses them, for its own purposes, originating a new ideological pattern" (23). What Schwarz calls "favour" operated through networks that cut across various organizations and official capacities, allowing power to move without record, as the law was selectively applied to one's allies within these networks. The perpetual exempting of one's self and friends from the inconveniences of the law led to a sense of collective bad faith with respect to liberal principles. Others simply flouted these principles, especially the regional agrarian bosses "who were proud of the fact that the law never entered the gates of their land" (Weffort 1988: 333). Popular cynicism about liberal civic virtue abounded, and this "cynicism [was] mirrored in the ironic smiles of the powerful, for whom the lack of popular expectations serve[d] as a license to act arbitrarily" (ibid.: 332).

The First Republic ended in 1930, when Getúlio Vargas, a clever military man, canceled the results of a national election and, in so doing, broke the backs of the regional oligarchs, submitting them to a central government that would promote industrialization. Vargas was able to situate himself at the nexus of various interests—domestic industrialists, anarchist-inspired communists, progressive unionists, left-wing lieutenants, and so on—playing them off one another. He eventually shored up a dictatorship by manipulating mass fear of a communist threat (Levine 1980: 59). His dictatorial New State (1937–45) established institutionalized labor legislation that allowed only for state-sanctioned unions. The idea was to suppress the communist and anarchist activists and make workers more "depend[ant] on the resources of the state" (Maybury-Lewis 1994: 14). In Vargas's rhetoric, this social arrangement (scholars call it "corporatism") originated with the state's generous "*outorga* [derived from *outorgar*, meaning 'to grant, confer, award or bestow']" (John French 1992: 49). In theory corporatism relied on a patronage chain in which benefits (e.g., medical assistance, sick leave, retirement packages) flowed from the Labor Ministry to obedient union leaders. Yet, would-be patrons within the Labor Ministry often lacked "any direct ties to the unpaid local union leaders," at least in industrial São Paulo (ibid.: 136). If corporatism entailed institutionalized patronage, that patronage often broke down in practice. At the same time, Vargas's labor legislation, even if designed to co-opt urban labor, provided legal protections for workers that empowered unions to take individual workers' grievances to the courts (ibid.: 111–21). In short, while institutionalized patronage characterized much of Brazil's midcentury labor regime, subordination to the state was a double-edged sword.

Vargas's New State lost much of its popular appeal when Brazil entered World War II on the side of the allies, and the glaring contradiction between Vargas's dictatorship and the democratizing rhetoric of the war motivated a return to free elections (Weffort 1988: 343). During the era of Populist Democracy (1945–64) that followed, Brazil saw the rise of competitive mass politics. Literate urban workers, an expanding population, had gained the right to vote. Populist politicians used new media (radio, loudspeakers, television) to appeal to the interests of a class that had once been excluded from political institutions. Scholars often allege that the populist politician's ambitions reflected his "narrow, parochial sense of satisfying his new 'clientele'" (Roett 1999: 32, 96–123). Yet progressive national policies and social movements periodically emerged during this era. The early 1960s saw a sharp increase in rural unrest prompted in part by the mobilization efforts of urban leftists (Bastos 1984; Morais 1997). Peasant Leagues emerged in the Northeast that called for the redistribution of unproductive lands and contested the armed encroachment of the sugar and cattle elite onto small properties. In 1963, the left-leaning president Goulart signed the Rural Workers Bill, legalizing rural unionization and including conditions that impeded landowners from dominating those unions (Cehelsky 1979: 43). Goulart also supported extending suffrage to illiterates, which would have led to an unprecedented inclusion of the rural masses in the political process, and he tried to push through a land reform bill that called for government expropriation of lands that would have forced wealthy landowners to lease their unused lands to the rural poor (ibid.: 56, 88–90).

As Goulart's politics took a "left turn," conservative Brazilians and the U.S. government grew increasingly wary of Brazilian populism. The Cold War had been in full swing for over a decade. During the 1950s, populist presidents had played on U.S. fears of a communist threat in Brazil to secure foreign aid. But aid was slow in coming, even after Fidel Castro's 1959 Cuban Revolution redoubled the Eisenhower administration's fear that South America was going red. Wary of the United States, Brazilian leaders during the early 1960s "demonstrated a sympathy for the basic tenets of nonaligned states—anticolonialism, coexistence with the Soviet bloc nations, ideological pluralism in the Third World . . . and a radical restructuring of economic relations between North and South" (Roett 1999: 194). In 1964, a U.S.-backed military coup responded by throwing out President Goulart, claiming that democracy had grown corrupt and chaotic. The generals who assumed power suspended elections for important executive branch offices, outlawed the formation of political parties, and hunted down activists in an effort to "restore the influence of the patrimonial regime" (ibid.: 127).[3]

It is perhaps because liberal institutions (however limited) eventually threatened economic hierarchy during the Populist Era that Brazil's underground leftist movements assumed that once they brought down the military dictatorship, a restoration of democracy would yield left-wing governance. They were sorely disappointed when the slow demise of the dictatorship brought a rash of civilian presidents who showed little interest in easing the suffering of Brazil's poor. As a result, many people on the left began to consider democracy to be an insufficient, if necessary, feature of social justice. During the decade following redemocratization, "socialism" (however ill-defined) became the Left's rallying cry.

THE PT, POLITICAL ETHICS, FOOD SECURITY, AND PARTICIPATION

During the late 1960s, a period of intense political persecution, urban unions (led by Lula among others), progressive intellectuals, outspoken students, peasant leaders, and other dissidents hid from the state security apparatus. They took cover in Christian base communities led by priests and lay clergy who were sympathetic to anticapitalist and antiauthoritarian struggles. A Christian base community was a group of neighbors who "belong[ed] to the same popular quarter, shantytown, village or rural zone, and [met] regularly to pray, sing, celebrate, read the Bible and discuss it in the light of their own life experience" (Lowy 1996: 48). Brazil, more than any other Latin American country, experienced a powerful surge of what Michael Lowy calls "liberationist Christianity" (a combination of liberation theology and popular Christian mobilization) that contradicted the Vatican's general endorsement of Brazil's military dictatorship (also see Burdick 1993). Brazil's liberationist priests and lay clergy spoke out against state torture and emphasized mutual aid among neighbors as the solution to social problems instead of appeals to the state or to private charity. Proponents of liberationist Christianity generally opposed "the three main political traditions of the country: clientelism . . . populism . . . and verticalism" (Lowy 1996: 89). The movement infused the Marxist and union activists with "the spiritual and ethical dimension of revolutionary struggle: the faith (mystical), the solidarity, the moral indignation, the total commitment at the risk of one's own life . . . an attempt to re-enchant the world through revolutionary action" (ibid.: 18; also see Burdick 1993). Thanks to the combined voices of secular and religious objectors, the dictatorship lost most of its legitimacy by 1973; a host of clerical, union, peasant, residential, and professional (e.g., attorneys) movements were organizing to bring back representative democracy.[4]

In 1980, this diverse group of left-wing dissidents founded the socialist Workers' Party (PT) with Lula as its leader. The PT called for popular elections, a break with the capitalist free market, a rejection of the Soviet model of top-down party control over workers, and strategic alliances with more conservative opposition parties in order to expedite the end of the dictatorship.[5] The PT's struggle to gain national office throughout the next twenty years proved that opposition to capitalism was impractical from an electoral standpoint. PT affiliates and sympathizers began to imagine a new kind of state policy that a Lula presidency would implement *in the context of* the capitalist market. The fight against hunger eventually fulfilled this purpose.

Wendy Hunter (2007) observes that while the party line officially remained one of uncompromising commitment to "socialism" during the 1980s, the PT's experiences in government at the municipal level (and some governorships) taught it the value of pragmatism. PT politicians, perhaps taking council from a senior generation of communist union leaders in their midst, realized that Marxist concerns with the long-term project of building socialism did not speak to the many single-issue social movements that had immediate, specific worries about housing, transportation costs, sewage, and so on (Keck 1992: 50–52). These officials had to make immediate practical decisions about allocating limited resources to conflicting segments of the population. Numerous municipal experiments in participatory democracy (especially participatory budgeting) both helped PT officials diffuse the grievances that came with such a task and deepened party members' thinking about the meaning of democracy itself (Hunter 2010: 96). The challenge, as leading PT intellectual Plinio de Arruda Sampaio (1986: 112) once wrote, was "to make democracy an inalienable space of everyday life and not just an instrument that one uses while it's useful to gain or maintain power." For many in the PT, this entailed deemphasizing the struggle against capitalism and focusing instead on the everyday concerns of the organized masses. Debates among the party's rank and file did not produce consensus on this point; many (Sampaio included) insisted that the party must continually remind movement leaders that "reformist struggles . . . will not resolve the deepest question of capitalist exploitation" unless they are linked to "the socialist program" and the "elevation of the level of political consciousness" (ibid.: 121). But, in general, the PT moved away from a concern with socialism, espousing "radical democracy" (later the name of a PT faction) and focusing on increasing popular participation in the political process (Chaui 1987).

The PT generally had a much easier time winning municipal (and a few state) elections in Brazil's industrialized South than in the more rural Northeast. The South had been recolonized in the late nineteenth century by literate, politically progressive immigrants from Southern and Central Europe whose admission had been integral to the federal government's plan of "whitening" the nation (Skidmore 1993). The liberal, anarchist, and communist ideologies that flourished in this region floundered in much of the rural Northeast (Soares 1973; Roett 1999; Kinzo 1988). According to Kurt von Mettenheim's (1995: 205) study of Brazilian voting patterns, "rural voters may express more interest in politics, but their notion of what constitutes acceptable political action is quite limited. Two or three times more southeastern and northeastern urban respondents approved of writing petitions, conducting strikes, and nonviolent occupation of public buildings, than rural respondents. . . . [This] confirms the underlying conservatism and passivity of rural political culture." Brazil's rural

Northeast generally lacked the new social movements, NGOs, unions, and professional associations found in cities. The exception lay in the Peasant Leagues and later the Landless Workers' Movement (Movimento sem Terra—MST) that militated for land reform "by law or by disorder" and committed their support to the PT (Hochstetler 2000: 176). The MST's immediate and constant support for the PT was a mixed blessing for the party. The affiliation gave the PT a foothold in the rural Northeast, but it also reinforced popular perceptions of the party's radicalism throughout Brazil.

At the national level, the PT pursued the practical steps needed to return Brazil to a formal democracy even before it enjoyed any real electoral success. The PT played a defining role in the convention that drafted the 1988 constitution as well as the popular Direitas Já movement that demonstrated (unsuccessfully) for an immediate return to popular elections in 1986 (Nylen 2000: 131). These efforts to expand democracy appealed to the party's changing constituency; the PT increasingly absorbed moderate professionals, artists, students, and business owners (Keck 1992: 193). Many of these people identified with the "new social movements" that fought for the rights of Afro-Brazilians, indigenous people, women, gays and lesbians, the disabled, and so on. For these groups, the dream of a full and dignified citizenship in a consumer society was more important than the fight against capitalism.

The PT's major ideological turning point followed Lula's failed presidential campaign in 1989. The campaign had been "an unapologetic effort by the PT to place Lula and his party firmly on the left and to identify them with the intention to bring about socialism, however ambiguously defined" (Hunter 2010: 110). When the center-right candidate, Fernando Collor de Mello, defeated him, the balance of power in the party shifted to the moderate factions. Combined with the collapse of the Soviet Union in 1989, these events led the party to jettison the fight against capitalism from its official rhetoric. If it retained anything from this rhetoric, it was a critique of a particular kind of capitalism, "neoliberalism," a term that referred to policies that privatized state businesses, reduced supportive services, prioritized the repayment of loans to the IMF, and in general submitted to foreign capital. Such were the policies of Brazil's presidents during the 1980s and 1990s, and the PT's factions seemed united against this neoliberal model—at least while the party remained in the opposition. As an alternative to this model, the PT developed an agenda that linked democracy and the fight against hunger, political corruption, and patronage.

With regard to the fight against corruption, the PT leadership tried to ensure that its officials resisted the temptations that come with elected office. For instance, the PT shamed its own members when they were (convincingly) accused of impropriety by "distancing" (*afastando*) them from the party's internal governance. Moreover, the PT's statutes required its officeholders to contribute 40 percent of their salaries to the party, a policy that discouraged capricious opportunists from entering the party to exploit its clean reputation (Keck 1992: 218). Indeed, Brazil's new multiparty system had quickly turned into a free-for-all; a highly fragmented and ephemeral array of nonideological parties that emerged around the personas of particular candidates (Mainwaring 1999; Samuels 2003; Nicolau 2002). The PT, by contrast, asserted party discipline over its representatives, making it the first postdictatorship party with a clear ideological identity. The PT's claim to clean politics was boosted by the quick discovery of President Collor's own corruption. Collor's misfortune allowed the PT to gain renown by mobilizing a popular grassroots "Movement for Ethics in Politics" that successfully lobbied for his impeachment (Weyland 1993: 1). Linking political ethics to grassroots participation established two of the three pillars that would define the PT's model of democracy.

The third pillar was the food and hunger movements of the mid-1990s. After Lula lost to Collor in 1989, those close to him in the party set up a think tank called the Citizenship Institute that was tasked with reimagining progressive social policy for Brazil. Rather than call for a total break with the free market, the Citizenship Institute, in consultation with the U.N. Food and Agriculture Organization (FAO), crafted a comprehensive "National Policy of Food Security," the blueprint for what became the Zero Hunger program roughly ten years later. A focus on food policy put the PT in touch with religious organizations and professionals in organized civil society who were already participating in international discussions on food-based development. Once such event was the 1996 World Food Summit held in Rome, where the concept of "food security" was defined as a situation in which "all people at all times have access to sufficient, safe, nutritious food to maintain a healthy and active life" (World Food Summit 1996). This definition, still used today, makes no reference to social equality, suggesting instead that a healthy, *individual* human body is the goal of food policy (rather than a restructuring of class and other collective relations). The political neutrality of the global "food security" movement played well with moderates in Brazil, but it also spoke to more left-leaning members who saw global enthusiasm for food security as an opening to discuss land reform, state crop purchase, enhanced rural credit, higher wages, and an end to all payment on Brazil's foreign debt (Balsadi 2004). The theme of food security thus gave common cause to people of very different political persuasions.

The PT's involvement with the food security movement went well beyond the Citizenship Institute. PT mayors and legislators experimented with local food security policies (milk-distribution programs, community gardens, small-scale irrigation projects, microcredit, etc.) that channeled funds and administrative responsibility to nongovernmental organizations (Gasques 2002). This earned the PT increasing renown among nutritionists, nurses, schoolteachers, agronomists, engineers, and other professionals prone to distrust state authority and champion "organized civil society." NGO activists were also inclined toward the more individualistic ideals of personal empowerment, capacity building, and self-sufficiency (Tranjan 2011). These had become the hallmarks of global development discourse during the 1990s (Chambers 1997; Cooke and Kothari 2001). By thematizing participation and food security and working with entities like the FAO, the PT established partnerships with powerful, "apolitical" international players who began to trust that a PT-governed Brazil would be moderately progressive, rather than radically anticapitalist. (Both the FAO and the World Bank later made large financial contributions to Lula's Zero Hunger and Bolsa Família programs.)

The conceptual link between food security and the fight against patronage came in the form of a critical policy discourse that this diverse set of social actors voiced when lambasting prior administrations. Food security activists often claimed that all prior state food policies had fallen victim to *assistencialismo* (see, e.g., L'Abbate 1988). The term *assistencialismo* can be translated as roughly "welfare statism," though it carries an added connotation of a citizen's accommodationist attitude toward the state. It is useful to examine the term's conceptual underpinning among members of the food security movement. From the political center, the late anthropologist Ruth Cardoso (2004: 43) defined assistencialismo as "a style, a way of doing something that creates a relation of submission and does not offer the tools for overcoming needs." From the political left, Reinaldo Pontes (2003: 4), an intellectual in the food movement and a PT supporter, wrote that assistencialismo "play[s] the role of conservative ideological cement, pinning enormous contingents of the population under the weight of political alienation. . . . [Yet assistencialismo] . . . cannot be defined by the type of service given to the population, but by the 'form' through which it is done." These definitions encompass both a market-oriented fantasy of the state withdrawing from the economy once its work is done, and a leftist preoccupation with "alienation," the mental slavery that impedes social revolution. Deeply akin to the idea of clientelismo, assistencialismo reconciled these two orientations, and the two terms often appeared together in various sympathetic texts that differentiated Zero Hunger from prior food policies (e.g., Yasbek 2003).[6]

The sophisticated discourse of food security and assistencialismo did not easily spread to Brazil's popular classes, but talk of hunger did. The PT-affiliated sociologist Herbert "Betinho" da Souza orchestrated the enormous "Campaign against Hunger and for Life" in which some 5,000 ad hoc "committees" cropped up around the country to engage in a variety of antihunger activities (Landim 1998). These committees included a wild cross-section of adherents ranging from private philanthropists, the state-owned Bank of Brazil, religious organizations, the PT and other parties, environmental movements, nutritionists, gay and lesbian movements, indigenous and black rights movements, and even military clubs (ibid.; Gohn 2004: 22; Cardoso 2004: 46; Vasconcelos 2005: 448). Betinho's transcendent, messianic rhetoric expressed the enthusiasm of the campaign in a way that defused ideological conflict among its many participants. In his missionary pilgrimage throughout Brazil (the "Caravan against Hunger"), Betinho said he "would speak with God and the Devil to resolve the problem of hunger," which, he maintained, was too urgent to leave to politics (Landim 1998: 261; also see Betto 2004). Despite these apolitical tones, Betinho's connection to the PT was indisputable. Much of his Christian discourse was borrowed from the liberationist priests who had sheltered leftists during the dictatorship. Christian discourse, therefore, led a double life in the hunger movement: for the general population it signaled an apolitical, humanistic appeal, while for people familiar with left-wing politics, it evoked a history in which the cloak of Christianity protected Brazil's progressive dissidents.

Having mobilized the population around the theme of hunger, the PT's remaining challenge was to politicize the policy solution to hunger in a way that was more widely accessible than the erudite critiques of assistencialismo. In 2000, Lula (already gearing up for his 2002 election) went on television and told the nation, "Unfortunately, in Brazil, the vote is not ideological. Unfortunately, people don't vote for a political party. And unfortunately, you have a part of society that, because of its great poverty, is led [conduzida] to think with its stomach and not with its head. That's why there are so many food baskets and milk packs distributed, because this is a kind of trade at election time. And in this way, you depoliticize the electoral process. . . . You have the logic of maintaining a politics of domination."[7] While words like "ideological" and "depoliticize" may have appealed only to the educated, Lula's reference to a population in poverty that "thinks with its stomach," that feels valued only at election time, and that is therefore "dominated" requires little study to comprehend. In Lula's formulation, hunger is not just an ill in itself; it perpetuates patronage and short-circuits democracy.

In short, by linking its challenges to Brazil's political system to the visceral problem of hunger, the PT was able to move toward the center of the political spectrum without sacrificing the revolutionary energy it had drummed up in the fight against the dictatorship. The party preserved its revolutionary charisma by trading its anticapitalist persona for an identity founded on a robust model of democracy in which the concrete goal food security was paramount. On October 16, 2002 (World Food Day), candidate Lula announced his intention to create a program that would "end the hunger of more than 40 million Brazilians" (Betto 2003: 4). He won by a landslide.

THE LULA ADMINISTRATION: A LEFT-WING NEOLIBERALISM

Because Lula's campaign discourse in 2002 had been far more moderate (on questions of privatization, trade, debt repayment, land reform, etc.) than in prior elections, it was unclear how much his policies would actually deviate from those of his immediate predecessor, President Fernando Henrique Cardoso of the Social Democratic Party. Stylistically, the two men were archetypal opposites, "the professor and the worker" (John French 2010). Cardoso's every word dripped with the erudition of São Paulo's intellectual elite, while Lula's voice elicited classist mockery for its stereotypical deviations from "proper" Portuguese—as one might expect from a northeastern metalworker who never finished elementary school. The two men had been fellow travelers during the darkest days of the military dictatorship, but Cardoso had taken a right turn toward neoliberalism in the 1990s, viewing austerity measures as the only way to steer clear of hyperinflation (which Cardoso had ended as finance minister prior to becoming president) and to stimulate economic growth. Cardoso privatized dozens of state companies, borrowed enormous sums from the IMF, loosened laws that protected workers, and further opened Brazil's borders to foreign investment. Many blame these policies for Brazil's increased

wealth gap, heightened unemployment (or underemployment), more con-
centrated agricultural ownership, skyrocketing utility costs, and higher
interest rates for middle-class borrowers—all of which occurred during
the 1990s (Amann and Baer 2002).

Lula and the PT interpreted Cardoso's administration as one of total
subordination to capital accumulation at the expense of social justice. Yet
as president, Lula never renationalized any of the businesses that Cardoso
(or Collor) had privatized; nor did he lower interest rates or erect trade
barriers against wealthier nations (Sotelino 2011). Rather than default on
Brazil's debt to the IMF (as he had said he would during the 1980s and
1990s), Lula paid the debt off quickly in order to lower Brazil's overall interest burden. In general, what Lula created was a kind of left-wing neoliberalism, what Glauco Arbix and Scott Martin (2011: 61) call a "neo-activist
state" based on "moderate, pro-market intervention via an active competi-
tiveness policy, joined closely with a much stronger role in providing social services and benefits . . . fostering market inclusion for the previously
underserved and excluded" (also see Font and Randall 2011; and Love and
Baer 2009).

Lula's social policies evince some continuity with those of President Cardoso, who in truth exercised his own brand of progressivism. Cardoso had
actively tried to fight institutional patronage in the party system by pushing through legislation that constrained the opportunistic alliances allowing parties to shirk ideological consistency (Fleischer 2011). Moreover, he
had created several cash transfer programs, mainly Bolsa Escola (School
Grant) and Auxílio Gás (Gas Assistance), which helped improve education
and health for the most impoverished. Like Cardoso, Lula created institutional spaces of cooperation between the state and private business and a
"tone of dialogue and . . . participation in a process of promoting public-
private alliance for development" (Arbix and Martin 2011: 66). Lula also
pushed forward on the tax, labor, health, and social security reforms that
Cardoso had begun, some of which the PT's labor constituencies strongly
opposed (Monteiro 2009; Michael Hall 2009; Leopoldi 2009).

Lula's main policy divergence from Cardoso lay in the extent of his
investment in the fight against poverty. Cardoso's program Bolsa Escola
insufficiently covered the poor,[8] and it only provided families with fifteen
reais (about five to seven U.S. dollars) per month per child. (Cardoso's
other cash grants typically paid them even less.) Lula's cash transfer policies extended to virtually the entire impoverished population, they were

far more generous, and they were linked to a more extensive set of social development initiatives.

Implemented in January 2003, Zero Hunger was Lula's first flagship social policy. It officially consisted of three types of policies: emergency, local, and structural (see table 2 in the appendix).[9] The convergence of the three pillars conformed with the popular adage, "Give a man a fish and you feed him for a day. Teach a man to fish and you feed him for a life-time." Emergency policies included a major cash grant and food baskets for indigent families. Local policies consisted of municipal projects (housing, literacy, sewage, electricity, community gardens, nutritional classes, microcredit to farmers, etc.) that addressed infrastructural problems somehow related to food. The structural policies were those that aimed to generate employment and attack the pillars of inequality through land reform, federal crop purchase, and milk distribution programs (cf. Belik 2003: 18). The structural policies never went very far. The crop purchase and milk distribution policies were very limited in scope, and land reform was simply too controversial for the administration to treat as a priority.[10] The local policies encompassed so many types of initiatives (housing, nutrition, literacy, sanitation, etc.) implemented by so many agencies (government at all levels, NGOs, multilateral development agencies, etc.) that they were impossible to keep track of, let alone evaluate. While Zero Hunger's local and structural components were intended to teach poor people "to fish," state officials claimed they needed to fish them as well; "Nobody learns new skills when they're hungry," many officials claimed. Zero Hunger's "emergency" component addressed these immediate needs with a cash transfer program called the Food Card (Cartão Alimentação), which Lula implemented alongside Cardoso's cash grants. Unlike the local or structural components, Food Card spread fast and far, reaching nearly 3,000 of Brazil's 5,684 municipalities before the close of 2003 (Balsadi et al. 2004: 88–90). The Food Card allocated fifty reais to one member of each family living in "extreme poverty" for up to eighteen months. Female household heads were prioritized as the cardholders, and they drew funds once a month from designated locations.[11] Food Card beneficiaries received green booklets, where they were to paste their receipts from stores that sold them food, kitchen supplies, or hygiene products, and they were supposed to submit these to a local management committee every month. In practice, this virtually never occurred, and civil society organizations throughout Brazil were so outraged by the grant's restrictions (calling them patronizing) that the federal government discontinued this feature when Bolsa Família was created in 2004.

Administrative problems befell Zero Hunger from the beginning. To oversee the program, Lula had created a new Special Ministry of Food Security (Ministério Extraordinário de Segurança Alimentar—MESA) and placed at its head a rural sociologist who had been involved in the Citizenship Institute, José Graziano da Silva. Graziano faced immediate criticism from many civil society representatives in the food security movement who objected to his technocratic and centralizing persona. They believed Graziano was prioritizing the Food Card over other component policies (Goertzel 2011: 70). Indeed, the MESA did prioritize Food Card when it came to its own budget. It did not have the funds to spread all of Zero Hunger's component policies throughout the countryside, so the Food Card became MESA's spearhead. Because the cash grant arrived in most places before any "local" or "structural" initiatives, civil society organizations railed that Zero Hunger merely "gave a man a fish rather than teaching him to fish," in other words, that it was guilty of the very assistencialismo its proponents had critiqued during the 1990s. (This critical phrase spread like wildfire among the general population; I heard it wherever I went, hundreds of times.) Graziano protested that the public was blind to the other Zero Hunger projects that were implemented in various locales, but he could not salvage his reputation (interview with Graziano da Silva, July 2005).

In 2004, the Lula administration relieved Graziano of his position and replaced MESA with another ministry. It stopped talking about Zero Hunger and recast its social policy under a new name: Programa Bolsa Família ("Family Stipend Program"). The irony is that Bolsa Família, Lula's new flagship social policy, emphasized the very cash distribution that so many civil society members had critiqued. It combined the fifty reais from the Food Card with the monies families received from the two prior Cardoso grants (Bolsa Escola and Auxílio Gás). Lula's motivations were understandable. Despite the critiques of assistencialismo, cash grants clearly improved the lives of the poor immediately, and they earned Lula (and the PT) popular support among this enormous segment of the population. Thus, Lula's removal of Graziano did not indicate the administration's desire to make cash transfers less central to its social policy; instead, it revealed the government's effort to placate the critical voices within civil society by putting a more diplomatic character, Patrus Ananias de Sousa, in charge of Lula's social policies.[12] This was apparent to many of the civil society representatives outside the administration who subsequently interpreted the administration's prioritization of Bolsa Família as evidence of Lula's reluctance to commit resources to anything but cash transfer policies. While some members of the food security movement insisted that such policies amounted to (empowering) "assistance" rather than (demobilizing) "assistencialismo," others were profoundly disappointed (Burity et al. 2010: 25). As one academic, N. N. Gomes Júnior (2007: 18), wrote cynically, "The Zero Hunger Program that was announced as the government's priority was reduced to the condition of a fantasy name. Food and Nutritional Security lost its relevance in the government's policy strategy, and an income transfer program [Bolsa Família] came to be our 'national savior'" (quoted in Pinheiro 2009: 187). Echoes of such accounts underlie a common left-wing frustration with Lula, a sense that he betrayed his roots by turning a group of former trade union leaders into bureaucrats who dispensed state patronage.

This perspective aligned with the neoliberal critique of the Lula administration that Anthony Pereira (2012: 780–81) attributes to supporters of Cardoso who believe Lula embodied "a regressive Latin American populist tradition" and a hypocritical embrace of "personalism, patronage, and clientelism." A major corruption scandal in 2005, in which high-level PT officials were caught buying off congressional votes, gave further popular credence to this perspective. While many scholars (e.g., French and Fortes 2012: 9) dispute the claim that Lula's regime "degenerated into populism and an amorphous cult of personality," the Brazilian middle class lost faith in much of his social policies. Within the food security movement, there was a growing consensus that Lula would not implement a comprehensive food policy. Food security activists eventually took their battle to the legislature, where they successfully lobbied for passage of the Organic Law of Food Security in 2006, which recognized food security as a human right and laid out the general principles of a national food security system. The legislation was sufficiently vague that it did not require any immediate policy shift from the administration (Pinheiro 2009: 188).

Bolsa Família has since become a model for antipoverty policy the world over. It greatly expanded poor people's consumption of food and other basic commodities. Along with Lula's use of the National Development Bank to finance small businesses and start-ups, his deployment of cash transfers helped to capitalize Brazilian markets and grow the Brazilian economy, which was stable enough to weather the global economic crisis of 2009 as well as any nation in the world (Leite 2011: 302; Sotelino 2011:

277). Policy analysts generally credit Bolsa Família with reducing Brazil's rate of extreme poverty as well as social inequality (Lindert et al. 2007; Soares, Perez Ribas, and Guerrero Osário 2010). Moreover, the conditions it places on its beneficiaries (school attendance, medical exams, vaccinations) have correlated with improvements in educational and health measures in some of the most destitute corners of Brazil (Lindert et al. 2007). Its proponents defend Bolsa Família against charges of assistencialismo by pointing to these indicators and arguing that they themselves constitute an extension of citizenship rights.[13]

As I see it, in order to understand the transition in Lula's social policies after 2003, we should avoid the temptation to contrast Zero Hunger with Bolsa Família. Zero Hunger was a collection of various projects that the erstwhile MESA coordinated with other ministries, state agencies, and private organizations; Bolsa Família was (and is) a single, albeit enormous, cash transfer program run entirely by the Ministry of Social Development (Ministério de Desenvolvimento Social—MDS), which replaced MESA.[14] They were apples and oranges. It makes more sense to compare the two phases of Lula's cash transfer policies (Food Card and then Bolsa Família), and then to study separately his administration's general policy orientation toward a given segment of the population (e.g., the rural poor) before and after 2004.

Regarding the cash grants, it is obvious that Bolsa Família gave families more money because its sum was combined with funds from the Cardoso grants. This sum further increased over Lula's two administrations because it was pegged to the federally established minimum wage, which Lula increased several times. It is also useful to compare the beneficiary selection mechanisms of the two cash transfer programs. Food Card's beneficiaries were selected by a municipal management committee (*comité gestor*) comprised mostly of locally elected civil-society representatives. The purpose of this structure was to deprive small-town mayors of the power to manipulate the disbursal of the grants (see chapter 7). When Bolsa Família emerged in 2004, Minister Patrus Ananias ended this use of the local management committees and created a special bureaucratic position within each municipal government that was tasked with beneficiary enrollment and compliance monitoring.[15] Critical to this shift was the expansion of Bolsa Família into a (de facto) entitlement program. Instead of municipal quotas on the number of beneficiaries who could receive a cash grant, all poor families were entitled to receive the grant.

Comparing Lula's early and later policies toward the rural poor, one sees a related shift. Under the aegis of Zero Hunger, the federal government sent a raft of one-time housing projects, short-term adult literacy projects, community gardens and women's cooperatives, and other small-scale, community development initiatives to towns and villages across the rural Northeast. These mostly ended by 2004, when the emphasis of Lula's rural development policy shifted to a focus on family microloans using the structure of Cardoso's existing Family Agriculture Support Program (Programa de Apoio ao Agricultor Familiar—PRONAF). By 2005, Lula had nearly doubled the number of beneficiaries receiving PRONAF credit and tripled the overall federal investment in PRONAF. He also redirected PRONAF credit to the poorest segments of the rural population (Guanziroli 2007: 304–5). The underlying pattern of this shift was a move away from projects that required collective management of communal resources and toward projects that took the nuclear family as the beneficiary unit. Moreover, the shift toward microloans indicated an increased emphasis on imparting the values and techniques of financial responsibility, whereas, under Zero Hunger, collective management projects focused on strengthening cooperation and accountability (avoiding graft).

These comparisons reveal a shift in the administration's vision of the state's role in social policy: instead of stimulating participatory democracy (under Zero Hunger), the state (under Bolsa Família) focused on including the poor as capitalist subjects, that is, as responsible small entrepreneurs and cash-empowered consumers. Bolsa Família was, at an institutional level, less intentional about fighting patronage or market individualism. Yet this shift in policy structure did not necessarily translate in the minds of the PT-affiliated state agents who implemented Lula's policies. Many of these officials lamented the termination of the management committees and intensified their commitment to dismantle local patronage in their face-to-face encounters with program beneficiaries. This is the side of Lula's antipoverty policies that I seek to illuminate in greater depth. Before doing so, I will sketch out the basic history and social conditions that characterized Passarinho, Piauí, when I arrived there in 2003.

A People on the Margins of a Corral and Slaughterhouse

The state of Piauí was symbolically and politically perfect as the locale for Zero Hunger's pilot municipalities. As a result of a political fluke, the PT had managed to elect one of its own as governor in 2002. With the PT affiliate Wellington Dias as governor, the federal government could be assured of state-level cooperation with its policies. More important, though, was Piauí's place in the national imagination; it was an icon of poverty, the state Brazil forgot, the state Brazilians knew they had forgotten. At the same time, Piauí's rural population was not renowned for violent clashes between plantation owners and rural wage laborers. Piauienses were generally viewed as peaceful "family agriculturalists" beset by the drought and famine so characteristic of the sertão. Piauí appeared innocent and romantic in its extreme underdevelopment.

While the semiarid sertão cuts across the interior of all the northeastern states, it defines Piauí more than any other. Unlike other northeastern states, Piauí is virtually landlocked, so its soils were too dry to support a colonial sugar economy. Settlement of Piauí came not from the coast but from the inland regions of neighboring colonial units. In the southeast of the state (where Passarinho is located), a few powerful ranching families entered from the Bahian sertão in the late 1700s and settled lands, having obtained royal titles to sizable holdings (Mott 1985: 50). The commercial activities of their large cattle estates were dictated by the interests of the sugar plantations housed in the neighboring colonial units: the captaincies of Maranhão and Pernambuco (Mott 1985; Brandão 1999: 114). Piauí thus became the "corral and slaughterhouse" of northeast Brazil, supplying these plantations, and eventually those of other states, with beef and leather goods (Mott 1985; Sobrinho 1946). The ranches were initially quite large, though they were always unproductive due to poor soil quality, low rainfall, and sparse water (Mott 1985: 71–72). Moreover, Piauí's ranchers neither sought nor received productive technologies from the Portuguese Crown or private investors.

These vast ranching estates required both highly skilled cowboys and peasant sharecroppers (slaves and freepeople), who lived on the fringes of the owner's lands (Mott 1985: 56). It was the leather-clad cowboy (*vaqueiro*) who came to occupy the symbolic center of this productive configuration and whose skill with a gun helped to decimate the "numerous and threatening indigenous tribes" (Sousa Martins et al. 2003: 41). The vaqueiro's coveted skills forced his employer to pay him well and treat him respectfully. The vaqueiro embodied the "code of the sertão," which called on a man to show courage, humility, and loyalty to his employers, as well as a willingness to resort to violence to solve disputes, exact blood vengeance, and protect the sexual honor of women (see Roniger 1990: 113; also see Marques 2002). This code of honor should be seen not as the transhistorical essence of *sertanejo* character but instead as a response to the historically specific threats to poor people's dignity brought by the economic dislocations of the late nineteenth century. The vaqueiro persona may have emerged in "the disjuncture between the ideal of patriarchal authority and the reality of insecurity in subsistence and familiar disorganization" such that he embodied a "public enforcement of patriarchy, often asserted through violence" (Santos 2012: 6).

As Piauí's large farms continually broke apart during the twentieth century, the vaqueiro became a figure of collective memory and nostalgia. The ideals of strength and autonomy still orient the identities of Piauí's rural men. During my time there, I saw men don the traditional leather cloak and hat of the vaqueiro on ceremonial occasions, and they sometimes asked me to take their pictures while they were mounted "cowboy style" on a horse or a mule. Even with the obsolescence of the cowboys, the code of the sertão endures. Most men I knew proudly claimed (honestly or not) that they never left their fields to seek work on the coastal sugarcane plantations that humiliated workers by submitting them to a boss (see, inter alia, Scheper-Hughes 1992; Freitas 2003; and Rogers 2010). Like other residents of the sertão, Piauí's rural families largely labored for themselves, recognizing their economic inferiority to regional elites "without becoming morally submissive" to them (Villela 2012: 14). Still, as of 2000, Piauí's cultivators had the lowest income in all Brazil, and they scored the worst on the Human Development Index (Fortes 2000: 24–26). They were both proud and destitute.

In the Brazilian imagination, Piauí's peasantry is politically docile by comparison to that of neighboring states, especially Pernambuco and Bahia. While some of Piauí's rural poor did mobilize in Peasant Leagues and landless workers' movements, these episodes of militancy are seldom mentioned in accounts of rural activism in the Northeast. What little scholarly work exists on the subject suggests that "social tensions in rural Piauí don't manifest as great armed struggles, owing to a dearth of peasant mobilization" (Mendes 1997: 19; Adad and Ferreira 1987). Lacking a coastal sugar economy, Piauí did not have a much of a rural proletariat, so unionization was slow in coming. Its peasant and slave underclasses were dispersed around large cattle ranches, consigned to living off poor soils. The low levels of peasant mobilization may partly derive from "the great dispersion of this population across Piauí's territory, creating enormous difficulties for contact among its inhabitants" (Sousa Martins et al. 2003:

87). In the 1970s, a process of conservative modernization of the countryside increased the concentration of land in the hands of mechanized agriculture, causing waves of immigration to the capital city, Teresina (Bandeira 1994). Yet Piauí remains a rural state with a large, conservative cultivator population.

The Piauí state government did little to ameliorate rural suffering throughout the twentieth century. During Vargas's reign, Teresina was electrified, hospitals were built, and running water was installed, but the only rural projects involved bovine productivity for the wealthiest ranchers. This trend continued during the Populist Era and military dictatorship, when the state-owned Bank of the Northeast created the Commission for State Development, which extended technical assistance to large estates (Moraes 2003: 12–13). (This was quite consistent with the rural elitist development strategy of the military dictatorship throughout Brazil.) Rural land distribution throughout Piauí changed significantly between 1950 and 1970. State-backed mechanization increased land concentration, and a more profit-centered mentality among landowners led them to expel peasant families from the fringes of their estates. The peasants were forced to squat on even more marginal unclaimed lands, which were further subdivided with each generation (Rocha 1988: 30–41). By 1972, three-quarters of the population resided on property of less than 100 hectares (ibid.: 35). Piauí became a state of highly impoverished small properties, with scattered medium-sized cattle ranches disbursed among them, and a few very lucrative mechanized soy plantations in its south.

Despite the historic lack of state support, some of Piauí's cultivators, including those of the Passarinho municipality, had some access to cash as a result of the cotton crop. Cotton production in the sertão had begun during the U.S. Civil War, filling the vacuum left by Confederate plantations (Rocha 1988: 30). The peasantry could plant the cotton alongside their corn and beans and sell sacks of the "white gold" to regional ranchers, who acted as middlemen. The ranchers had to compete for the cotton by offering higher prices, and by treating peasant families with a modicum of dignity. Unfortunately, the price of northeastern cotton dropped in the late 1930s due to competition with São Paulo's farmers, who went into cotton production after the collapse of Brazil's coffee economy (Ianni 1984: 37; Coelho 2004: 154–55). The crop was later dealt a deathblow by the boll weevil infestation of the 1980s and 1990s. The region then spiraled into a depression from which it has never recovered.

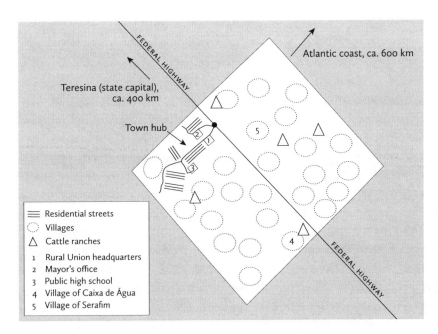

Legend:
- ≡ Residential streets
- ⌣ Villages
- △ Cattle ranches
- 1　Rural Union headquarters
- 2　Mayor's office
- 3　Public high school
- 4　Village of Caixa de Água
- 5　Village of Serafim

Map labels: Atlantic coast, ca. 600 km; Teresina (state capital), ca. 400 km; FEDERAL HIGHWAY; Town hub; FEDERAL HIGHWAY

FIGURE 2 Field map of Passarinho municipality.

PASSARINHO'S SOCIAL STRUCTURE

The settlement of Passarinho municipality (originally part of a larger municipality in the southeast of Piauí) followed the building of a train line that transported cotton to the neighboring state of Pernambuco for export. Passarinho's area is quite large (about 1,000 square kilometers), but it is very sparsely populated. When I first went there in 2003, the railroad tracks were rusting idly, and most of the roughly 5,000 inhabitants who resided in Passarinho (by then an independent municipality) lived in poverty. It was largely a village-dwelling, rural municipality; only 13 percent resided in the small town hub. There were only a half a dozen or so large farms (more than 500 hectares each), all of which belong to men who claimed descent from one of the two ranching families that colonized the region. About 15 percent of Passarinho's farms were medium-sized (100–500 hectares). Roughly 20 percent of properties were between 50 and 100 hectares. About 50 percent fell between 10–50 hectares, leaving 15 percent of properties with less than 10 hectares (Census 2000). Most families (those with 50 hectares or less) were barely reaping enough crops to feed themselves. The vast majority of the money that flowed to the town came to the few ranchers who sold cattle to market middlemen.[16]

The cultivators of the small farms (100 hectares and fewer) raised goats, pigs, and chickens but devoted themselves primarily to their corn and bean fields. What little was left over from their own consumption they sold in local markets. At a secondary level, they cultivated small patches of sugarcane and manioc to produce sugar candy (*rapadura*) and meal (*farinha*) that they used, gifted to kin, or sold to known persons in town. Labor was generally divided by gender: Men worked in the fields with the crops, goats, and (a very few) cattle. (They used hand tools and draft animals to plow.) Women, in addition to tending to the household (cooking, cleaning, caring for children, and fetching water), also cared for the chickens and pigs in the immediate domestic area. Households averaged about six occupants but ranged widely. Kinship was bilateral and either spouse's parents or junior siblings sometimes resided under the same roof. Most marriages occurred within the village, often between cousins. Strong patriarchy meant that married women were careful not to converse with other men, and they fed their husbands first, followed by the children, then themselves. (Male privilege was less pronounced in the town center.)

Corn and bean subsistence is extremely difficult on these soils without irrigation. Only the town hub had running water, thanks to a massive reservoir in a nearby city that was built during the 1970s by the Superintendency for the Development of the Northeast, a very important federal development agency that President Cardoso shut down in 2001.[17] In the villages, open watering holes were the most common source of drinking water, because, despite Piauí's massive underground water reserves, there were very few wells. (Digging them was expensive and risky.) The women and children thus had to fetch water by hand (or draft animal) from rain-fed watering holes often quite distant from their homes. The water problem was related to the lack of electricity in the villages; only the town hub had a power grid. Without electricity, villagers could not buy water pumps. (Gas and diesel pumps were too expensive.) This meant that not only did families not have running water inside their homes, they also could not set up inexpensive, small-scale, garden irrigation for fruits and vegetables. The lack of electricity also meant no refrigeration and thus considerable labor time for women in the kitchens. It also created expenses, such as radio batteries and gas-lamps, which burdened this already cash-poor population. (By 2006, the Lula administration had furnished electricity to Passarinho, and most other municipalities, through the program "Light for All.")

Opportunities for cash were increasing in Passarinho by 2003 but so

FIGURE 3 A village boy fetching water during the dry season.
Photograph by the author.

was the need for it. After the 1988 constitution, the federal government finally gave all rural workers retirement pensions (Schwarzer 2000). About 14 percent of Passarinho's population received these monies (equal to one month's minimum wage) monthly. The constitution also expanded municipal jobs by decentralizing education, health, and later social assistance so that these functions became part of municipal governance.[18] Opportunities for formal employment thus revolved around the 120 municipal jobs, such as security guards, janitors, school lunch cooks, schoolteachers, and so on. Since 2000, the state-owned Brazilian Agricultural Research Corporation (Empresa Brasileira de Pesquisa Agropecuária—EMBRAPA) had also enhanced local access to cash by encouraging Passarinho's villagers to convert some of their crops to rentable pasture. Some families also benefited from the Cardoso grants. Yet these measures did not afford most people enough money to buy the food they needed for their households.[19] After Brazil's currency finally stabilized in the mid-1990s, factory-made goods (sugar, pasta, rice, manioc flour, shoes, metal cookery, clothing, radio batteries, furniture, motorcycles, and gasoline) flooded into local stores and enticed the population to give up many artisanal goods (e.g., sugar candy) for these new commodities.

While the population's plight went largely unaddressed, some antipoverty initiatives did both ease their material affliction and reshape the organization of village life. One of the most important development projects underway in Passarinho in 2002 involved the World Bank in the building of household cisterns that captured rainfall for drinking water. The World Bank's Fighting Rural Poverty Project began during the 1990s as part of the decentralization of the bank's development funding. In conjunction with each state government's bureau of planning, the bank funneled a certain number of cistern projects to the Municipal Community Aid Fund (Fundo Municipal de Apoio Comunitário—FUMAC), whose councils then selected the villages to receive them. The FUMAC leadership was elected by assembly, and council positions were highly sought-after by municipal politicians. At the village level, Passarinho's inhabitants organized themselves into "community development associations" in order to become legally qualified beneficiaries of such development projects. These village development associations were heir to the Catholic mobilization efforts of the liberationist priests and lay clergy who were active from the 1960s to the 1980s. They met in the village chapels and sometimes read from the Bible before initiating monthly meetings.

Racism against darker-skinned residents was subtle but pervasive during my time in Passarinho. Like most Brazilians, the people of Passarinho show traces of Portuguese, African, and Indigenous descent. Most everyone denied any kinship with the "wild Indians of the underbrush," who were confined, expelled, enslaved, or massacred by the colonizers (Mott 1985: 128). They usually referred to themselves as white (*branco*) or brown (*moreno* or *mulato*); the word for black (*negro*) was mostly used as an insult. Polite talk about race entailed referring to a dark-skinned person in a way that situated them in the middle of a black-to-white racial continuum—a subject of considerable academic debate (Harris 1956; Wagley 1963; Skidmore 1993; Hanchard 1994; Sheriff 2001; Sansone 2003; Mitchell 2013). But older people still recall a time when the racial divide was sharp, when town dances occurred in two adjacent salons: one for brancos, the other for negros. Moreover, while cordiality among people of all skin colors was generally the norm of street culture, racist assumptions about nonwhites (promiscuity, laziness, stupidity, deceitfulness) abounded.

Any overview of Passarinho would be incomplete without mentioning the problem of hunger that became so focal for the Lula administration. Hunger appeared to be a genuine problem in Passarinho during my stay. I saw its traces most days, but I never attempted to quantify it. Representing hunger numerically is always messy anyway. Scientists have many ways of classifying hunger into types and subtypes, and the meaning of their terms ("famine," "light"/"medium"/"severe hunger," "acute"/"chronic malnutrition," "wasting," "starvation," "food insecurity," etc.) differs among researchers. Even terms that are defined with precision cannot be diagnosed with precision because there is no objective caloric minimum below which life and activity may be jeopardized. No single medical test can reveal an individual's level of nutritional deprivation. Tests for hunger-related symptoms, such as stunted growth, presuppose a normal body size, but genetic variation means that a well-nourished body of smaller stature can be mistaken for a malnourished one. Despite these problems of measurement, it may be useful here to consider a basic conceptual distinction between chronic and acute food deprivation (even if scientists sometimes use different terms to gloss this distinction). People suffering from acute deprivation do not ingest sufficient calories to function actively throughout the day. They will at some point experience the physical sensation of hunger, even though this sensation may actually subside as the condition progresses (Sorokin 1975: 63). People suffering from chronic deprivation (i.e., malnutrition) may eat enough food to function for days or weeks, but their diets lack sufficient nutrients (due to either low quantity or poor quality of food) to ensure sound health and development over months and years. They may or may not feel actual *hunger* in their stomachs, but they are prone to fatigue, headaches, anxiety, or delirium, and they grow susceptible to disease (Castro 2003 [1952]: 191; Scheper-Hughes 1992: 128–67). In practice, the line between acute and chronic deprivation blurs, but the distinction nonetheless helps us to understand the face of hunger in Passarinho.

The Zero Hunger program's own nutritional diagnostic (done in early 2003) pointed to a prevalence of chronic "malnutrition" in Passarinho that was twice as bad as that of northeast Brazil in general, and 3.5 times worse than Brazil's national average (CESACF 2003: section 5.2.1.2). Chronic malnutrition was nearly twice as prevalent in the rural zone as it was in the town hub and probably affected about 10 percent of all village residents. The data also suggested that women and children had higher rates of chronic hunger than adult men.[20] These data probably masked racial disparities in hunger. Villages comprised of Afro-Brazilians tended to be farther from the municipal hub, their residents had smaller plots of lands, and they often lacked land documents. In the town, darker-skinned people lived in poorer houses farther from the main commercial strip, and often outside the town's power grid.[21]

In general, Passarinho's residents were very concerned with the poverty that circumscribed their lives. They wanted "to advance" in both their physical infrastructure and their mentality, which they often claimed was backward and "ignorant." Wealth and knowledge were associated with the city, though active membership in a development association also carried the implication of "forward-looking" personhood. Virtually everyone in these villages greeted outsiders with the hope that they would bring some tangible resource to the community and their modern aura would rub off. This attitude extended to the Zero Hunger agents, and to me.

My Place in Passarinho

My own involvement with these matters began in Rio de Janeiro in the summer of 2001. A graduate student still fumbling with my Portuguese, I had found my way to the city's PT headquarters, where the general secretary and other staff befriended me. By late 2002, I had resolved to write an ethnographic study of the party's institutional culture and the mechanisms its leadership was using to marginalize its more radical factions. I abandoned that project after my father died in the spring of 2003. Pursuing it would have meant falling into the flirtations of Rio's tourist-oriented south zone, where I would have buried my guilt at having spent his last few years away from home. I was about to quit my graduate study when I learned that Lula would pilot his flagship social policy in the desert. Hoping to find solace in the sertão, I applied for funding to study Zero Hunger "on the ground." The desert didn't bring the peace I had hoped, but it let me feel part of something meaningful.

When I arrived in the town adjacent to Passarinho in June 2003, Zero Hunger's regional contact person was nowhere to be found. But I did find a local development consultant, Benedito, who befriended me and took me around town. Benedito was one of the two de facto leaders of Passarinho's Zero Hunger Management Committee (see chapter 7). He was also deeply involved in local politics, which had begun to "heat up" in anticipation of the 2004 municipal elections. Benedito took me into Passarinho's rural zone while he collected information about villagers that the committee then used in considering people's eligibility for the Food Card. Along the way, he introduced me to his "friends," two of whom proved very important to my research.

The first was Jorge, a town-dwelling man my age who became my field assistant, and whose father, godfather (a town councilman), and twelve siblings adopted me. Jorge hated the erstwhile mayor, Rodrigo. He had been working as a municipal security guard when the mayor asked all municipal employees to sign a waiver of their right to three months' wages that had gone unpaid because the mayor's son-in-law had robbed the municipal coffers. Jorge refused and the mayor banished him to a remote, largely Afro-Brazilian village that I will call Caixa de Água, where Jorge was assigned to guard a malfunctioning well. Jorge facilitated my entry into this village and several others that became very important to my research. While I was away from Passarinho, Jorge collected genealogical information about the villagers. He didn't like that work. Jorge much preferred to talk to me about local political intrigue, the aid that his godfather had given to families, the opposition candidate for mayor, Rodrigo's malfeasance as mayor, and the foibles of his would-be successor. Jorge told me these stories as loud as he could, inviting others to listen and chime in, and knowing that his own prestige was rising because he had the ear of the American. When I left the town hub to live in the outlying villages, I asked Jorge to keep a journal on these matters and others related to Zero Hunger's implementation in the town. He enjoyed this far more than the kinship diagrams, and he did not feel jeopardized by it. I told him not to write anything in the journals that he would not want others to see. He agreed but made it clear to me that I still needed to exercise discretion when speaking of matters he recorded.

The second of Benedito's friends was Henrique, a semiliterate rancher (and market and butcher shop owner) who had lost two elections to the incumbent mayor, Rodrigo, and was gearing up for a campaign against Rodrigo's successor in 2004. (I mentioned him in the introduction.) Henrique was laconic and beguiling. He spoke with oblique metaphors that presupposed my allegiance to his political faction. When I first entered his truck and looked for the safety belt, he stopped me. "The safety around here is us," he said with a wink. Henrique assured me of his imminent electoral victory: "The sun rises and sets. Today Rodrigo, tomorrow Henrique." He courted my friendship for strategic reasons. He was, like many Passarinho politicians, out of his element when it came to the increasingly technical discourse of development and public administration. He communicated very well with the cultivators from the region, but he grew awkward and self-conscious when it was time to "talk pretty" in the presence of state agents and urban sophisticates. Generally speaking, it was good for Henrique to be seen around town with me in his truck. Keeping my company made him look forward-thinking, technocratically savvy, and—though he never used the word—democratic. Aside from my accent, he barely noticed my nationality. He once told me, "In my mind you are like Paulo [the visiting development agent from the neighboring state of Bahia]. You two are here not to mix into politics but just to help the people." Still, he knew that just as our friendship made him appear more modern, it also made my persona more partisan.

When I returned to Passarinho for my main field stint (January 2004– December 2005), I tried to avoid close contact with Henrique in order to maintain political neutrality, professional objectivity, and cordiality with Rodrigo's faction. I was also facing an ethical problem: While anthropology's code of ethics permits exchange relations with informants, especially when it accords with the informants' own morality, many of my peers considered patronage relations to be a form of political oppression. Did my friendship with Henrique support his patronage network and thus undermine the democratization of Passarinho? If so, was I working against the interests of my informants—something our code of ethics certainly does prohibit? The situation was further complicated by the fact that I was also dealing with another group of informants, the Zero Hunger officials, who I argue were trying to dismantle intimate hierarchy in the sertão. Was my friendship with Henrique and others undermining their mission? If so, perhaps I was guilty not only of betraying their confidence but also of imperialism—a U.S. citizen sabotaging a progressive Latin American government's effort to bring social justice to an oppressed population.

Still, I was drawn to Henrique. I had much to learn from him, and he felt familiar. He was my father's height and build, and the two were both prone to elliptical speech and sentimentality. As a labor lawyer, my father had represented Jimmy Hoffa's teamsters in the 1950s (and other unions since). His was a world of heroes who fought for working people, and his own heroism involved creative legal thinking that bent the letter of the law in the service of its spirit. Both men took pleasure in their cleverness and crafty subversions of the regulations that would have kept them from "helping people." Like Henrique, my father had also struggled to navigate a world that changed faster than he could keep up. I felt protective of Henrique. His political adversary had a college education and a greater facility with the urbane registers of development. I never tried to help Henrique win the election in 2004, but I may have nonetheless. And once he won, I helped to broker his relationship with Zero Hunger officials from the capital.

To some extent, my factional identification was out of my hands. In the sertão, factional identity resides not in one's mental interior but rather in one's position within a configuration of social relations. As soon as I started walking around with Henrique, Benedito, and Jorge, members of the opposing faction greeted me as ready-made enemies no matter how impartial my talk. The mayor refused to shake my hand, and his allies looked away when I approached. Even those who liked me personally would not speak with me inside their homes but only on the porch, where everyone could see that we were not talking politics. Conversely, even the people from Henrique's faction who did not like me became my friends when I needed them, transmitting messages and materials, and rushing me to the hospital during an ugly bout of dysentery.

I did insist to Henrique on my full independence in relating to the Zero Hunger officials from the capital cities, especially those from Brasília and Teresina. Henrique's position vis-à-vis Zero Hunger was friendly but complicated. The mayor, Rodrigo, had been a longtime enemy of the PT, and Henrique's sister led the PT's local chapter in Passarinho. But Henrique himself had broken away from the PT in 2002 and joined a local right-wing party (though he did not think about politics in terms of a left-right political spectrum). With respect to the Zero Hunger officials and the state-level PT, Henrique practiced the old *jogo de cintura* ("game of the waist"), the art of "managing in the shadow of an apparent smoothness to irritate as little as possible . . . [finding] the middle term . . . perfect equilibrium" (Amado 1947: 122–23; quoted in Schmitter 1971: 71). As a result, I feared that the state officials would consider me a local liability, but they did not. They understood the fluidity of local political alliances and party affiliations. Moreover, they wanted me to examine the system of *clientelismo* from "the inside," and they took advantage of my familiarity with the many local Zero Hunger initiatives to use me as a guide when they visited the municipality.

The officials invited me to offer constructive criticisms of Zero Hunger, which I did when I traveled to Teresina (about ten hours by bus). I would spend days loitering about their office in the city center and sharing with them information about which aspects of their programs were "working" in Passarinho and which were not. This was tricky. I didn't want to do anything that would cause the state to withdraw investment from any local community. When I made this concern clear to them, they honored it, saying that their goal was just to refine the program models that would be implemented elsewhere. I believe they had a right to use me to evaluate the effectiveness of their projects. After all, they had given me formal interviews, private confessions, total access to documents, and introductions to federal officials in MESA. The closer my relationships with the officials became, the more we quarreled like colleagues. As I became an insider, I took it on myself to defend Zero Hunger's image to the outside world. The few times when the popular media interviewed me about Zero Hunger (as an "objective outsider") my remarks were polemical, highlighting the existence and success of Zero Hunger "local policies" to counter allegations of assistencialismo. I was even combative in a televised interview when I thought the reporter was fishing for dirt on the program.

Eventually, I think the state officials in Teresina intuited that my entanglement with local patrons was politically advantageous to them. If Henrique were to win the municipal election in 2004 (which he did), the officials would eventually have to work with him. My connection to him allowed me to "make the bridge" between the PT state government and Henrique's administration. I later reinforced this "bridge" when the local PT forged a surprising alliance with Rodrigo's faction, giving Henrique added incentive to criticize the Zero Hunger program. My continual vocal support for Zero Hunger in Passarinho dissuaded him from doing so. Had I been I allied with the local PT (or Rodrigo), I would have proven politically redundant to the state officials.

As for my relationships with the cultivators living in villages, I was a source of humor, hope, and disappointment. Few villagers knew where the United States was, or even that it existed at all. I had come to them from someplace far away like the Japanese and Israeli agronomists that some of the men had met while working seasonally on irrigation projects in Petrolina, a city in the neighboring state of Pernambuco. But they realized that I was not smart like those men; I knew nothing of farming except what they told me. My saving grace was my "good heart" (also the mark of a good patron), which was manifest to them by my choice to live in their villages "at the end of the world" and to help them "move forward." This I did by convincing politicians to sponsor the documentation of people's lands and to pay for the identification cards that people needed to register to vote. I also tried and failed to coordinate a small-scale irrigation project in one village.

The thing I did that most pleased my village friends was to build two Catholic chapels and refurbish two more. (The funds came from the Catholic congregation, Calvert House, at the University of Chicago.) These chapels were the only public space in the villages where the development associations could meet. Only one village had an Evangelical church; the congregants of the Assembly of God largely resided in the town hub, and their pastor frowned on any secular use of his churches. He did not appreciate my chapel renovations, but when I told him I was a Jew with no interest in supporting Catholicism except as a means to promote rural development, he relaxed his opposition. Being Jewish was useful. Very few people knew what Judaism was, and it puzzled them that anyone could believe in God but not Jesus. This was disarming for the people who were invested in religious rivalries, and thus it was helpful to me. I could tack back and forth between Catholic mass and the Evangelical services. I could discuss notions of divinity with them without inciting conflict, and they stopped trying to convert me when I told them that "my people understand being Jewish as a born condition, like being a man or a woman."

A final issue merits mention: I mostly refrained from giving money to people even if I believed they were hungry. I found it hard to refuse the few people—mostly alcoholics—who asked me directly. I would simply hide from them, as did many villagers who knew those neighbors who were likely to corner them with such requests. I did, however, give people gifts of food (usually a couple of kilograms of rice or beans) if they received me in their home for a visit or gave me an interview. These I framed as repayments to them so as not to engender a sense of debt. There were also a thousand other favors given and received, other exchanges that I brokered, and plenty of practice for my own jogo de cintura. I relate some of these in the pages that follow.

Fieldwork in this context was ethically and emotionally disorienting. I've tried to turn that experience into a book that is intellectually and politically coherent in its appreciation of intimate hierarchy, and state policy toward it. The reader will no doubt observe that there are some ambiguities that I cannot resolve, and some forms of intimate hierarchy that still unsettle me.

CHAPTER TWO

Hunger, Envy, and Egalitarianism in Passarinho

One day I was sitting with a very impoverished, middle-aged village man, Adenísio, when I heard his teenage daughter, Fátima, crying violently from inside his doorless house. Her mother had scolded her after learning that a group of village women had gossiped that Fátima's hunger-induced envy might have been responsible for the death of a neighbor's cow. Fátima cried out, "I didn't do anything. I did look at the cow, but I didn't admire it. Looking is one thing; admiring is another. Mama, I wasn't admiring it! Old, ugly cow! I didn't even stop for one minute. I went straight to the field to bring Papa his lunch."

By the time this event occurred, I was already aware that in Passarinho many believe that people are constantly battling internal forces that can slip out of the body and destroy certain kinds of property. They express this belief through talk about the evil eye. A person who emits the evil eye performs no rite, utters no spell, and possesses no medicines. The act is a psychic one, the outward consequence of an inner emotion: envy.[1]

Envy for Passarinho's villagers was (and still is) an ocular experience. It was tied to a system of intravillage household stratification that was based on visible and visually impressive forms of wealth, what I call "ocular wealth." As was the case in many other rural societies where evil eye belief was present, the giver of the eye did not necessarily feel any ill will toward the possessor of a coveted object (Maloney 1976: vii–viii). Rather, the eye responded automatically to the emotion of envy. It reacted by distending (invisibly) into the airspace surrounding the desired object and polluting this air with a profane miasma that dried crops, slayed cattle, spoiled food and water, caused houses to collapse, and even killed small children (Kearney 1996: 180; Rebhun 1994: 375; Ansell 2009: 104). People whose bodies were in good force (*força*) were better able to contain their envious impulse to emit evil. Both physical exertion and hunger undermined the body's inner force and thus facilitated the spread of envious evil. Hunger both spurred the envy of others' food and weakened "the blood," reducing the body's capacity to contain envy within its borders. The body's força could also be drained by the temptation caused by attractive property, which led people to "admire" such ocular splendor, and thus destroy it. Because the unfortunate owner of the stricken ocular wealth understood that well-intended people can emit the eye, he or she typically did not seek direct retribution from the suspected offender. Rather, the victim dealt with the evil eye by paying local prayer-sayers to remove the sickness (especially for afflicted children) before death occurred (cf. Rebhun 1994: 371–73). Yet, in practice, suspicions regarding the culprit always made their way into local gossip that could have real effects on the suspected party.

As I sat on the plank of wood outside Adenísio's house mutely taking in Fátima's drama, I tried to imagine her carrying a cup of salted rice and beans to Adenísio—the family had virtually no access to meat—and seeing the magnificent cow on the road, somebody else's beef. I imagined the smell of the meal in her hands perking up her appetite, making her want to eat her father's food to take her mind off the cow. I imagined her bringing the humble lunch to Adenísio, feeling guilty that it contained no meat for him, guilty that she wanted to take his food, and angry that he could not provide beef for her like the owner of the cow could for his daughter. And I imagined Adenísio thinking about the gossip, worrying that suspicions like these would make it difficult for him to find labor partners. Indeed, I noted that he always worked alone in his field.

"Never have I come to anybody's house" (*Nunca cheguei na casa de ninguém*) was the stereotypic boast that Adenísio and other rural people used to attest to their virtue. The phrase is a euphemism for "asking for charity," as well as a literal description of the way people approach the open doors of others' houses at the dinner hour in a wordless appeal for food. I had never seen Adenísio "come to anybody's house," but I had seen his wife and daughter do just that. Did they ever tell him where they were? Did he send them? Was this the silent trauma of their household? Did their wanderings from door to door reflect only on them or on Adenísio as well? Was this the reason the other men didn't want to work with him? Rather than answering these questions directly, let me situate this family's predicament in the context of village life.

Most of the cultivator families who I came to know did not live their lives in hunger as Adenísio's family did. But they witnessed his hunger and that of a few other families around them, and they harbored memories of bad droughts when they themselves experienced hunger. They knew that fortune could change and that they might one day know hunger again. Just as important, cultivators feared the hungry people who lived among them, or rather, they feared the evil power that they ascribed to these people. Thus, most people went to great lengths to avoid being suspected of hunger.

The stigma the cultivators placed on hunger impacted their engagement with the Zero Hunger program both directly and indirectly. I observed its most direct effects in the unwillingness of impoverished people to identify themselves as "hungry," and thus to step forward and receive Zero Hunger resources such as the Food Card. More subtly, hunger (and its stigma) fit into a broader array of practices that cultivators used to manage the emotions, labor, and goods that circulated in their villages. This general logic of signs, sentiments, and actions also shaped the way people responded to state antipoverty policies like Zero Hunger and Bolsa Família. In the remainder of this chapter, I elaborate this logic in order to depict the tone of interhousehold relations in Passarinho's villages.

No anthropologist can write about hunger in northeast Brazil without acknowledging Nancy Scheper-Hughes's enormous landmark study *Death without Weeping: The Violence of Everyday Life in Brazil* (1992). The book is a trenchant and moving treatise on hunger in a shantytown in Pernambuco's sugar plantation zone. At its heart is an attack on a cultural relativistic anthropology that "sidesteps entirely the question of the ethical" (21). Scheper-Hughes faults scholars who "sanitized and aestheticized" human suffering by casting hunger and famine as "symbolic categories used in organizing relations, ordering experience, or expressing or mediating contradictions" (131–32). Her alternative is to confront the physical harshness of hunger, especially among poor mothers who deny "compassion, emphatic love, and care" to their starving babies (22). Even a mother's love, she claims, can be deferred until she believes her baby will survive. If she thinks it will die, she practices "selective neglect," allotting scarce food only to her viable children. In short, hunger disrupts the deepest of human sentiments, a mother's love.

Many of Scheper-Hughes's insights into hunger in the lush *zona da mata* apply to the arid sertão. Especially valuable is her claim that rural Brazilians see their bodies as a "battleground" where the life force (*força*) that is the source of their "strength, grace, beauty and power" must contend with the debilitating labor that uses them up, waists them away, sucks them dry, and renders them worthless and disgraced (187–89). In Passarinho, similar ideas undergird people's anxieties about the body's emission of an evil force that destroys family wealth and erodes the moral fabric of interhousehold relations. Another critical insight of Scheper-Hughes's argument is that "food separates the self-respecting poor . . . from the miserable and the truly wretched," and that this distinction promotes the stigmatization of hunger (158). This point holds true for Passarinho as well. Finally, Scheper-Hughes convincingly asserts that the medical arm of the Brazilian state has been complicit in misrepresenting rural hunger by treating its symptoms (anxiety, nausea, fatigue, etc.) as an independent medical condition rather than as a basic problem of access to food. Her book should thus be regarded as an important contribution to the food movement of that decade discussed in my chapter 1.

Yet the ethnographic account I offer in this chapter differs from that of Scheper-Hughes in my interpretation of shared labor, interhousehold sociality, and the place of hunger in the ethno-anatomical beliefs of Passarinho's cultivators.[2] Scheper-Hughes depicts rural people's collective labor (mutirão) as an assertion of solidarity in the face of everyday hardship. I am reluctant to affirm her characterization of collective rural labor as an "open and balanced reciprocity" expressive of rural poor's "generosity of spirit" (98). This romantic description serves two functions in Scheper-Hughes's ethnography: First, it mitigates her harsh depiction of selective child neglect and other ugly survival tactics. Second, it supports her condemnation of patronage. I argue that it is misleading to idealize egalitarian labor as an "ethic of open and balanced reciprocity" that "enhances class solidarity," just as it is misleading to reduce vertical exchanges to "servility, dependency and loyalty to those who oppress and exploit" the poor (98).[3] In fact, Passarinho's villagers are very apprehensive when they forge egalitarian labor relations with one another for reasons that pertain to their ideas about the body and its uncontrollable forces. These exchanges may be "balanced" but they do not indicate "class solidarity." And if by "open" Scheper-Hughes means a spirit of all-inclusiveness, then the data from Passarinho refute that claim as well. These issues are important because, if we acknowledge the delicate politics of horizontal work arrangements in village life, then we must recognize that it is not only the state and the dominant classes that hide and stigmatize hunger; Brazil's impoverished villagers do this as well. Moreover, once we see that such depictions of rural life are grounded in a very modern nostalgia we can understand why Passarinho's villagers were confused when state officials attributed to them labor arrangements that seemed quite alien.

Collective Labor:
State Fantasy, Rural Reality, and Social Change

The Brazilian sociologist Antonio Candido (2001 [1948]: 88) wrote romantically of collective labor in the sertão when he defined the term *mutirão* as "essentially a meeting of neighbors, invited by one of them in order to complete a given job: burning the underbrush, field-clearing, planting, harvesting, building a house, etc. Generally the neighbors are called and the beneficiary offers them some food and a party when the job is over. But there is no direct remuneration, unless one counts the moral obligation of the beneficiary to respond to similar calls to assistance in the eventual future." The hearty image of peasant villagers working together in harmonious unison is hardly unique to the Brazilian imagination. It is typical of a global fantasy in which people living outside of, or prior to, capitalism live in warmth and mutual support (Kearney 1996).

Like many progressive projects throughout history (e.g., Russian populism of the late nineteenth century), Zero Hunger's designers would find in this image a "political quality of the peasant . . . that worked to convert the so-called backwardness of the peasant into a historical advantage" (Chakrabarty 2007: 48). In reference to rural India, Dipesh Chakrabarty explains that in this fantasy "the peasant, uncorrupted by the self-tending individualism of the bourgeois and oriented to the needs of his or her community, was imagined as someone already endowed with the capacity to usher in a modernity different and more communitarian than what was prevalent in the West" (ibid.). It's probably fair to say that Zero Hunger officials were tempted to adopt this attitude toward the rural beneficiaries.

The image of "the peasant" as a collectivist creature at odds with capitalist individualism is ironically compatible with the neoliberal effort to extract value from small family farmers. Neoliberalism, whatever else it may entail, is also a project defined by the search for economic value in the sentimental spaces of everyday life (Muehlebach 2011). Brazilian state officials regarded the mutirão as the warm sentimental architecture needed to shift Zero Hunger's center of gravity from "emergency" policies to more "structural" ones, in other words, to those that involved collective management. This would allow the state to terminate its cash grant policies. (This logic was later rescinded with the advent of Bolsa Família.) The term *mutirão* thus came to saturate Zero Hunger discourse. Virtually every Zero Hunger initiative that involved cooperation among beneficiaries framed that cooperation as "mutirão," and national Zero Hunger rhetoric characterized the citizen's volunteer contributions to the program as participation in a "great mutirão against hunger." But Passarinho's cultivators did not experience mutirão labor as a happy outpouring of community fraternalism.

First of all, in rural Passarinho, mutirão labor made up only a small portion of the cultivators' agricultural practices. The mutirão was associated primarily with the processing of sugarcane into rapadura (artisanal sugar bricks) and the processing of the manioc tuber into farinha (manioc meal sprinkled on food to make it more calorically robust). However, sugar and manioc were declining in importance in 2003. The growth of local grocery stores and increased access to cash had made refined sugar and factory-made farinha more popular in the region. This represented a substantial vitamin and mineral loss; the artisanal varieties were richer in nutrients (Oliveira et al. 2007). The old wooden *engenhos* (sugar-presses) and the *casas de aviação* (manioc-processing facilities) had deteriorated. I only saw them on the property of older people, and none had been built after the 1980s.

The mutirão practices involved in sugar and manioc processing had never been entirely egalitarian, nor did they unite entire villages in a shared activity. These processes had hierarchical aspects and gave rise to competition within and across extended families. The senior man of an extended, patriarchal family commanded the labor process, telling his sons and junior brothers when it was time to prepare the harvest for the mutirão (which lasted between one and three days). For the manioc mutirão (the *farinhada*), junior siblings, sons, sons' wives, daughters, and daughters' husbands would bring their tubers to the senior man's property, where he would direct the women and children in peeling the tubers and the men in grinding them into thick pulp. The women and children squeezed some of the pulp into cheesecloth allowing the finer strained bits to collect into *tapioca*, which could then be used to make a few rich pancakes (*beiju*). The rest of the pulp would go into a large press to drain the water and would then be cooked over an enormous grill. The patriarch then divided up the product (dried meal) among the adult participants and sent gifts of beiju to his married children's in-laws. These gifts were not so much expressions of generosity or gratitude as they were tokens of reconciliation, proverbial olive branches, given by one rival to another. The rivalry between a couple's fathers revolved around the fate of the young couple's manioc tubers. In theory, children would bring to one father only the tubers grown on his (and his wife's) fields, fields to which he allowed

FIGURE 4 A village woman grating manioc as part of farinhada mutirão.
Photograph by the author.

the couple usufruct (use and fruits) rights. So young married couples typically participated in two farinhadas with their two stocks (the wife's side and the groom's side) of manioc, but of course they could prioritize either father by bringing to his mutirão some or all of the tubers harvested from the fields of the other father. By showing up with a large basket of tubers, young couples sought to induce a father(-in-law) into giving them a better piece of land than he would allot to their siblings. Competition among fathers-in-law in the mutirão thus also implied competition among siblings and siblings-in-law. It is no surprise that fights between siblings and their spouses often occurred at such events, though they were often blamed on the alcohol that accompanied them.

During my fieldwork, I found that adults between thirty and fifty years old expressed ambivalence when recalling the days when mutirão labor was more common in their lives. Many said that they were glad to be out from under the control of their fathers, and to be able to make decisions about planting and harvesting as they saw fit. Yet some people seemed remorseful about the matter. One woman from town fondly recalled the rapadura mutirão, not so much for the event itself but because "Father would take money from the sale of our rapadura and buy me a new dress. My brothers wanted it for themselves, but Father would look out for me. . . . we have lost respect for our fathers [parents] now." Such comments were typical of people who missed their parental protection, and I suspect that some even felt guilty for paying less respect to their parents. As I will later show, both their positive and negative feelings about collective labor affected rural people's engagement with Zero Hunger development projects that sought to induce their nostalgia for the bygone era of mutirão cooperation.

Rather than collective mutirão, it was the dyadic (two-person) labor arrangement that predominated during my fieldwork. Each year, two men formed a "day-trading" compact (*troca de dia*); one day the two would work together on one man's field, and the next day they would work on the other's field. (This was especially common for men without grown sons.) Men traded days with kin and nonkin alike, and sometimes angled for good partners to become brothers-in-law by marrying their sisters. Conversely, sisters would encourage their sweethearts to trade days with their brothers in order to increase their romantic access and family endorsement. Several times, I observed one man playfully refer to his day-trading partner as "brother-in-law" in front of the other man's sister. The man may have been flirting with his partner's sister or teasing his partner, or both. Either way, the brother-in-law and day-trading partner relations are close analogues. Both imply structural equality and shared interest, as well as rivalry and divergent interest (a common formula for joking behavior throughout the world) (Radcliff-Brown 1965).

The divergent interest separating day-trading partners relates to the norm of household independence. Despite their actual dependence on day-trading relations, the cultivators' everyday speech idealized the productive autonomy of their households. A key component of cordial, sociable conduct in village life consisted of recognizing the autonomy of one's fellows, especially nonimmediate kin. Even though households possessed different amounts of land and cattle, household autonomy (i.e., having enough to eat) was the condition that allowed an etiquette of equality to prevail among households. But this was not an equality of intimates. There was a tension between families because, beyond mere autonomy, some fared much better than others.

The tone of social relationships among people of different households could be felt in the forms of address they used during visits to one another's homes. Men and women often addressed one another by their complete first names: Maria do Carmo, José Carlos, José de Sousa, and so on. When inside one another's homes, even siblings and in-laws would use this form of address with one another, regardless of birth order or wealth. When they would pass one another on the side of the road they were more likely to use nicknames, which nearly everyone has. Thus, use of the full first name inside the home gave a tone of formality to interfamilial interactions that evoked the structural tension between families that the house came to signify. The emphatic character of this full-name formality was reinforced by the fact that people would use the full first name multiple times in a single sentence instead defaulting to a pronoun ("you"—*você* or *tu*) after the first use of the proper name. In Passarinho, the conspicuous repetition of someone's first name as a substitution for a second-person pronoun indicates a kind of midlevel respectful form of address.[4] It falls somewhere between the more respectful use of a title (*senhor/a, doutor/a,* etc.) and the more familiar name-then-pronoun. (And it's certainly far more formal than nicknaming.) This use of the repeated first name suggests that the basic tone of interhousehold sociality combined warmth with "diffuse enmity" (Marques 2002: 22).

Ana Claudia Marques (2002) observed during her work in the sertão region of Pernambuco that people from different households interacted cautiously with one another, because the constant, low-grade rivalry they felt could potentially erupt into violence (also see Santos 2012). A code of respectful distance guided relations among households to prevent these rivalries from exploding into long cycles of blood feuding.[5] In Marques's field site, people often said, "Here everybody is friends, each in his [or her] own house" (51). Applicable to Passarinho, this phrase expresses a distinct mode of relating across households that is predicated on a noninvasive mode of sociability, a kind of minding of one's own business that emphasizes the need to steer clear of the other's (ocular) wealth. Thus, people in Passarinho often affirmed their well-mannered sociability by saying, "I want only what is mine." This code of respect does not preclude the existence of friendships among the members of different households, but it suggests that these friendships do not revolve around liberal notions of "expressive individualism," in which one reveals one's inner feelings and thoughts to one's friends (Bellah 1985). Friendship in Passarinho's villages was lived as shared joyfulness (*alegria*), harmony, and festivity.

It is partly because of this idealized household autonomy, and the diffuse enmity that underlay it, that day-trading relationships tended to be ephemeral and fragile, especially when they occurred between men who were not close kin. João, my most important consultant in the village of Caixa de Água, told me that many of his day-trading arrangements had "not turned out right," so he found other men with whom to work in subsequent years. When I probed, he would tell me only that he "didn't like to speak ill of others," and I would let the matter drop. Yet I wanted to know what caused these breakups. I took stock of the individuals João had worked with in the past, and got the impression that a couple of them were gaunt, haggard, and frequent customers of a little bar down by the village reservoir. Once, when João and I stopped at the bar for a few drinks, a man he had once worked with approached us boisterously. "João and I used to work together every day," he exclaimed. "It was me on his field and him on mine, and I hope we can do this again!" João replied with some light, diplomatic affirmation, but when we left he told me that he didn't want the man on his field. The sun was going down as we walked out together. I remember sensing that João was feeling indebted to me that day for lending him my motorcycle. And so I took advantage of his integrity to probe him on the matter again. "Why did you not reinitiate your day-trading relationship with the man in the bar?" "Because he's bad for my crops," João said. These cryptic remarks were not euphemistic references to personal quarrels; they stemmed from deeply entrenched concerns that cultivators had about the danger that a labor partner can pose to living property.

The Visibility of Hunger and Nonhunger

The general fear of hungry people was most easily seen in the mocking language applied to those who were unable to control their urge to eat: they were *comilões* or *esfomeados*. An adolescent boy defined the first term for me: "A *comilão* is that guy who comes to your house while you're dining and eats all your food really fast like an animal. He can't help himself. He can't stand the hunger. He can't control himself." The comilão is a figure that violates the fundamental moral principle of interhousehold life captured by the phrase "I want only what is mine." People who came to bear this stigma often failed to find or retain day-trading partners. Their chances of marrying a desirable spouse—and thus for inheriting good lands from in-laws—diminished. Their parents usually opted to live with other siblings, so they forfeited the benefits that came from a senior resident's rural pension. Falling into drink and despair, these people became *desmantelados* (broken-down people) who begged for food or *enrolões* (tricksters) who swindled or stole food and money from others. Thus, the stigma of uncontrollable hunger isolated them from labor partners in ways that exacerbated hunger itself.

This was one reason why rural people who lived with hunger often hid their neediness. They sometimes stole away from their homes to eat "wild foods" (*comida braba*) such as cactus, roots, bark, eggshells, all of which people regarded as unfit for the dinner plate. Eating "wild foods" publicly was tantamount to an admission of hunger. Yet partaking of such nourishment helped men to ready their bodies for a hard day's work, and to avoid giving off the signs of hunger (fatigue, dizziness, or nausea). One of the few ways I could induce villagers to speak about their hunger was to ask them how long they could work without eating. Most men answered with pride that they could work for two or three days without food. But when I asked them when was the last time they had to do so, they would avoid answering. One man simply laughed and wagged his finger at me.

The concealment of hunger was not a free-standing practice; it fit within a broader set of abstentions, misdirections, avoidances, and other elusive practices by which people protected themselves from evil and the suspicion of evil. For instance, cultivators refrained from talking about all ocular wealth outside the household, and they did not ask members of other households direct questions about such property (Rebhun 1999: 61). They did not stand looking at another's field; they never boasted of any livestock or harvest of their own.

Curiously, cultivators did not seem to exhibit the same concealing behaviors toward their cash. Indeed, they told me that, while it was never good to show off money, the contents of one's purse were not susceptible to evil eye danger. Cash, checks, government welfare cards, all of which I simply call *purse* wealth, were more resistant to evil. Perhaps this was because the different quantities of cash that households possess were a generally poor indication of the underlying distribution of wealth among them. Cash accounted for far less of most families' wealth than crops or livestock, and the distribution of cash was more even across households than holdings in land or cattle.[6] Their more limited concern over purse wealth may also express the fact that ocular wealth reflected one's food and family-oriented labor, whereas cash earned though wages was often spent on booze and prostitutes. This differential susceptibility to evil may partially account for the cultivators' willingness to discuss membership dues, account balances, and the cash in their wallets within the development associations even though they never discussed individuals' land and livestock (Ansell 2009). As I discuss further in chapter 5, when these associations became the beneficiary units of Zero Hunger's participatory development projects, the association members struggled to discuss project details that related to livestock. I would even say that the cultivators' different attitudes toward ocular and purse wealth partly accounted for their preference for Zero Hunger programs like the Food Card (and later Bolsa Família) that channeled cash to them.

The hygienic containment of one's own envy did more than maintain one's personal reputation; it protected the community as a whole. The evil that came from envy had social repercussions for the entire village. Once evil was released into the air, "the wind" could blow it around to the fields of neighbors. Gossip thus condemned ambitious people or braggarts for eliciting others' envy, just as it did to those suspected of emitting envy. The movement of the winds, however, was no accident; God (the Father) regulated the moral order of the village by affecting the weather. God punished people by withholding rain or by blowing the envy-polluted winds in their direction, thus bringing to their doorstep the aggregate community evil to which all villagers, at some point or another, contributed.[7] This may account for the fact that when state officials introduced development projects into the villages I studied, the presidents of both village associations opted not to invite the neediest residents (including Adenísio's family) to join the project. Adenísio "would never be able to make it work," one villager explained to me. "He'll fail and cause other people to fail."

Food-Giving Practices

Despite the cultivators' idealization of their autonomy and their concealment of hunger, they did occasionally provide food to members of other households. These practices were delicate and fraught with the possibility that the helpful party would offend the recipient of charity. Two practices exemplifying this dilemma were dinner invitations and the care-taking of sick women.

As I mentioned earlier, when I dined with João, Elena and Fátima (Adenísio's wife and daughter) would occasionally approach João's doorway. (In fact, João received many similar visits from others at the dinner hour.) The event would always provoke a curious hospitality ritual. João would invariably tell them, "Come in. Eat." Almost always the visitor would refuse, waving him off. "No, no! I ate just this moment before leaving my house!" Whether or not visitors would eventually sit down and join us depended on two things: how sincere they perceived João's invitation to be and whether they could resist the hunger they were feeling. When sincere, João would speak his invitation as soon as the visitors approached. He would smile and look at them as they spoke and not turn back until the other party had either accepted or satisfied him they had already eaten. When João was insincere, he would mumble his invitation a few seconds following the visitors' approach (he often did this with Elena) and speak hunched over his own plate, shielding it from sight with his body. When the visitors declined, he made little effort to cajole them into entering.

This invitation ritual, well-explored in the ethnography of rural Brazil, protected both guest and host from the social stigma and spiritual danger that could easily arise from such a desirous interaction (Candido 1979: 187; Scheper-Hughes 1992: 160). Hosts could not be envied if they shared what was theirs with another. Guests could not be considered *esfomeados* if they refused an invitation to eat. Together, the two parties performed their morality for one another and then felt their way gingerly toward a resolution. But Elena found it hard to perform the obligatory refusals to João's insincere invitations. She would just stand silently, looking into space. I felt very uncomfortable during these moments. So did João and his wife, who usually stood in the kitchen while he and I ate. None of us spoke while Elena lingered in the doorway. We just sat in silence, pretending not to recognize the epic battle that Elena was fighting within her own body.

Food-sharing practices also took the form of caring for the sick, though these practices seemed less frequent than dinner visits. The few times I followed up with questions, I learned that the women's symptoms included anxiety, diarrhea, eye problems, stomach aches, headaches, dizziness, nausea, delirium—all symptoms of chronic hunger (Sorokin 1975: 64; Castro 1952: 229–32; Scheper-Hughes 1992: 167–213). I suspected that women sometimes claimed sickness as a strategic way of getting food to their children without shaming their husbands and jeopardizing their day-trading relations. A woman's declaration of sickness implicated herself, not her husband, in an immediate food problem, as if she were simply too weak to cook food, rather than lacking enough food to prepare. When women brought food to one another they never gave uncooked items; this would perhaps imply that a husband could not provide for his family. Given that a man's successful labor in the field determined the esteem of his household, a woman who claimed sickness to feed her children protected the reputation of her family as a whole (Heredia 1996; Scheper-Hughes 1992: 50). In these cases, then, the dangerous inner state (hunger) remained concealed behind a less threatening one (sickness). That said, the beneficiaries of the food-sharing practices I observed were not the neediest women in the villages. The women who received helpful gifts of food during their sickness seemed to be women who were well-ensconced in extended families that occasionally labored together in mutirão, or they were the wives of men who traded days. The most desperate women (e.g., Elena) seemed isolated and marginalized.

Scheper-Hughes (1992) attributes these egalitarian charity activities to women's critical awareness of the social relations responsible for their hunger. She notes that often women who are taken sick describe their condition as *nervos*. While easily translated as "bad nerves," this folk ailment, Scheper-Hughes argues, expresses a "critical reflection by the poor on their bodies and on the work that has sapped their force and vitality. . . . But *nervos* is also the 'double,' the second and social illness that has gathered around the primary experience of chronic hunger" (195). For Scheper-Hughes, Brazilian doctors warped the folk notion of nervos by treating it as a free-standing psychological condition, rather than a product of hunger. They "transformed [nervos] into something other: a biomedical disease that alienates mind from body and that conceals the social relations of sickness" (1992: 169). Perhaps. But for the folk category nervos to express a robust "critical reflection" on the social causes of hunger, it would also have to include a self-critique. In Passarinho, poor people reinforced the stigma of hunger, and this stigma isolated the poorest members of a village from the shared labor relations that could otherwise have helped them escape hunger.

Reckoning with Culpability

I do not mean to blame the poor for the problem of hunger in northeast Brazil, though I acknowledge opening myself to that accusation. Passarinho's structural circumstances—the size of the cultivators' fields, the price of their crops, their access to water and other resources, and so on—are the root causes of their suffering. But acting within that structural context, which they generally saw as natural, they treated some of their fellows with honor and compassion and others they left to fend for themselves. The tone of this neglect was not callous but anxious. It derived from an experience of community in which kinship, poverty, and morality were linked together such that the fate of the village as a whole hinged on the containment of evil.

My objection to romantic characterizations of egalitarian interhousehold relations is that they displace the violence within community life to the outside. They are attempts at purification, and as such they invite the scapegoating of some other group, such as the state doctors, market middlemen, or patrons. These groups certainly do play a role in reproducing village poverty. But the intricacies of the part they play, the structural conditions they're responding to, and their constructive engagements with poverty are too easily obscured by misplaced hostility that results from romantic orientations toward village community. In the next chapter, I examine villagers' relationships with local politicians, the very hierarchical intimacies that the Zero Hunger program sought to dismantle.

CHAPTER THREE

Intimate Hierarchy and Its Counters

In 2004 the conservative mayor, Rodrigo, had served his maximum two terms and could not run again. The man he chose to succeed him was less popular, so the opposition candidate—the wealthy rancher, Henrique— had his first real chance to capture the mayoralty. With a particularly vital contest brewing, municipal politics ran "hot" that year. Family members with different allegiances grew estranged, casual acquaintances became the best of friends, and day-trading partnerships between people with different allegiances strained and sometimes broke. The informal rules of engagement generally discouraged physical violence, but a few boozy fistfights had broken out in the town hub as the campaign approached its climax in October, the voting month.

The political season (*época da política*) occurs once every two years in Brazil, where elections for municipal office alternate with those for state and federal ones. Yet it is only during the municipal elections (once every four years) "that these municipalities divide themselves . . . with a factional distribution of the very physical spaces of the city . . . more radical than can be imagined" (Palmeira 1996: 43–44; also see Heredia 1996; Chaves 2003; and Villela 2005, 2012). In practice, the municipal political season begins several months before the onset of the official campaign (July through October). The sociology of egalitarian and vertical relations transforms during this period. If during normal time individuals can engage in vertical exchanges with rival elites, no such option is available during political time. Rather, the political contest among elites "polarizes the life of the localities [villages] in the [rural] interior between 'incumbency' and 'opposition,' especially in the town centers" (Palmeira 1996: 42). Any new or rearranged alliances that have formed during the prior three years as a result of favors, fights, affairs, lawsuits, and so on, have to be either abandoned or integrated into one of the two warring factions that emerge. Thus, two voting factions form in the town, each of which has a rival mayoral candidate at its head, though the hierarchy is vague from there on down. Participation in these factions is public and boisterous. People often post stickers of their preferred candidates on their doors and motorcycles, announcing their affiliations to the world, but the secrecy of the actual voting act is honored.

In addition to this sociological transformation, there is an emotional shift during political time. During the political period, vertical alliances between common people and politicians (and also egalitarian alliances among the politician's supporters) reach their most intimate phase. People share embarrassing secrets with one another, including criminal activities that could cost them face in their communities or forfeit elections for politicians. The flip side of this intimacy is a feeling of wrath toward those "of the other side." In 2004 a kind of paranoia set over the municipality, such that accidents and other things that go wrong were frequently attributed to the shadowy malfeasance of the rival faction. "They [the other faction] know only how to destroy things," people would say. "Our side knows how to work." When they reflected on the social divisions that set in during this time, most people claimed to despise the political season. But when I pressed one man on the matter, he confessed that the political season was the time when he felt most alive.

While chapter 2 was concerned with the horizontal relationships among cultivator households, this chapter examines the vertical exchanges through which relatively wealthy municipal politicians (most of whom resided in the town hub) provided poor people with material resources in exchange for their political support.

The PT officials who condemned such exchanges drew on the scholarly work of Brazilian social historians, who had an arsenal of terms derived from investigations of rural politics during the twentieth century. The most famous was *coronelismo* ("the politics of the colonels"), Victor Nunes Leal's term for the power dynamic of the First Republic (1889–1930), when the rural bosses (to whom the emperor had once awarded the title of colonel) gained votes from the poor by channeling to them state and federal resources, and thus managed to cling to power despite their declining private wealth (Leal 1977 [1948]). Other terms from Brazilian social history included *voto de cabresto* (literally a "bridled vote"), the practice whereby "colonels" hired mercenaries (*capangas, pistoleiros*) to coerce peasants to vote as they commanded under threat of violence from local strongmen, and the related *curral eleitoral* (literally, "electoral corral"), which referred to the region where people's votes were under the colonel's control. These terms date back an era before the secret ballot was initiated (1925), when regional agricultural bosses owned substantially larger portions of land and peasant families often lived on those lands by the grace of their patrons, and literacy requirements for voting (lifted only in 1985) either excluded the rural population from the polls or greatly facilitated their manipulation by local bosses (Holston 2008: 102–3; also see Nicolau 2002). Thus, I argue that these terms provided an outdated caricature of Passarinho's electoral relations that failed to grasp the shape of those relations in the early twenty-first century.

Another discursive current among Zero Hunger officials (and some local activists) described all vertical electoral alliances as "vote-buying" (*compra de voto*). While vote-buying and coronelismo seem intertwined, vote-buying does not presuppose any relationship between the two parties other than an immediate transaction. Thus, when state officials alleged that local politicians turned the vote into a "commodity" (*mercadoria*), they evoked not the classical image of land-oligarch patronage but the perils of a pure market relation between individuals who cared nothing about one another aside from what they could glean in their transaction. Both ways of looking at political exchange were flawed in my view, either anachronistic in the case of the language of coronelismo, or a projection of the commodity form in the case of "vote-buying." (The term *clientelismo* seemed to float back and forth between these two frames of meaning.)

The state officials overestimated the role of both elite coercion and commodification in rural political exchange. In so doing, they ignored the moral distinctions that Passarinho's citizens used to evaluate different vertical exchange relationships. The people of Passarinho distinguished between honorable and dishonorable varieties of hierarchical exchange in electoral politics. Honorable exchanges emerged from, and in turn constituted, intimate (i.e., mutually vulnerable) ties between unequals; dishonorable, commodified exchanges allowed for no such intimacies. These distinctions between intimate and commodified exchange are crucial because they impacted people's engagement with the Zero Hunger program. State officials generated confusion when they equated all such exchanges with "vote-buying" or old-style coronelismo. In the following sections, I explore the conventional distinctions that Passarinho's inhabitants make between intimate and commodified political exchange, as well as the recent disruptions to this conventional system. I deepen my analysis of these different types of exchange by looking at features related to their temporality (time dimension). I then explore recent shifts in political exchange that have coincided with the monetization of Passarinho's economy and the emergence of grassroots activism.

The Cycles and Scales of Politics

Factionalism runs so much deeper during the municipal election because it is at this local level that the electoral contest directly involves known persons, and because it involves them in the distribution of limited goods (e.g., municipal jobs). Goods are limited either because they come from finite informal funding streams that originate with higher-up legislators (state or federal) or because they consist of official government projects that are scarce. Either way, people tend to see the mayor's office (*prefeitura*) as a space where these resource streams pool, and where they get redistributed. In parallel to the prefeitura's general reservoir, political figures opposed to the mayor tap into specific resource streams from allies at higher levels who may or may not hold public office at a given time and channel these to rural families. From the perspective of Passarinho's inhabitants, the local allocation of all these resources works through local, transgenerational relations that they see as distinct from the networks that determine resource flows at higher levels of government. For this reason, reference to "the government" (*o governo*) excludes the prefeitura and the town council (*câmara*). It is as if people imagine the municipality as a separate animal whose functions are sustained through several umbilical cords.

For this reason, poor people's votes at higher levels of the polity are often determined by their local allegiances; allied politicians suggest that their supporters vote for certain legislators (state and federal) because these are the local politician's benefactors who send down resources that allow the local politician "to work for the people." Yet local politicians exercise far less influence over poor people's choices of president and governor, because these executive posts are more removed from the small resource streams that come into local individuals' control. The population uses television and radio media to decide its executive votes, and this results in a splitting phenomenon: left-wing politicians like Lula captured over 65 percent of Passarinho's votes in 2002, while the same population repeatedly elected the PT's conservative adversaries to both local office and to legislative posts at the state and federal levels. Passarinho's residents see nothing unusual or contradictory about this pattern, but schol-ars of Brazilian politics generally believe that this system of political in-tegration shores up the power of conservative state oligarchs throughout the sertão and the Northeast in general (Leal 1977 [1948]; Samuels 2003; Woodard 2005). Certainly left-wing executives come to office with very little support from conservative legislatures, and so they tend to imple-ment progressive policies by executive decree, rather than through legisla-tive channels that generally produce longer-lasting decisions.

Legally, the two rival factions are multiparty coalitions. The parties themselves are registered in Brasília, but they are highly ephemeral and fragmentary. The "ideological" convictions of small parties are a matter known and debated mainly by the urban elites and middle classes (Main-waring 1995: 376). In the small, northeastern municipalities, ideological designators like "left-wing" and "right-wing" are known and used by only a few people. (I will discuss this toward the end of this chapter.) As such, political parties (organizations ostensibly bound by left- or right-wing ide-ological convictions) make no sense, and so people treat them as a joke. "Do you vote for the party or do you vote for the person?" people asked rhetorically. Local candidates simply affiliate with the parties of their state-level benefactors as a means of signaling their personal allegiance.

Henrique, who became Passarinho's mayor in 2005, had tried to affili-ate with the PT in 2003 as the party rose to power in Piauí, but when he learned that its statutes would force him to wait two years before running for mayor, he allied with a federal deputy (congressman) from a nearby city and affiliated with his small, conservative party. Henrique justified the alliance by claiming that the young deputy "worked" and did not just "eat money" (also see Chaves 2003). Henrique expected his deputy to channel him money, work-hours on a private tractor, development projects, and hospital beds for Henrique to redistribute.[1] When his deputy came to Pas-sarinho to take part in the celebratory initiation of a government project, Henrique expected to be mentioned honorifically as his "friend," even if the privilege of standing onstage beside the deputy belonged to the erst-while mayor. In return, Henrique would try to convince his supporters to vote for the deputy, but he needed evidence that the latter actually sent resources down to Passarinho: "There's no harder thing to do in politics then get votes for a legislator who doesn't work," he told me. When I asked him what he thought about the PT (President Lula and Governor Dias), he replied, "If I'm elected, I stand ready to work with whoever wants to work. But I tell you I have a critique: They call themselves the Workers' Party, but others like me are also for the workers." Such were Henrique's notions of political rectitude in his dealings with higher-ups. Let me turn now to his relations with Passarinho's less fortunate.

A Day with Many Exchanges

One day in July 2004, Henrique learned that the mayor's faction was throwing a mass rally in town, complete with meat, drink, and entertainment. Henrique decided to do some damage control by throwing a smaller counterparty of his own in the village of Caixa de Água, where I was living at the time. He chose to hold his party at the house of a middle-aged widow, Mailda. He provided drink, food, and music piped in on amplifiers loaded onto the back of his son's pickup. Before the party began, Henrique's truck made several stops at particular houses, and Henrique entered them alone and stayed for perhaps fifteen minutes in each. The houses he entered were those of the better-off families in this otherwise impoverished village.

The first was the house of Josevaldo and Maria, a respected middle-aged couple. Henrique stood at the edge of their property and shouted smilingly, "O Seu Jorge!" (The title *Seu* is a colloquial abbreviation for *Senhor*.) Josevaldo and Maria emerged from the house, and Josevaldo returned, "O Seu Henrique!" Thus far, the forms of address were more formal than those that villagers used when talking with the heads of other neighboring households (full first naming). Then, both parties dropped the formality:

HENRIQUE: How are the two of you [*vocês*].
MARIA: We are fine, thank God.
JOSEVALDO: Get out of the sun. The sun is hot. (This is typical hospitable phrasing for an invitation to enter one's house.)
HENRIQUE: Okay, good. Perhaps a little word [*palavrinha*] with the two of you. I cannot stay long because time is short.
JOSEVALDO: I know. You [*tu*] are rushed. Right, Henrique? [Josevaldo smiles.]

Then the three went inside the house.

Outside the house, a small gathering of curious villagers stood in groups of three or four looking at the ground silently or making an occasional joke to relieve nervous energy. The jokes all somehow involved a person of high position who was tricked out of money by a beggar, who otherwise revealed himself to be a buffoon despite his wealth, or who was somehow knocked down a peg by a clever poor person. I inferred that Henrique's presence was generating anxiety, perhaps related to the mystery of the negotiation ensuing inside. Later, I asked my friends in the village what they thought might have transpired there. One man replied: "Only three know: the two men and God." I suspect that the women of the house were also present for these discussions, and that their participation was retrospectively elided. One thing was clear: the information that people shared with politicians in these private encounters would be socially disruptive if uttered in public.

What struck me about the interaction was the degree of symmetry and informality in Josevaldo and Henrique's form of address to each another. And this was fairly typical of the three or four other households where Henrique stopped before attending the party. At two houses, no honorific titles were used even to preface the encounter, and on several occasions village families attached the diminutive suffix *inho* to Henrique's name (i.e., Henriquinho). I had expected a far more asymmetric pattern in which the cultivator household heads would address the politician as "O Senhor" and the politician would address the family heads by their first names—reminiscent of the days when wealthy ranchers would have owned the lands on which poor people like Josevaldo and Maria worked.[2] Sérgio Buarque de Holanda (2012 [1936]: 117–18), an important twentieth-century theorist of Brazilian culture, understood these linguistic informalities as exemplary of Brazil's archetypal "cordial man," whose "rich and overflowing emotional base" is grounded in "the desire to establish intimacy." I suspect that these greetings set the tone of the mutually vulnerable closed-door negotiations that I did not witness.

Henrique finally made his way to the widow's house, and the family heads with whom he had met privately followed shortly thereafter. As the group enjoyed the festivities, Joaquim, the village's most pitiable *desmantelado* (broken-down man), approached Henrique several times over the course of a few hours to solicit money in exchange for his vote. With no pretense of discretion, he called out in his slurred voice, "My patron gives me food today and liquor to make the pain go away. But tomorrow I will be hungry. Give me money so I can buy liquor tomorrow and I will vote for my patron. Give me money and wherever my patron walks, he will be blessed." Henrique clearly felt embarrassed by Joaquim's antics. Joaquim had put him in an uncomfortable position. Whereas most villagers concealed their hunger at all costs to preserve their dignity and their social relations, Joaquim had no dignity left to protect, no farther to fall. His direct reference to his hunger made Joaquim's plea for cash difficult for Henrique to deny; Henrique, after all, wanted to appear generous to the small crowd. Yet, to give Joaquim cash in public would be to engage in an exchange that "doesn't build a man's respect," as Henrique later told me—never mind the fact that selling his vote to Joaquim would directly violate electoral law, and that such a violation could have cost Henrique the election if someone from "the other side" happened to be there "spying" on him. My eyes on Henrique may have affected his choice in this moment as well. He looked at me before responding, "Joaquim must vote for the one who works for the people. I work for the people. That is why you should vote for me." Joaquim tried to repeat his appeal but he was shouted down by his fellow villagers, "Leave the man alone, drunkard!" Mailda went over to Joaquim with a cup full of booze and a conciliatory word, "Here, drink, my Joaquim."

Next up was Matteo, a more violent man with a reputation for trickery. Matteo worked his angle more privately. Whenever he could get Henrique's ear, he whispered complaints of a hand injury he had sustained. He even uncovered the festering wound to substantiate his need for cash "to feed my family until I can work again." The other villagers saw this private conversation and looked away from him in disapproval, but nobody denounced Matteo audibly. Henrique avoided giving him cash as well . . . at least at that moment.

When the party was over, Henrique crammed me into the cab of his truck alongside a village woman he was driving to the town hospital for a prenatal exam. We were slowly rolling away when I dodged a pair of intruding hands shoved through the window. They belonged to Matteo. Henrique pulled out a wad of cash from his breast pocket and gave it to him. He placed another wad into a second pair of hands, maybe Joaquim's, and then into a third. Henrique never brought the truck to a total stop, and when he finally looked at me he had a grimace on his face, "What can you do?" he asked fatalistically.

The next day, I asked Josevaldo (who had attended the party at Mailda's) for his take on Henrique's behavior. Josevaldo did not speak of the private interactions that occurred behind closed doors, but he expressed disapproval of the quick cash exchanges that had occurred on the way out. He explained, "It looks ugly, a man taking cash. I've taken cash, but it's not right. Henrique should know we value his heart, not just his wallet. It didn't used to be like this."

For Josevaldo, to value Henrique "for his heart" did not preclude engaging in a private exchange with him, so long as that exchange was honorable. Likewise, Henrique boasted of his good character by speaking of how he "worked for the people" by gifting fencing wire, seed, fertilizer, pesticide, sacks of cement, tile roofing, emergency trips to the hospital for injured workers and parturient women, and (later as mayor) municipal employment. But when Matteo asked Henrique for cash, he was soliciting an amoral gift.

Josevaldo's critique focused on the narrow instrumentality of cash exchange. Henrique's closed-door negotiations with independent households—which may also have involved cash—posed no moral problem for Josevaldo. But why then had those closed doors stirred anxiety among his peers? It may be that the kind of information that people share when they negotiate political exchanges in private would be scandalous if shared among their peers. This is because it involves the forms of "ocular wealth" that point to enduring status differences among households and provoke cosmological danger by inciting envy. Some of my field observations suggest that villagers make themselves vulnerable to politicians behind closed doors when they reveal to them information about their thriving and dying cattle and livestock. The vulnerability that a villager shares with a politician presents itself as the flip side of the respectful distance that villagers maintain with one another. Perhaps it is because the information that the villager discloses would bring suspicions of envy or hunger among neighbors that its revelation to the politician brings the two parties closer together. At the same time, politicians make themselves vulnerable to certain voters during these negotiation sessions. In fact, politicians' vulnerability has two aspects. First, and most obvious, in making a deal in which they promise private goods in exchange for political support, politicians risk the legal forfeit of their candidacy if they are reported. Second, candidates, in negotiating for the commoner's militant support (rather than just the simple vote), must reveal the fragilities and deficiencies of their electoral base. Politicians' admission of their vulnerability is suggested by the stereotypical phrase attributed to them during their private interactions with commoners: "Help me now and I'll help you later." Let me try to substantiate these claims.

In June 2012, on a return visit to Passarinho, I asked a candidate for mayor if he ever discussed his deficiencies of support with potential electors beyond the using the general phrase "Help me now." He responded enigmatically. "You have to talk about it. But not with everybody. Each case is unique [*cada caso é um caso*]. You have to know how to treat each person according to . . . You understand? [I nod but say nothing, trying to encourage him to continue.] There are people of confidence in each community. There are people who it's just smiles, good day, and goodbye. Some people you indicate, 'It's this way, that way. . . .'" His voice trailed off musically in a local register of vagueness.

What this candidate referred to as "people of confidence" are also called *cabos eleitorais* (literally "electoral cables"), a regional colloquialism for the avid local supporters of a politician who try to drum up votes on the politician's behalf within their communities. Scholars and activists often regard this practice as a kind of class betrayal, one that enables what Susan Stokes (2005: 318, 316) calls "perverse accountability," an antidemocratic scenario in which politicians "insert themselves into the social network of constituents" to "make good inferences about what individual voters have done in the voting booth and reward or punish them conditional on these actions." But what's also indicated here is a sliding scale of intimacy, one in which politicians gauge an elector's degree of trust in them based on his or her revealed vulnerability and then respond in kind. From the politician's perspective, a successful negotiation will result in the commoner's patching the holes in the electoral fabric by campaigning stridently, putting the candidate's sticker on his door or motorcycle, attending campaign rallies, singing musical satires of the adversary, and generally drumming up support.

Yet the commoners' support for a politician is not solely a matter of drumming up votes and making noise. The vocal support of common people testifies to the candidate's moral worth, indicating that the candidate's electoral success stems from more than just his or her command over money. It is a curious feature of many market democracies that the money on which campaigns depend becomes a symbolic liability to the extent that it signals the distance between a candidate and the general public. In northeast Brazil, this logic extends beyond the electoral context; intimate hierarchy is based on a humble recognition that everyone's life energy (*força*) is finite and insufficient to the monumental tasks they hope to accomplish. It must be supplemented by those they hope to help. Patrons, to be moral beings, must manifest their need of their clients, and the clients must reveal their heroic capacity to protect or rescue their patrons. Consider John Collins's report (2008a: 246) of a Bahian crack addict, "Denilson," who relied on a local nurse ("Conceição") to channel him state and NGO resources connected to the restoration of Salvador's historic Pelourinho district: "According to Denilson, Conceição risks assault by treating the excluded. He once gave her a silver crucifix so that 'the bad guys (a malandragem) will see her and know that she's mine, that she's under my protection.'" The amulet that Denilson gives to Conceição may appear to be a token gift from someone who has nothing else of value to offer, but it perfectly captures the essence of the client's value to a patron. The client spreads out his or her moral and spiritual energy across an elusive, intangible space (a magical field, a social network, etc.) so as to create the conditions for the patron's success.

Politicians do not enter these intimate relationships with people like Joaquim and Matteo, because such people cannot or do not direct their força to work for their patrons' interests. Politicians engage in intimate, vulnerable arrangements only with people who have the wherewithal to maintain honorable decorum, that is, properly self-contained, self-directed people, not drunks, tricksters, or those unable to conceal their envy or hunger. Demonstrating command of one's inner forces points to a person's general capacity to influence one's community and broader network, and this is of great interest to politicians. This became clear to me about a week after the party when a village man, Sérgio, asked me to broker a request he hoped Henrique would grant: "Aaron, I was hoping to request that Aaron speak to Henrique and ask if he would give me a ball of fencing wire. He knows that here in my house, we all vote for him. Will Aaron do this?" I wondered why Sérgio had not met with Henrique in his own house to make his own request prior to the party as others had done. As it turned out, Sérgio was switching politicians that year and wanted the support of an esteemed intermediary to vouch that he was a self-respecting man. The next time I saw Henrique, I told him that Sérgio's cornfield seemed like it needed some fencing wire. Henrique smiled at me, instantly inferring what I was up to. He asked me if Sérgio was a "good worker" (bom trabalhador). I didn't know what to say. I told him I knew very little about Sérgio's expertise with his crops or the number of hours he worked each day. I told him that I knew Sérgio maintained a day-trading arrangement with another man from the village, and that I had seen him grilling manioc flour in a mutirão that included his brothers and sisters-in-law. "This is what matters," Henrique said. "I know Sérgio knows how to work. I know everyone here."

Henrique, like all politicians, looked for signs of interhousehold cooperation among villagers for several reasons. First, those who sustain cooperative relations can influence the votes and general support of their labor partners. They are, as Moacir Palmeira (1992, 1996) calls them, "electors with multiple votes." Shared labor arrangements with people from other households extend a person's influence beyond the boundaries of the home. Traditionally, rural men have controlled the votes of their wives and coresident children; the father and husband "represents [the household] to the outside world" (Heredia 1996: 58). As such, a man's honor has depended on the unity of his family, and "the unity of the vote exemplifies the unity of the family" (ibid.: 59). Not only are men who are well-regarded in labor arrangements more likely to receive this "respect" from their children but they also draw loyalty from extended or junior kin from other households. "Where you go, I go" (*Onde você entra, eu entro*) is the stereotypical phrase by which one person indicates such a willingness to follow another's lead in forging political alliances. By 2004, however, when I was conducting my research, it was rare for fathers to fully command the votes of any children who had moved out of the house, and there was mounting dissention even among coresident children. Yet fathers still held sway over these children, wives, and other coresident junior kin.

By withholding material favors from these "electors with multiple votes," a politician like Henrique risks creating resentment in a key person that will elicit the sympathies of labor partners, and thus result in a loss of multiple votes. Perhaps most important, a villager's cooperation with his or her neighbors also indicates an ability to form enduring alliances, the kind that politicians hope to form with people they can trust. Long-term, intimate alliances between politicians and electors are the building blocks of *moral* power and prestige. The moral value people attribute to these exchanges contrasts sharply with their devaluation of vote-buying, a distinction that can be better understood by reflecting on the relationship between morality and time as they intertwine in different forms of electoral exchange.

Time and Intimate Exchange

The moral distinctions that Passarinho's inhabitants make in the electoral arena relate primarily to the temporality of their transactions. This is nothing new to anthropologists, who have generally found that people around the world consider exchanges that have greater temporal depth to be more ethical than those that are of shorter term. Maurice Bloch and Jonathan Perry (1989) posit that people associate long-term exchanges with the reproduction of a virtuous cosmic order underlying all social and spiritual relationships. To engage in long-term exchange is to sustain the moral structure underlying the world. Short-term exchanges, in contrast, are associated with selfishness. They stifle the circulation of objects, prevent a person's renown from spreading over space and time, and generally contract the scales on which the dramas of social life play out (also see Munn 1986). Anthropologist Jorge Mattar Villela (2004: 269), who writes of sertanejo municipalities in the neighboring state of Pernambuco, argues that the exchange of votes for "money, in its purest monetary form, makes instantaneous and finite a relation (elector-candidate) whose prolongation as creditor/debtor is often more desirable."

It is useful to distinguish between two temporal dimensions of any act of gift-giving. First, there is the duration of the social relationship that a particular gift presupposes; and second, there is the duration of the activity that a gift sponsors.[3] In considering the importance of the duration of an exchange relationship, recall how Henrique shoved cash into Matteo's hands after the latter had promised him a vote. The amoral nature of this exchange (as evaluated by Josevaldo) derived not from the cash medium per se but from the fact that it implied a one-time transaction. Henrique gave Matteo some money in return for the implicit promise that Matteo would vote for him in the upcoming election only. Villela (2005: 273) puts the matter well when he writes (of rural Pernambuco) that "to sell the vote to a candidate on the day of the election implies an emptying of credit that one could otherwise enjoy in the future." (As Villela suggests, the customary context for such buy-offs is the evening prior to the actual election, when candidates send out their cronies with wads of cash to buy their votes.) The cash-carrying compatriots are often *aventureiros* or *pistoleiros*, men known for violence, womanizing, and lawlessness. They ride their motorcycles off the main highway, taking the back roads into villages— the same roads used by contrabandists to bypass state checkpoints. By all accounts, they carry guns not to threaten the electorate but to protect themselves from one another.

One such aventureiro (later turned town councilman) proudly recounted the following tale over drinks: "I was on the road into [a village] with my cash to get votes and [another pistoleiro] passed me. He saw what I was doing and he drew his gun and said, 'Go home.' I looked him over and drew my gun and said, 'I'm here getting votes, same as you.' And he said, 'This business of politics is no good for any of us.' And he put his gun back and he rode off. Here we understand that politics is no reason for violence." I gathered from his brash, boastful tone that he was telling the story to build his reputation for bravado, not to assert his moral standing as a self-respecting man. Not surprisingly, a woman who overheard his story later told me that the man was "courageous" but "had no future" (*sem futuro*), or, in Villela's (2012: 9) terms, "morally dissociated."

These buy-offs are commodity transactions insofar as they do not initiate an open-ended cycle of gifting and countergifting. The parties to this commodity transaction do not face one another as "persons" whose respective location in a larger social order shapes their dealings with each other; they are "individuals," faceless and interchangeable, the mere conduits of generic currencies, such as votes and money (DaMatta 1991 [1979]). The price of a generic person's vote standardizes in relation to inflationary and market conditions. In 2004, it was fifty reais (about twenty U.S. dollars).

Of course, the relation is not entirely instantaneous in that it entails some trust by politicians that the elector will actually vote for them in the ballot box. A cunning friend of mine, who was hired by a candidate to buy votes en masse, spoke to me of this matter.

> FRIEND: I did this for him [laughs]. I got into the car and passed out his little photo [*santinho*] to whoever would take it! Guess what? Each photo had fifty reais under it. Everybody knew what it was.
>
> ANSELL: Did everyone accept?
>
> FRIEND: No. Maybe half.
>
> ANSELL: Do you think those who took it voted for [the politician]?
>
> FRIEND: Ah, nobody knows, do they? But our people are honest here. Sometimes they would shout to me from where they were lined up to vote: "Give me a little photo and I'll vote for who you want."
>
> ANSELL: When you passed them the money did they smile?
>
> FRIEND: You want to know if they felt bad. I don't know. Some smiled. There are many shameless people, though.

My friend's responses to my questions highlight what struck me as a curious possibility: some of the same people who were "shameless" enough to smile while selling their votes may also have been "honest" enough to vote for the one who buys them. I suspect that many feel that their fulfillment of the verbal contract redeems them from the degradation of a cash sale that presupposes them to lack intimate commitments and territorialized kinship obligations (Villela 2004: 274).

By contrast to cash, booze, and other short-term transactions, an alliance solidified through moral gifting implies not a finite exchange but an ongoing relationship characterized by periodic gifts and favors, a generalized exchange relation. Here the term "general" does not imply a group of people who exchange with one another, only a lack of "record keeping," that is, one does not necessarily wait to receive a countergift before gifting a second time. The gifts that comprise this mode of exchange typically include farm inputs (seed, tools, watering holes) and municipal jobs. These are the gifts that moral cultivators negotiate behind their closed doors. While these negotiations may only bind a family to vote for the politician in the upcoming election, they have more far-reaching implications. They lay down the tracks for an ongoing relationship, creating a default expectation that, unless interrupted, the alliance will recur ad infinitum (albeit under freshly negotiated terms each campaign). Consider that the implicit terms of such an open-ended alliance call for the politician to rush to the aid of a supporter during times of need, regardless of whether that politician has already made his electoral gift to the family, regardless of whether these emergencies occur before or after the election, and regardless of whether the politician wins public office. Usually these are health emergencies; rushing parturient women and injured workers to hospitals and using contacts with deputies to ensure their treatment. The elector also has a reciprocal obligation to show up when called to public events that honor his or her allied politician regardless of when these occur, and to run small favors for him or her when asked. These favors bring esteem (*prestígio*) for the elector, just as emergency assistance does for politicians (Villela 2004).

A young friend of mine whom I interviewed on a return trip to Passarinho in 2012 proclaimed of his own campaigning, "When I declare [my vote] to someone, I go right ahead and declare to everyone. It's a flag and photo and this year I will put up the name. . . . Wherever Henrique goes, I'm with him. If he says so, I'm with him. I'm together with him. I'm like— Henrique need only say, 'Your path is this one here' and I say, 'I'm with you, sir, wherever it is. And what's the best curve for us to follow?'" He and others around him laughed as he drew to a close. The young man's statement locates his use of campaign photo-stickers in a broader field of practices that convey his bold, big-hearted loyalty to Henrique, the incumbent mayor. His agentive obedience restores whatever masculine decorum might otherwise be sacrificed by his submission to another man, and makes him worthy of more favors than those who merely vote for Henrique.

Because not all gifts self-evidently fall within the category of short- or long-term exchange, politicians use their talk about gifts to indicate the kind of transaction they hope to generate. My assistant, Jorge, once casually relayed to me how a town councilman, long retired from public service, had used some of his pension to pay for a private tractor to dig a reservoir for his native village. When one of the village men asked him what he could do for him in exchange, he allegedly replied, "No, down the line, you'll set it right [*acertar*]." His use of the word *acertar* (to set right) rather than *pagar* (to pay) demonetizes the obligation, pushing it away from a commodity exchange. Also, there is a temporal ambiguity surrounding the obligation; the councilman postpones the settling of accounts, citing only a vague future. Of course, all this may have been said with a wink that implied both parties knew that the currency of repayment would be the vote, and the time for repayment would be the October election. Still, the ambiguous framing preserves the possibility that an enduring relationship is on the horizon.

The ambiguity surrounding the repayment of gifts flattens out the relationship between exchange partners over time into a continuous "friendship." As this happens, the character of the exchange shifts in such a way as to admit new, spontaneous acts of generosity outside the campaign period. These acts have the dual effect of detaching such exchanges from the narrow confines of elections, while at the same time ensuring a family's electoral support of a given politician during each subsequent election.

Only in the context of these open-ended exchanges can a politician hope to shape a commoner's voting in the state and federal elections. Common people vote for the legislators of their patron's choosing both to sustain this resource flow and to show respect for a politician who engages in moral exchange. One man who idealized this norm explained to me that "as children we vote for the mayor our fathers like, we vote for the senator our mayor likes." (Brazilian "children" are allowed to vote at age sixteen.) In contrast with the influence that local politicians have on voters with whom they engage in long-term exchange, little influence follows from short-term exchanges. When a politician gives away cash and booze, the elector has no reason to care about whether that politician will receive resources from allies higher up. Long-term alliances build upward-looking ties and become part of morally significant resource circuits, but short-term buy-offs affirm people's exclusion from those circuits, making their enactment a kind of mutual disgrace—like a regrettable one-night stand.

The second temporal feature of exchange relations pertains to the duration of the activities sponsored by the politicians' gifts. In moral and intimate transactions, the sponsored activity is figured in years. For example, seed, fertilizer, and fencing allow the household to successfully complete one or more harvest cycles. Medical assistance (emergencies or routine treatments) allow for the perpetuation of individual and family life across generations.

By contrast, the activities sponsored by amoral exchanges are of short duration. People in Passarinho say those who accept cash payments made on the eve of the election "ate the money" right away. Here the term "ate" need not literally refer to the purchase of food. Money spent on booze or sex is also "eaten." Like the pangs of hunger, these shamefully immediate needs evoke the specter of an envious and ravenous person (comilão, esfomeado, etc.) who cannot control his or her bodily urges. This is how politicians justify their immoral cash transactions. After all, what other means does a politician have of reaching someone who lives off the bottle? One woman impressed the political stupidity (and unreliability) of booze-taking electors on me with a little story: "Luiza said she didn't know who she would vote for this year. Suddenly, Tomás showed up and gave her a big bottle of liquor saying it was from Rodrigo. She said she would vote for Rodrigo. She told me all the way home how she adored Rodrigo. Then later that night she [accidentally] knocked the bottle down and it broke. 'I don't like Rodrigo anymore. I'm not voting for him,' she said. This is how absurd some people are, Aaron." Accurate or not, the story speaks directly to the relationship between political right-mindedness and the duration of whatever activity is sponsored by a politician's gift. It aligns activities of short-term benefit (drinking booze, or in this case, not even getting to drink it!) to deficits of loyalty and common sense.

In distinguishing short- from long-term exchanges, I should note that no concrete currency is ever rigidly locked into one or the other transaction order. Money itself has "diverse forms," as Villela (2004: 276) argues; it "doesn't necessarily transform the electoral process into a (commodity) market." Indeed, Villela argues that cash gifts can establish enduring ties of protection, especially between state-level politicians and their municipal counterparts (274). In Passarinho, cash gifts do not become moral unless they are immediately converted into concrete goods or services. My friend and assistant, Jorge, produced a contrastive example of moral versus amoral cash transactions on one occasion. He was singing his godfather's praises to another man in the effort to get his *padrinho* (godfather) reelected as councilman:

My padrinho, Leandro, he digs watering holes for communities with tractor hours that Renato [a state deputy] gives him. And last election, Renato offered my padrinho money for him to deliver his supporters to Renato, but my padrinho wouldn't take it. He said, "Give me more hours with your tractor, so I can work for the people. I don't want money." And he doesn't have money! All the money from his pension is gone. There are days when I ask him to buy me a soda, but he doesn't even have a real in his wallet. He gives his money away for people's medicine, for travel to Teresina so people can visit family!

The cash offered by the state deputy (Renato) is an amoral gift because, while Leandro could theoretically use it to do good things for his supporters (such as digging watering holes), Renato does not specify such good uses. Jorge's narrative implies that Renato would not mind if Leandro spent the money on himself, so long as he delivered to the deputy a bunch of votes. Jorge contrasts the cash offered by Renato with the cash that Leandro gives for medicine and family-oriented travel. In his padrinho's hand, money does not function as a means to immediate ends but as a means to ensure the continuity of a family.

In sum, short-term transactions imply no obligation to rescue commoners in times of need, to give them work, goods, and favor, and to help them access assistance from state programs, municipal officials, and others. More intimate, lasting alliances increase politicians' obligations to rescue their "friends" in times of need, thereby affording commoners more security in the areas of life that matter most to them. The temporality of the exchange determines the extent to which it creates friendships in which interest and emotion, calculation and vulnerability, coincide.

Commoners are clearly better able to utilize long-term alliances to escape the devastating consequences of drought and the resulting downward spiral into chronic hunger. However, commoners cannot necessarily choose whether to engage in intimate, long-term alliances or brief, episodic transactions with a politician. "The reputation of an elector, or of their household, determines the type of relation that he or she can establish with the candidate" (Villela 2004: 277). Many impoverished people would gladly shift from cash transactions to more intimate and lasting alliances, but they tend have a difficult time doing so. Rarely do the poorest of the poor become influential "electors with multiple votes," and their imputed desperation may cost them a politician's trust or regard. They remain, in most cases, isolated within their villages—in part because others find their hunger threatening. Thus, stronger horizontal relations among villagers foster a form of patronage that is locally considered to be moral, whereas weaker lateral ties tend to reduce vertical reciprocities to immoral cash or booze transactions.

Changes and Contestations

The norms described above distinguish more and less intimate varieties of hierarchical exchange, and these are the norms that predominated in Passarinho during my fieldwork. But they did not go unchallenged. Even before Zero Hunger's arrival, social forces were already pushing against the conventional admiration for intimate hierarchy. The increasing prominence of cash, newly formed village associations, and grassroots movements headquartered in the town hub have changed the dynamics of political exchanges. Greater tolerance of vote-buying, decreased paternal authority, and a new rhetoric of "insurgent citizenship" (à la Holston 2008) that contrasts hierarchy and egalitarianism were all colliding in Passarinho.

The increasing importance of cash in the municipal economy has pushed against the conventional distinctions between moral and immoral political exchange (Palmeira 1996: 48–49; Villela 2005: 271–73; Barreira 2006: 152). Taking cash, even on the eve of an election, is increasingly destigmatized as people come to prize cash over other forms of wealth, especially land and cattle. Cash also gives people access to new prestige commodities (e.g., clothes, televisions) that help them feel cosmopolitan. Access to cash makes young people increasingly independent of their parents, facilitating the decline of paternal authority related to the decline of the mutirão labor activities discussed in chapter 2. Children's increasing agricultural independence may have also contributed to the rise of independent voting among coresident children. Both trends are no doubt related to the monetization of Passarinho's economy. One village man in his twenties told me about the time he voted for a politician who was not to his father's liking. At the time, he was nineteen years old and still living at home, but he wanted to marry a woman and build a house with her. His father's candidate of choice promised the family a certain amount of seed for all the votes in the household, but "I wanted to marry Roselma, and Roberto [the adversary] offered me the cash I needed to build a house. Papa was enraged, but what could he do. I was born naked, but by then [he laughed] I was dressed." The man offered no apology for defying his father's wishes and taking (use-specified) cash from the politician, Roberto. The exchange he entered into disrupted his father's alliance with Roberto's rival by reducing the value that his father's allegiance had historically afforded the household. With fewer descendants voting at his command, the speaker's father could not expect the same amount of resources and attention from his patron. The increased independence of offspring makes such incidents common.

Overtly anticlientelist discourses have emerged in some pockets of Passarinho. From the 1960s through the 1980s, liberationist priests from Germany and Italy settled in the nearby city and began organizing some villages into Christian base communities. The priests taught villagers to "rely on one another" rather than on "the big people" (os grandões). While liberationist Catholicism generally declined during the 1990s, the development associations emerged to take its place. The associations became the unit of interfamilial collective discussion, meeting in the local chapels and often beginning their meetings with prayers. These associations stand ready to implement community development projects channeled from the World Bank and other multinational agencies through the state government and ultimately to them. Their members wait patiently, but most never see any such project.

While the local activists who organize today's associations deploy the liberationist rhetoric of self-reliance and instruct villagers "not to let politics" into the association, the association itself offers politicians opportunities to experiment with new kinds of reciprocity. Candidates often try to court association members' support much as they do that of traditional patriarchal households. They deposit cement and building supplies at the doorsteps of the village chapels where the associations convene and sometimes pay the association's federal registration fees. People like Henrique deny that such actions corrupt the associations. Rather, Henrique claims that making such gifts shows that he is a "forward-thinking man" (homem pra frente) who stands for development and progress. An emerging point of confusion for politicians and commoners alike is whether gifts and services rendered to an association should be considered substitutions for or supplements to the gifts or services done for individual families. One politician told me that development would come much faster if all he had to do was exchange with the associations. Yet not all villagers trust the association; some complain that their president "eats" the members' dues. As a result, gifts given to associations before the election rarely determine a village family's electoral allegiance. However, they do operate as overtures of goodwill, as openers to exchange relations with independent village households.

In addition to stimulating the formation of the associations, local activists also founded Passarinho's chapter of the PT and Rural Workers' Union, turning both into sites where words like *clientelismo* were used to criticize the status quo. Another related locus of left-wing dissent is the regional Black Movement, also known as the Quilombola Movement (the term *quilombo* refers to a community of escaped African slaves or their descendants, while *quilombola* refers to the people (singular or plural) living in such a community; see chapter 6). These pockets of democratic, Marxist, and race-based militancy would later serve as pockets of receptivity to the Zero Hunger's assault on intimate hierarchy in a locale whose residents otherwise found that project alien.

There were two ritual contexts in which the insurgent ideology of these new movements stimulated commoners (villagers and townspeople) to rethink intimate and commodified exchanges. Auctions and pilgrimages revealed the way Passarinho's citizens tried to make sense of the transformations occurring within their political system. Through these rituals the population is increasingly absorbing the left-wing ideological premises that guided Zero Hunger state officials, especially the notion that hierarchical and egalitarian solidarities were mutually incompatible, or at least antithetical.

Even before the intervention of the liberationist priests, commoners from this region of Piauí had undertaken annual (or multiannual) pilgrimages to one of several central municipalities, including Oeiras, Santa Cruz dos Milagres, Santa Cruz do Piauí, or Juaziero do Norte (in the state of Ceará). They often walked or rode their horses or mules to these locations, where they set candles and notes in the church grottos, requesting the intervention of saints to heal sick children or to bring prosperity to their families or communities (Barreto 1986). Some scholars have argued that the relationships that these pilgrims established with saints in the religious context mirrored their alliances with local patrons. For instance, devotional "exchanges" with the saints expressed pilgrims' "obedience, humility and even suffering," leading to a "sacralization of the earthly patron-client relationship" (Gross 1971: 136, 145; also see Greenfield and Cavalcante 2006). Patricia Pessar (2004) argues for a slightly different interpretation, claiming that pilgrimage and other folk Catholic movements during the twentieth century occurred when northeast Brazilians lost faith in their patrons' moral worth, as these men failed to make good on reciprocal obligations. Pilgrims turned to messianic figures (Padre Cicero, Pedro Batista) out of "raw desperation for a good patron" (ibid., 88). Whether pilgrimages sacralized patrons or pointed out their failings, they clearly affirmed patronage reciprocity as an underlying ethic. But that was then. Recent practices of pilgrimage led by left-wing activists now call into question the underlying ethics of hierarchical reciprocity.

During the 1970s and 1980s, the liberationist Catholic priests encouraged poor urban residents of a neighboring town to engage in local religious processions. These processions usually culminated at private homes, where owners would auction private livestock to the crowd. They allegedly gave their proceeds to the Church in order to "pay their promises" to a saint who had answered their prayers in the past year.

In 2000, more than a decade after the practice of small-scale processions had dwindled out, a few liberationist priests (those who retained their positions) from other municipalities in Piauí began holding new large-scale pilgrimages that explicitly thematized issues related to democratic citizenship (e.g., forced labor, women's rights, environment, etc.). For example, some are now carried out under the banner of the national Romaria da Terra e da Água (Pilgrimage of Land and Water). These new pilgrimages connect Passarinho's inhabitants with members of the Pastoral Land Commission (a Catholic agrarian reform movement) and the Quilombola Movement. Given that these movements have consistently railed against clientelismo, there is little doubt that participation in them has caused rural people to reflect critically on the terms of their political alliances.

One such context in which this reflection occurs is the auction. During the 1990s, the older private auctions connected to local processions slowly morphed into charity auctions held on behalf of village development associations. The associations now hold these every year, usually between June and October, the period that overlaps with the official campaign season during election years. (Not surprisingly, auctions are far more lucrative during election years.) Candidates for office purchase the prizes, show up to overbid on plates of cooked food and booze, and then distribute their winnings to the commoners who gather around them. Rival politicians engage in bidding wars with one another to prove their força (strength) to the crowd. Booze and goods gifted directly at auction events bear no stigma whatsoever and politicians speak of the practice as "sharing with friends" and "supporting [association-based] development." Framed cynically, politicians launder their cash, booze, and cooked food into moral gifts that reflect their status as "men of good heart" who desire long-term moral alliances with common people.

At first glance, therefore, the charity auction seems like a ritual of patronage that reinforces the domination of the rich. But politicians are not the only people who bid at these auctions. Friends, siblings (and siblings-in-law), work partners, association members, and fellow social movement activists go to auctions in small groups and bid on prizes with money they pool together. When they win a prize, they adjourn to the perimeter of the gathering to share it among themselves. For these informal groups, a successful bid signifies their egalitarian "unity." Sometimes commoners pool together to bid against their patron's rival candidate, putting this person into the kind double-bind I mentioned in the introduction: either the candidate wins and appears like a bully who "bids against the people" or he or she withdraws from the contest, which may suggest weakness and thus provide the rival with a victory by proxy. In either case, popular participation in the auction provides an opportunity to build egalitarian solidarities and a ritual format for reflecting on the coexistence of egalitarianism and hierarchy (for further analysis, see Ansell 2010).

Sorting Out the Local Culture of Patronage

Clearly, Passarinho's inhabitants were already becoming increasingly aware of alternative ideas about politics before Zero Hunger officials arrived in their municipality. They were rethinking these relationships both through explicit critiques uttered in the spaces of organized civil society (e.g., union headquarters) and through implicit ratiocinations melded with auction gamesmanship and pilgrimage devotion.

It is ironic that the critical reassessment of political values is playing itself out in the context of increasing commodification of patronage exchange. Yet both processes converge insofar as they replace the socially embedded "person" with the disembedded "individual" (à la DaMatta). These are the twin—political and economic—aspects of liberalization. But Passarinho's inhabitants are not simply on a path toward liberal subjectivity. Monetization and grassroots organization have stimulated their critical engagement with the local workings of power and will probably give rise to new standpoints of critique irreducible to market fundamentalism, patronage, or social-democratic ideology.

When Zero Hunger's campaign against patronage entered Passarinho, it intersected with a conventional mode of politics in which various political exchanges assumed different moral valences, a cash-prone political universe losing its stigma. It also intersected with an emergent antipatronage activism that was quite friendly to the ideas of the state officials. This complex context poses challenges to any straightforward description of "what locals thought of Zero Hunger" when it entered their world. In the remaining chapters, I foreground the friction between the officials and the conventional way of thinking about and "doing" politics in Passarinho, while trying not to ignore these newer countercurrents. Any account of these encounters would need to problematize the subjectivity of the state officials themselves—pushing deeper than a simple description of their hostility toward patronage. In the next chapter I examine the mindset and emotions of Zero Hunger's frontline agents who brought the program to Passarinho in 2003.

CHAPTER FOUR

The Prodigal Children Return to the Countryside

Moving from the perspective of Zero Hunger's beneficiaries to that of its implementers, I now turn to the program's frontline agents in the state of Piauí. For these state officials, the local distinctions between long- and short-term modes of exchange that separated moral and amoral political relationships were neither visible nor meaningful. For them, all such transactions were characterized as patron-client exchange, and such clientelismo contributed to food deprivation. And so while these urban officials admired what one called the "beautiful system of family agriculture" from which their own families had derived, they nonetheless worried that in the rural interior, "our people there are still slaves in a certain way."

As individuals, state officials saw many of the nuances of political exchange, including its intimacies and benefits to the poor, and yet the master discourse that guided their collective action was one in which contemporary politicians were little different from the coronéis of old, local elites who preyed on the physical hunger pangs of poor clients by giving them food, alcohol, medicine, cash, or other hunger-relieving goods in exchange for their votes. Accordingly, hunger was not only the perverse outcome of clientelismo but also a condition that made people unfit for democracy and participatory development. The rest of this book is primarily devoted to explaining how the state agents sought to remedy that problem. To set up that project I show how the state officials typically related to the beneficiaries. I argue that these officials acted as if they were the beneficiaries' descendants, children of the countryside who had gone to the city and left their less fortunate parents and grandparents in a warm, though oppressive, world. A longing to return to the rural heartland infused their technical policy pursuits, leading them to experience their administrative excursions as a spiritual rediscovery of themselves.

Here I argue that the subjectivity of Zero Hunger's frontline officials should be recognized in its full ambivalence. The officials both identified with the beneficiaries' authentic rural tradition and sought to introduce modern ideas from the city to alter traditional rural culture. They held these two sides of their position in balance through a spiritual narrative of Zero Hunger's implementation in which they were "prodigal liberators" (my term, not theirs) who, having left the countryside, would now return to redeem their own authenticity and rescue their kin from patronage. I find evidence for this argument in the master imagery and narratives of the Zero Hunger program that President Lula himself choreographed, in the daily routines of project implementation involving the officials from Piauí's Zero Hunger office (the Coordenadoria), in the reflections of state personnel from allied bureaus, and in the diffuse usage of traditional communication media (the *literatura de cordel*, or pamphlet literature) to broadcast Zero Hunger–related messages. I then take up the related issue of how some of Passarinho's (middle-class) townspeople came to act and think as agents of the state, albeit with priorities, anxieties, and understandings of patronage that distinguished them from the officials from the state capital, Teresina.

President Lula's Misery Tour

Less than one week after his inauguration in January 2003, President Lula gathered over twenty of his newly appointed federal ministers and went on a Misery Tour (*Tour de Miséria*). Part of Zero Hunger's propaganda campaign, this camera-friendly tour featured Lula's well-dressed, light-complected statesmen hiking through the brown-skinned reality of Brazil's destitute Northeast: the Vila Irmã Dulce in Teresina, the shantytown Brasília Teimosa in Recife, the Vale do Jequitinhonha in the north of Minas Gerais, and Zero Hunger's other pilot town in Piauí.

Throughout this entire photo-op campaign, Lula represented himself not only as the initiator of the tour but also as its guide. His biographical persona naturally lent him his desired credentials—the poor caipira from the backlands of Pernambuco who left his town to seek his fortune in the city. Lula narrated his biography in terms of the life-cycle of hunger itself: beginning as a skinny backland toddler whose mother struggled to keep him fed, growing to a scrappy kid who learned how to get by on his wits, and then becoming a desperate teen whose hunger forced him to leave home in search of work. The theatrical Misery Tour "was a search not just for popularity but for the urban and privileged in Brazil to understand the feeling [*sentido*] and get engaged with programs like Zero Hunger"

(Cruvinel 2003: 2). Minister José Graziano da Silva (Zero Hunger's chief architect) and his team of superb economists, policy experts, and agronomists were crafting a modern, erudite, and technically sophisticated program, but the spectacle of pilgrimage evoked Zero Hunger's more visceral character. Harking back to Betinho's Caravan against Hunger during the 1990s, it both uncovered the face of suffering in Brazil's symbolic heartland and dramatized a redemptive return of privileged Brazilians to the locus of tradition and humble simplicity.

With Lula at its head the tour had a messianic aura. His ministers followed him around like disciples ready to reform their ways. Together they modeled a Brazil ready to accept its accountability and shatter out of its selfish materialism and volunteer to help. In that sense, the tour also had an allegorical quality: the return of the prodigal son to his honest humble origins, a narrative that Lula performed as he walked through the town of his birth (Garanhuns, Pernambuco), kissing kin and hugging old friends.

The Misery Tour and other high-profile Zero Hunger events influenced the way the program's frontline officials in Piauí thought and felt about their administrative practices. It acted as a dominant narrative through which the frontline state officials could interpret and represent their own travels from the urban capitals to the interior municipalities like Passarinho. For the state officials in Piauí who launched many small Zero Hunger projects and who founded many Zero Hunger management committees throughout the municipalities of the interior, such narratives of pilgrimage and nostalgia energized their administrative work with spiritual meaning and helped them to cope with logistical and political challenges.

By emphasizing the state officials' narratives of nostalgia, redemption, and personal renewal, I try to complement a scholarly tendency to explore how development encounters are regimented by an orderly field of statements—knowledge categories, forms of expertise, modes of diagnosis, and so on—that "target populations" internalize (e.g., Ferguson 1990). The "development apparatus" may reform "aboriginal" populations, bringing their behavior in line with modernist models of efficiency and productivity, but it also summons developers' nostalgia for a time before such discipline was necessary. The practice of development taps into modernist desires to reclaim a time before disenchantment, such that the best of developers must reconcile the desire to bring the comforts of modern life to marginal peoples with the romantic fantasy that somewhere outside the modern city there remains a world not yet overrun by the wheel of industry. The need for this reconciliation is at once socially general and profoundly personal. It is animated by the immediate experiences of people whose jobs put them face to face with the populations that represent their own imagined past. Among Zero Hunger officials, biographies of faith-based activism energized frontline agents to confront the practical and political challenges of program implementation (cf. Bornstein 2005). Let me elaborate these challenges by locating Piauí's Zero Hunger officials in their social context.

The Social Location of Zero Hunger's Frontline Officials

The same year Lula was elected president, Wellington Dias became the first PT governor of Piauí. His victory was something of a fluke; the reigning centrist Brazilian Democratic Movement Party (Partido Movimento Democrático Brasileiro—PMDB) had split, paving the way for a temporary coalition between its center-right faction and the PT.[1] The federal government's choice to pilot Zero Hunger in two of Piauí's remote rural towns thus may have been motivated by Lula's knowledge that he had an allied governor in that state.

Once in office, Governor Dias created an ad hoc body within the Piauí state government called the Coordenadoria de Segurança Alimentar e Erradicação da Fome/Programa Fome Zero (The Coordination Office for Food Security and the Eradication of Hunger/The Zero Hunger Program; hereafter, Coordenadoria), which would experiment with Zero Hunger's various component projects in the two pilot municipalities. (See table 1 in the appendix for details on the policies implemented in Passarinho.) Housed in Piauí's capital city, Teresina, the officials within the Coordenadoria would figure out the best way for the federal Ministry of Food Security (MESA) to administer Zero Hunger's Food Card grant, as well as coordinate food basket distribution, housing, water, sanitation, development, literacy, and other "local" initiatives administered by various state and federal agencies. The twenty or so Coordenadoria workers based in Teresina made frequent car trips to Passarinho and the other pilot town located a few hundred kilometers from Passarinho. They acted as the primary intermediaries between the MESA agents from Brasília and the rural poor, middle-class townspeople, and municipal politicians in the two pilot municipalities (and elsewhere).

Most of the Coordenadoria's agents supported the Lula and Dias administrations, and many were formally affiliated with the PT. Only seven or so were government employees. Their respective bureaus signed their paychecks but loaned them out to the Coordenadoria. Alongside these employees was a set of contracted personnel with backgrounds in various social movements and civil society organizations. All of the Coordenadoria agents were young, between twenty-five and forty-four, and most had been inspired by liberation theology and had participated in urban movements (e.g., street children's defense movement). Many had been (and continued to be) politically active as university students, flowing in and out of the Catholic student organizations. Some considered their informal education in these base Christian communities to be as important to their intellectual development as their college courses in social work, social science, nutrition, accounting, administration, law, or philosophy. They sprang from Teresina's politically engaged lower-middle class—bohemian in their aesthetics but very serious of mind. Most lived in Teresina's periphery, former squatter settlements now "regularized" by the state. Like the neighborhood activists that Holston studied in São Paulo's autoconstructed peripheries, they used militant discourses in which they represented themselves as rights-bearing citizens. One had been a seminarian engaged with the Pastoral Land Commission that championed the cause of landless rural workers. They hung out after hours in a sexy, gay-affirmative bar scene that revolved around an open-air amphitheater (Boca da Noite) in the center of Teresina, and they attended weekly rock concerts, plays, political rallies, and poetry readings there. This generated some intergenerational friction within their homes. Most lived with more traditionally Catholic parents who had been raised in the countryside as subsistence cultivators and had migrated to Teresina in the twenty years following the "Brazilian economic miracle" of the 1970s. Their extended kin still residing in the state's interior often teased them for becoming hoity-toity city people. These rural kin visited them after the harvest season, bringing enormous sacks of beans and corn and occasionally spending a few days recovering from hospital procedures in their urban family's home.

The Prodigal Return to the Backlands

The officials in the Coordenadoria began their work without pay, and with only one (rather dubious) car at their disposal for trips into the countryside. (When Governor Dias took over control of Piauí in 2003, the state government was suffering a budget crisis.) They had to hitch rides with other government agents who for other reasons happened to be driving from the capital city into the interior. The general lack of resources was a constant source of frustration, and some vented their exasperation, as in, "What kind of priority is this Zero Hunger program if it lacks equipment in its main office?" Yet there was a silver lining to the cloud—the resource deficiency fed into the agents' narratives of their own devotion to the fight against hunger. As the head nutritionist in the Coordenadoria recalled, "We went to the municipalities without wages, with only strength [força] and courage and we did not even have the promise of good salaries."

The practical challenges that the agents encountered, including basic transportation between the two pilot towns, helped them to experience solidarity with the program's beneficiaries. As one agent told me, "When you go to talk to someone from the interior, you need to do it with humility. I'm not better than anybody. I know what it's like to work with no pay, to depend on other people's generosity to go anywhere. We all do. That's what makes this team [the Coordenadoria] special. This program [Zero Hunger] has no money. It's all through force of will. But we're making it work." The agent's lack of resources lent an air of Christian miracle to the Coordenadoria's achievements in starting up Zero Hunger. While most of the agents did not attend mass regularly, their talk about Zero Hunger contained allusions to God (Christ and the Father) and faith. In a few instances, the Coordenadoria members used biblical stories and parables to add meaning to their journeys, such as the story of Jesus' multiplication of fish and bread (John 6:1–15). In the Teresina office, the agents would begin each day's work by holding hands in a circle and praying for God to help them fight the hunger of "our people" in the interior.

One afternoon, I was lunching with Eugenia, a Coordenadoria consultant, in the center of Teresina by the Complexo Cultural where an NGO had built a life-sized mock-up of a colonial era waddle-and-daub sertanejo homestead. Eugenia had previously traveled to Passarinho several times, and there I had given her tours of Zero Hunger projects. I remember the warm serenity of her smile as she ran her hand across the structure's outer wall:

EUGENIA: My parents came from the interior. My uncles still live there. Aaron, we enjoy a much easier life in the city, with running water and electricity and schools and Internet. But everybody in this office has a parent or an uncle or a grandparent still working in that beautiful system of family agriculture, still living within those beautiful homemade brick walls.

ANSELL: Is everything there beautiful in your eyes?

EUGENIA: No, not everything. Principally because our people there are still slaves in a certain way. You as a Jew certainly know the story. They have the mentality of slaves. And we need to free their minds if we are going to solve the problem of hunger.

Eugenia both romanticizes her parents' bucolic home and pities those who still live "enslaved" there. The quaint houses seem cozy and their inhabitants warm in their ways. She yearns to be part of that world and supports her claim to an authentic place in it by referencing her family past there. Yet in her eyes, the people of the rural interior (her kin) lived under the boot of hunger-profiteers to whom they gave their loyalty. Zero Hunger, she admitted "will not be able to reverse 500 years of oppression, but it is our dream. It is a daring dream."

Spreading Zero Hunger throughout the Government

It would be easy to dismiss the Coordenadoria as an isolated pocket of youthful idealists were they not so influential on state employees from other sectors of government. Most Zero Hunger projects were administered by a mixture of several state bureaus and federal ministries, and while working together, they too came to believe in Zero Hunger's redemptive promise to reconnect with the heartland.

The context of these joint ventures merits mention. In Piauí, Governor Dias often found his own department heads resistant to his various policies. He had been forced to appoint many conservative leaders from other parties to these positions as a concession in exchange for their parties' legislative support. Members of the Coordenadoria suspected that these department heads wanted Zero Hunger to fail. In practice, much of the success of these interdepartmental efforts rested on the frontline government employees who answered to those potentially hostile directors. The Coordenadoria officials came to see low-level government workers from other social service–related departments as potential allies. When they planned projects or traveled together, they established their commonality by collectively bemoaning the corrupt administration that had plagued much of Piauí's history. According to Coordenadoria officials, many of these other state functionaries came to identify with the Zero Hunger program; they began to narrate a shift in their professional activity from fatalistic complicity with the "broken machine" of governance to hopeful and efficacious poverty intervention. (However, they did not necessarily shift toward the political left in the sense of greater sympathy for the PT.)

The Coordenadoria officials generally offered a different explanation for the "broken machine" than did their counterparts from other departments. While other department agents blamed corruption on the innate selfishness intrinsic to humanity, the Coordenadoria officials more often attributed corruption in northeast Brazil to the neoliberal present. A fixation on commodities and money had caused people to forget their shared history of suffering during the military dictatorship and the economic struggles of the 1980s. As one agent said, other government workers had "also gone through the CEBs [comunidades eclesiais de base, or base Christian communities], like us, even if they left the dream behind." By imagining a similar youthful Catholic militancy in their peers' biographies, the Coordenadoria officials were able to make their task one of rejuvenating the idealism of these agents, rather than convincing them of left-wing ideological positions associated with the PT. In this way, they invited their peers from other departments to partake of the same prodigal return to the rural heartland as they imagined for themselves.

On one trip to Passarinho (done as part of a Zero Hunger territorial development project), representatives from the state Bureau of Planning, the Rural Extension and Technical Assistance Company, the Brazilian Agricultural Support Company, and the Zero Hunger Coordination Team visited the house of a village woman. Dona Emília had volunteered her cornfield for an experiment in sustainable development called the "dead cover."[2] After touring and photographing the experiment, the group returned to Emília's house and spoke to her over the coffee she provided. I was seated at the table trying to transcribe the interaction in English as it unfolded. Below is a revealing stretch of the conversation (in which CDR = the representative of the Zero Hunger Coordenadoria, EMATER = the representative of the state Technical Assistance and Rural Extension Company, and EMBRAPA = the representative of the Brazilian Agricultural Research Corporation).

CDR: (To Emília) I first want to thank Dona Emília for her hospitality. It's like my grandfather always said, "We have to put coffee in front of anyone who comes under our roof." He was passionate for his crops. I think Dona Emília knows that we value her field and that she understands that the cash grants are not the principal actions we're doing. They're only one element. We have other actions, like this participation, and Senhora is helping us spread this idea to others. . . . All of us in the Coordenadoria say this all the time, but the presence of the other agencies here, it's what makes it Zero Hunger.

EMÍLIA: It's what makes it Zero Hunger. Indeed. There are times when I see people saying, "This Food Card doesn't feed us," and I say "My people, don't say this." Because I always say he who says this doesn't need it. Right? [Group chuckles.] For me it was a great help. Zero Hunger was a big help. We also want projects like this one, so we can have some resources that come from ourselves, too. Right?

CDR: A better life . . .

EMBRAPA: Let me say, like our companion from Zero Hunger, that we are very grateful to you for opening your house and your field. We can tell that Senhora is a person with the courage to dream for a better life.

EMÍLIA: Indeed.

EMBRAPA: We from the interior are strong for work. Father says that before I was old enough to remember I used to stand at the foot of our donkey to help Mom get water. I know Senhora sees my soft hands and perhaps doesn't believe . . .

EMÍLIA: I believe, Senhor.

EMBRAPA: . . . but I grew up where water wasn't piped in. . . . I have to say, you're a very elegant woman to receive this group of strangers into your house.

EMÍLIA: Oh, I was very satisfied. You're always welcome.

[About a minute of talk passes.]

EMATER: Now, if Senhora will excuse us. It was a long day. We need to be returning home before nightfall.

In the interaction above, three speakers from different government institutions establish their solidarity with one another in two ways. First, they share a nervous laugh at an embarrassing moment when Emília praises the Food Card policy instead of picking up on the CDR representative's suggestion that she (and other beneficiaries) value Zero Hunger's more "structural projects" in addition to its cash grant. Recall that mainstream critics from the political right and left were generally attacking Zero Hunger for being mere "assistencialismo" (welfare statism). Because the right-wing version of this critique asserted that the (lazy) poor would choose to remain dependent on the state's handouts, the state agents here tried to solicit an opposing discourse from Emília only to hear her affirm only the cash grant. Emília is unaware that the round of smiles that broke out across the group is a reaction to their shared failure to constitute her as a self-activating development subject. The moment of embarrassment reminds the agents of the cultural distance that separates them from Emília.

Yet as the interaction moves on, the agents move in the opposite direction. They recover from their embarrassing experience of cultural distance by closing the gap between themselves and Emília. In two instances this is done through references to parents and grandparents: The Coordenadoria agent's initial comments affirm that he and Dona Emília have similar senior kin who impart shared values of hospitality ("We have to put coffee in front of anyone who comes under our roof"), and the EMBRAPA agent talks about his hands to substantiate his claims to a childhood spent on the farm, and his submission to a labor regime controlled by senior kin. The very honorific reference to these senior kin sustains the traditional hierarchy of the rural family, a tradition whose stereotypical absence in the capital city is the cause of rural distrust of urban people. The EMATER agent's polite withdrawal under the pretext of "returning before dark" plays to a village sensibility as well. In actuality, the government agents had no concern about driving between towns at night in sturdy cars with strong headlights, but the agent correctly surmised that villagers preferred not to traverse the highway at night.[3] While the agents' words address Emília, they keep their eyes on their colleagues from other departments, validating their rural roots for one another as much as for her.

Many encounters like this one turned administrative forays into spiritual pilgrimages. They were ritual moments whereby state agents used specialized speech forms (e.g., the rotating oratory of formalized graciousness) to turn their mundane labors into moments of personal transformation. The encounter above exemplified precisely this tendency for developers to enchant their development practice, a tendency that seemed so natural due to the geographic dislocation and the physical hardship they undertook in their trips into the state's interior. It is in the nature of pilgrimage, as Victor Turner (1973: 193) once theorized, to produce a "non-utilitarian experience . . . of fellowship" among "pilgrims" by removing them from the statuses and structures of everyday life. As "the pilgrim moves away from his home, his route becomes increasingly sacralized" (204). The hardships of the journey come to signify the divine destruction of a previous life and the beginnings of pure possibility. Pilgrimages involve ritual construction of new identities, new social ties, and new relationships with the social and cosmological order. Frequently, this entails a broadening of one's group of allies through the establishment of a higher-order commonality that transcends the petty divisions of everyday life. For Zero Hunger's interdepartmental implementation teams, the many unplanned stops in the homes of beneficiaries such as Emília became opportunities for improvised ritual. The state agents acted on their shared impulse to express and consecrate the changes they felt occurring inside themselves during these trips.

These administrative pilgrimages were effective at generating new forms of identification and shared mission among officials from various state agencies. Even government workers involved only tangentially with Zero Hunger projects began to adopt narratives of personal redemption after their contact with the Coordenadoria agents. In early 2004, during a car ride from Teresina to Passarinho, one worker within the Bureau of Planning (SEPLAN) explained, "It works like this. The state deputy has some pull with the government because he voted for some law. So he gets the governor to give a Productive Project to a community he likes. He channels the money to a private enterprise that knows jack shit about the community. The company comes in with a predefined project. The mayor plays it up. Everybody skims money off the state, so it gets to the community underfunded. It fails in the end, but the deputy still gets the votes. . . . *That was my life before Zero Hunger. I was part of that machine. I'm not going back to that shit.*" This narrative and many others like it resembled stories of spiritual conversion more than shifts in political or technocratic outlook—the difference being that people experienced themselves as reconnecting with a virtuous yet long-dormant aspect of their being, rather than as merely changing their mind about world affairs after receiving new information or experience.

I do not know if these experiences of redemption and renewal endured more than a few days following the government agents' contact with Zero Hunger. My point is not that Zero Hunger irrevocably changed the culture of government in Brasília or Teresina but that it became a subculture within the government that prompted reflection among people in a variety of adjacent institutional settings. The redemption it offered entailed the government agents' rediscovery of their own rural origins and washed them clean of their complicity in the "broken machine" of state governance.

Speaking in a Sertanejo Voice

State officials closed the social distance between themselves and the beneficiaries by translating policy messages into the stereotypical folk media of the sertão. They used the genres of popular sertanejo culture to transmit information about Zero Hunger to the general population. Government entities involved with Zero Hunger, such as the parastate energy company, Petrobrás, sponsored program propaganda in the form of literatura de cordel. The *cordel* (literally "string" because merchants once hung the pamphlets on strings) is a genre of written verse designed to be read aloud. It's printed in small paper booklets with covers illustrated in woodcuts and sold for cheap in open marketplaces and bus stations (Campos 1998: 81). Iconic of northeast Brazilian tradition, cordel literature dates back at least to the late nineteenth century and is derived from much older folk culture (troubadour ballads, chapbooks, improvised verse, etc.). Illiterate people often heard the verses at markets and took a pamphlet home in search of a literate person who would help them memorize it. On the large cattle estates, "the landowner or his wife would often retell stories to their tenants" (Slater 1982: 34), inscribing the genre in cozy patronage hierarchies. Over the years, state and federal governments have used this traditional genre to communicate political and policy messages, including information about the peasant-leagues, President Vargas's suicide, and regional development programs (Lessa 1973; Slater 1982; Campos 1998). The stanzas they contain often merge news and entertainment, history and romance. They translate "new and often puzzling information [from the cities] into a familiar form [that] tended to make it more acceptable and less threatening" (Slater 1982: 35). On occasion, sertanejos still sing these poems at markets, and the verses are increasingly played over local radio.

I came across one of Petrobrás's sponsored cordel pamphlets at Teresina's intermunicipal bus station sometime in 2004. It was titled simply *Programa Fome Zero*. Its thirty-two stanzas described the Zero Hunger program as Lula's creation, explained the program in terms of Lula's effort to end hunger, implored "the people" to participate through donations and volunteer work, asserted that Zero Hunger was a long-term solution rather than merely charity, and emphasized the importance of education and health services as components of Zero Hunger (probably in reference to the mandatory schooling and medical visits required by the Bolsa Família program). The lyrics themselves were uncontroversial. No mention was made of clientelismo or local corruption. In fact, one stanza inducted state and municipal governments into the program, calling on them "to organize in response to the needs of each region and community." I found five or six other cordel booklets like this one that addressed specific components of the local Zero Hunger programs, usually sponsored by NGOs and other parastate entities.

When I spoke to my friends in the Coordenadoria about these booklets, they claimed that the cordel literature "spoke to the people of the sertão in a language that they could understand," one that "our tradition has prepared us to hear." As one man told me, "the sertanejo expresses himself in song. It's his way of venting [desabafar]." The term desabafar can mean to air a complaint or even to discharge an evil, pointing to a self that struggles to contain emotions and that occasionally fails to do so (see Linger 1992: 77–80). Alexander Dent's analysis of Brazilian caipira music is useful for understanding how rural Brazilian popular culture expresses the dislocations brought about by urban anonymity, technical expertise, and the relentless march toward progress. Caipira music counters urban progress through the figuration of "torn-up male" singers who embody a "country epistemology . . . a way of knowing by doing" by which rural people teach themselves that "individuals must experience both pain and joy[, that] tears represent the past moving through one" (Dent 2009: 49–50). Often sung in duet by brothers, the performance of caipira music embodies the reconciliation of the brothers' hierarchical and egalitarian relation, and, by extension, allows them to drape the ethos of the countryside over the city's modernist fragmentations (Dent 2009: 73–80; also see Draper 2010 on the nostalgic aspects of forró music). The genre of caipira is metrically and thematically similar to the cordel chapbooks. If Dent is right to see the folk forms emanating from the countryside as an implicit critique of neoliberal democracy, then it's ironic that officials would redeploy one such folk form (the cordel) to further that very democratic project.

All irony aside, a closer look at the cordel poem that Petrobrás sponsored suggests that the officials tried to envelop the state within the symbolic universe of rural tradition. In the Zero Hunger cordel composed by the poet J. Borges, the term mutirão (traditional collective labor) appears over and over, indicating the unification of beneficiaries, officials, and the general Brazilian citizenry into a sentimental community.

Então vamos nos unir	So let us unite
Em forma de mutirão	As a mutirão
Ajudando ao governo	Helping the government
Resolver esta questão	Solve this problem
E dando alimentação	And giving food
É preciso se falar	One needs to speak
Dos componentes do mutirão	Of the components of the mutirão
Contra a miséria e a fome	Against misery and hunger
Com grande mobilização	It is through great mobilization
Que o Fome Zero propõe	That Zero Hunger proposes
Em forma de organização	In the form of organization
É um mutirão de todos	It's a mutirão of everyone
Governo e sociedade	Government and society
Para os que são bem cultos	For people who are cultured [read "high culture"]
E os que têm necessidades	And those who are needy
Quem quer aprender a ler	Those who want to learn to read
Chegou a oportunidade	The chance has arrived
Pessoas que nada têm	People who have nothing
Mas têm a compreensão	But they have clear-headedness
Podem dar um incentivo	They can give incentive
Ao bem da educação	For the sake of education
A participar do grupo	for group participation
Que forma o mutirão	that forms the mutirão

As a stereotypically rural mode of cooperative labor associated with small-scale social interactions and hardy communalism, the mutirão epitomizes the positive features of rurality that make the beneficiaries worth rescuing from the clutches of patronage. The state officials are themselves "components" of this mutirão, which is so authentically Brazilian that it can encompass "people who are cultured / And those who are needy." The text extends a rural tradition into a national one. In so doing, the state officials tell themselves that it is not too late for them to recapture the pristine tradition of Brazil's heartland. The woodcut image on the cover of pamphlet (see figure 5) features an image of two men, one giving the other both a fish and a fishing rod, capturing Zero Hunger's promise to both feed people and teach them the skills that will make them independent.

Perhaps in parody of the state and President Lula, popular disapproval of the Zero Hunger program was also expressed in related caipira genres. Witness, for instance, some verses from the caipira song "A Fome Zero Zerou" (Zero Hunger Came to Zero) by the famous country duo Caju e Castanha in 2005:

A fome zero zerou,	Zero Hunger came to zero
E a fome zero zerou,	And Zero Hunger came to zero,
Tem gente passando fome	There are people going hungry
E a comida não chegou.	And the food didn't come.
Eu vi um cabra falar,	I saw a guy saying
Agora o Brasil acertou.	Now Brazil got it right.
Este homem é metalúrgico,	This man is a metalworker
Pobre e trabalhador.	Poor and a worker.
Conhece meu sofrimento,	He knows my suffering,
Meu lamento e minha dor,	My regret, and my pain.
Ele um dia até falou	He one day even said
Que se viesse a ganhar	That if he ever won
O salário dobraria para	Salaries would double and
a fome acabar,	hunger end,
Mas comprou um avião	But he bought an airplane
Só pra ele passear.	Just so he could travel.

FIGURE 6 Cândido Portinari's famous painting *Os Retirantes* (1944), depicting the tragedy of drought in the Northeast. Reprinted with permission of João Cândido Portinari.

The lyrics undermine Lula's effort to use his sertanejo and working-class identity to curry favor with the rural underclass. Not only does Zero Hunger never get to the poor but Lula also has the audacity to use federal money to buy himself a new airplane (the Brazilian equivalent of Air Force One; International Viewpoint 2005). Worse than Brazil's run-of-the-mill

FIGURE 7 Cartoon parody of Cândido Portinari's *Os Retirantes*, featuring President Lula flying over a famished sertanejo family in his new airplane. Courtesy of the archive of the Projeto Portinari.

politicians, from whom venal corruption is expected, Lula is made to look despicable for having led the public to believe in his authentic connection to Brazil's underclass. A more visual example of this same grievance can be seen in a parody of Cândido Portinari's iconic painting of a drought-stricken sertanejo family that roams the countryside in search of food (see figures 6 and 7). Such parodic critiques of Zero Hunger undermined the state's claim to a primordial connection to the sertanejo population through a countermobilization of the art forms associated with the sertão.

If the state officials never fully belonged to the rural world, this imperfect belonging actually afforded them a double-sided position from which they could engage in cultural engineering. On the one hand, they retained enough high-status urbanity to remain in a didactic posture vis-à-vis the beneficiaries; the state-sponsored Zero Hunger poem deploys words ("components," "mobilization," and "society") that are rarely heard in the everyday speech of the rural underclass. On the other hand, the officials belonged to the rural world *just enough* to make those didactic assertions look like helpful advice from one compatriot to another.

The Curious Position of Passarinho's Townspeople

Fostering a sense of commonality with residents of small rural municipalities was strategically important. Beyond the issue of beneficiary compliance, the state officials needed to induct Passarinho's townspeople into the administrative structure of the Zero Hunger program. The townspeople's understanding and identification with the officials became a matter of great concern for the program's implementation.

The town's middle class played a role in determining which of their compatriots would receive Zero Hunger's cash grant (Food Card), and which villages would receive development projects. One might say that state officials deputized the town's middle class as "state agent." Coordenadoria officials created a local management committee comprised of church leaders, shopkeepers, administrators, union officers, and other members of the town middle class to allocate Zero Hunger's limited resources (see chapter 7). Other townspeople found themselves contributing to Zero Hunger's implementation in less formal ways. One shopkeeper signed a concession to let the state government place a cash machine in his store so that Food Card beneficiaries could draw their monthly cash grant in Passarinho rather than traveling to the larger neighboring town. Two town agronomists were hired as temporary consultants with EMBRAPA and EMATER respectively, to work with projects connected to Zero Hunger. Leaders of the Rural Workers' Union became the Coordenadoria members' de facto municipal contacts, because union personnel were assumed to oppose municipal patronage, and because (in the case of Passarinho) the union people were affiliated with the PT. The union office also served as the headquarters for the Management Committee, which increased the union's general prestige and contact with the population. The leader of FUMAC (a body comprised of Passarinho's village development associations) became responsible for overseeing, and even for designing, joint Zero Hunger–World Bank village projects. All of these people eventually came to recognize themselves as part of the administrative structure implementing and overseeing Zero Hunger, whether or not they supported the PT at the state or national levels. Yet if the state officials imagined their partial belonging as a nostalgic return to the rural world, Passarinho's townspeople imagined their cooperation with the officials as an escape from the stigma of caipira backwardness epitomized by their family and friends in the municipality's rural zone.

The nature of the Zero Hunger program, as an ostensibly plural, de-centralized, and empowering initiative, exacerbated the ambiguity about who was and who was not an implementer of the Zero Hunger program. To some extent, this is probably typical of "participatory development" projects everywhere. "Participation" has become a cultish buzzword in the international development milieu. Participation is allegedly about in-stilling in members of a target population the idea that they have local authority over the development process, that they are "partners" rather than "targets," and that one of their duties is to "convert" others (to a modern mentality) once they themselves have been converted. To the ex-tent that this conversion spreads ("multiplies") throughout target popula-tions, the governments and NGOs that pay for development projects save administrative costs. The converted populations thus perform free admin-istrative labor. It is no coincidence that participatory development rose to prominence during the neoliberal 1980s, the exact time when states and businesses cut back on personnel, privatized, subcontracted, or otherwise downsized to save their skin. And it is no coincidence that the meaning of "participation" in Brazil has grown complex and contentious. For some, it refers to open and public deliberation; while for others, it points to a process of "acquiring marketable training through training in projects and programs" (Junge 2012: 420). In the case of Zero Hunger, the implicit dep-utizing of the town middle class offered its members a chance to enter a conversation with state officials as near-equals, while reproducing a cari-cature of the beneficiary population (their neighbors) as the passive tar-gets of state assistance.

Recall that for virtually all of 2003 and some part of 2004, the mu-nicipality of Passarinho was featured in Brazil's newspapers and on its TV news channels. Passarinho, together with another Piauí municipality, served as one of Zero Hunger's laboratories, chosen especially for its low per capita income. To some extent, this disgraced the town middle class, even its members who supported the Lula and Dias governments. These townspeople were all too ready to reaffirm the distinction between them-selves and the Zero Hunger's *true* beneficiaries: the members of the rural underclass who lived only a few kilometers away.[4]

When I interviewed local townspeople about the needs of their munici-pality, they offered suggestions regarding the social policies that the PT *should* have been carrying out in Passarinho. One person proposed build-ing a particular stretch of road to connect a set of adjacent villages to the main highway, thus allowing farmers to truck their crops to markets more easily. Another argued that reproduction rates should be limited by law to two children per couple, so that family fields did not get continually subdivided. Others suggestions were more focused on basic schooling and job creation, and older people often voiced their hope for increases to the minimum wage that would have the effect of increasing their federal retirement pensions. Many comments were explicitly critical of the PT while others framed their ideas as complements to Zero Hunger. Regardless, most people grounded their authority on a combination of their local knowledge of the poor and their privileged status as Passarinho's (high school) educated elite.

The state officials' idealization of a golden age of peasant-style agricultural production occasionally generated tension with the townspeople. For example, one government agent from EMATER devised a project that would enhance village production of small animals by employing an irrigation technology that he claimed people of the region once practiced long ago, but which no villagers seemed to remember. The technology was called a "level curve," and it relied on gravity (rather than electricity) to distribute rainwater to fields and gardens. (Before 2005, most of Passarinho's villages had no electricity.) Upon hearing about the project, a local agronomist railed against it: "Name me one place that developed without electricity!" The local agronomist firmly believed that the Lula government needed to provide electricity to the interior (which it later did). The EMATER agent's vision of development revolved around agricultural self-sufficiency and ecological harmony, linking both to a bygone local tradition. Key to this fantasy was the active role of villagers themselves, who would be responsible for taking the initiative to build these level curves once the EMATER agent taught them how. By contrast, the town agronomist's rejection of the level curve revealed a modernist impulse toward mechanization, electrification, aquifers, extraction, and centralized coordination. In his mind, villagers were not the builders of irrigation channels but the rightful recipients of technologies introduced from the outside.

In addition to their specific administrative functions, townspeople also became self-proclaimed experts in local culture, not as "native specialists" but as impromptu anthropologists whose own cultural makeup was aligned with the rational West rather than its savage Other. Their explanations of rural culture emphasized ignorance of proper custom and etiquette, as well as a general condition of disorder. One shopkeeper told me that "the people of the fields don't know how to eat. You go to their houses, and they eat in whatever which way. You listen to them talk, you can't understand them. They use words in whatever which way." Such critiques of the people of the interior often bled into a condemnation of alcoholism, laziness, and uncontrolled sexuality (especially among dark-skinned people). As such, the figure of the welfare-supported villager seemed to align with that of the quintessentially amoral elector who took cash or booze in exchange for votes.

The subject of political exchange sometimes arose in conversations between townspeople and state officials. Showing themselves to be "forward-thinking people," members of the town middle class would lament their village-dwelling countrymen's sale of their votes and their general lack of consideration for the future. Hearing this, the state agents seemed at first to express euphoria that some of the locals shared their condemnation of clientelist exchange, but soon an eerie confusion would follow. Emboldened by the state agents' approval, a townsperson might expand on her or his remarks to proclaim that moral politicians "worked for the people," "taking money from their own pockets when they needed to," and moral electors were those who knew the value of a politician who truly helped them in times of need. Puffed up with pride, feeling like a standard-bearer of political virtue, the townsperson might then perceive the agent's disillusion but not understand it. Several times I saw such remarks (often made in small groups on sidewalks or in family-owned stores) lead to awkward silences and the swift, polite departure of the government official.

The townspeople's understanding of local politics differed from that of the Coordenadoria agents. At times they affirmed intimate hierarchy in contrast to the increase of short-term cash exchange, but they occasionally expressed frustration with the "persecutions" that went along with intimate, factional politics. The town middle class assimilated the agents' antipathy toward clientelist intimacy into a preexisting local discourse that lamented the factionalization of families and villages during the political period.

In speaking of his work on the Management Committee during the 2004 municipal campaign, a town schoolteacher explained to me why villagers ineligible for the Food Card grant often blamed him personally for excluding them: "You must understand the mentality of the people of the fields. You and I have a certain citizenship [*cidadania*]. We're friends. You vote for one person, I vote for another. Doesn't matter, we're still friends. Not so with the people of the fields. You vote for the other guy, you're their enemy. Their world is black and white." The schoolteacher implied that the "people of the fields" attribute all bureaucratic decisions about program eligibility to the local political alliances of the decision makers. If I follow his logic, he was saying that the people of the fields believe that if they do not receive a benefit, it is because someone from the rival faction is persecuting them; if they do receive it, somebody "from our side" has intervened on their behalf. The schoolteacher aligned himself with me (an urban type) not by suggesting that our political practices are impersonal or egalitarian, but by affirming our shared ability to keep our factional politics in perspective and to compartmentalize our political selves such that we can remain friends with those who vote differently.

This emphasis on passionate factionalism does not line up perfectly with the anticlientelist rhetoric of the state agents. The Zero Hunger–affiliated agents were preoccupied by intimate hierarchies they imagined as dyadic (two-person) relationships arrayed into pyramids. The schoolteacher, in contrast, worried more about fanatical horizontal intimacies at war with one another. He did not critique intimate exchange per se, only the factionalizing consequences of political intimacy. At the heart of this critique was a call not for liberal democracy in the backlands but rather for tranquility in the context of a "hot" campaign.

While the townspeople appreciated that the state officials were trying to improve local politics in addition to fighting hunger, they generally misunderstood the officials' grievances with existing political practices. They did not so much internalize the state's antipathy toward clientelismo as project their own critiques of short-term electoral exchange and factional persecution onto the officials. While the state officials were troubled by private, hierarchical exchange relations, the townspeople recoiled from the alleged irrationality of their village-dwelling compatriots. This irrationality was discussed in terms of the villagers' laziness, their uncontrollable urges, or their passionate (often bellicose) devotion to a politician. For their part, the officials seemed to have read the affirmative nods of the townspeople as evidence of their shared criticism of intimate hierarchy when, in fact, the townspeople were nodding because they misperceived the state officials' intended critique. Both parties to this miscommunication spoke of democracy, citizenship, and development, and both imagined some linkage between underdevelopment and local political culture. Their ideas about the nature of these linkages, however, separated the two groups in ways they rarely acknowledged explicitly.

Sorting Out the Officials' Image of Themselves

The state officials' nostalgic attitude and imagined kinship with Zero Hunger's beneficiaries helped them reconcile their cultural engineering with their admiration and longing for a return to rural tradition. Perhaps their narrative of a prodigal return to the countryside afforded them some relief from a guilt that they never fully articulated: their abandonment of kin still living in rural poverty, their deviation from their parents' conservatism, their complicity in a world of urban consumption, and so on. In any case, the messianic energy of the Coordenadoria agents made them irresistible, both to their peers from other state departments and to the people of Passarinho.

The townspeople who took up positions within Zero Hunger's implementation structure approached the program differently. They sought from Zero Hunger not a return to rural tradition but an escape from it. Moreover, their idealized history celebrated certain forms of moral, intimate hierarchy, and so they did not always comprehend, much less share, the state officials' social engineering project. I think both parties often felt that they were *almost* communicating, but they were often unable to pinpoint what it was that made them feel awkward in their interactions. Like the feeling of talking to someone who looks at your nose rather than your eyes, everything was just a little bit off.

In the next three chapters, I examine more closely the interactions between Zero Hunger officials and the program's intended beneficiaries in Passarinho. I further explore the techniques by which the officials attempted to dismantle what they saw as patronage. The argument I've just presented in this chapter is crucial to that endeavor because all three of the techniques I'm about to discuss emerged from the officials' sentimentally and spiritually charged experiences of themselves as prodigal liberators.

CHAPTER FIVE

Induced Nostalgia

During one of my first trips to Teresina (Piauí's state capital) I met with the staff from the Zero Hunger Coordenadoria in its small office in the government district. It was still early in 2004, which meant that the federal administration of the program was undergoing serious changes—a new ministry led by a new minister, a "migration" of beneficiaries from the Food Card to the new Bolsa Família program, and a general shift in emphasis away from the once celebrated "local" and "structural" policies toward the "emergency" (i.e., cash transfer) policies. In point of fact, Zero Hunger was giving way to Bolsa Família. The Coordenadoria office was thus responsible both for implementing Zero Hunger policies in tandem with other state agencies and for overseeing this general transition in Piauí. In a modest office at the end of the hall, I met the Coordenadoria's (interim) director, who engaged me in an hour-long conversation about the various Zero Hunger projects at work in Piauí and the challenges faced by his team. He offered me a place at their plenary meetings and virtually gave me a key to their archives. As I walked away, I told him that I would help his team if I could but that, like any researcher, I would need to express my critiques of the program in my writings, despite my admiration for it. He nodded and smiled, and I suddenly felt small and selfish.

I was nearly out the door when I turned to ask him if there was anything in particular that he thought I should investigate during my stay in Passarinho. His eyes lit up, "Yes, see if the people there can actually . . ."—his voice sputtered and trailed off, but his hands were talking. In a series of short, clasping motions, he brought both hands together, touching one set of fingertips to the other in front of his chest. He animated the gesture for several seconds as he struggled for words. "See if they can come together with each other. If they can actually come together. They've lost that. We've all lost that, I think."

In chapter 4, I argued that the Zero Hunger officials experienced a personal and political nostalgia for the sertão and its people. In this chapter, I argue that the officials pursued their assault on intimate hierarchy by inducing the beneficiaries to feel nostalgia themselves. At the heart of this technique was an idealization of the mutirão collective labor arrangement, which came to stand for a bygone era of egalitarian warmth in which rural families worked alongside one another in the fields and shared the fruits of the soil. The decline of this Edenic period coincided with the increase in exploitative patronage exchanges with town politicians, or so the story went. Zero Hunger development projects would ostensibly reverse this trend by resurrecting the mutirão, replacing vertical with lateral reciprocities.

Most remarkable about this nostalgia was that virtually none of the state officials, when I asked them directly about the region's history, ever spoke of a golden age before patronage. When they engaged me (and one another) as university-trained intellectuals, they spoke of the old semi-feudal *coronelismo* that had historically deprived the region's underclass of any dignity. (Indeed, Zero Hunger rhetoric at the national level often framed the program as a solution to a 500-year-old problem of inequality, exploitation, etc.). Yet in their offhand comments, they sometimes spoke *as if* egalitarian transactions (symbolized by the mutirão) had diminished over time in proportion to the increase in villagers' vertical dependence on politicians. Moreover, built into the very administrative procedures of Zero Hunger's policies was a "structural nostalgia," not in individual's considered beliefs, but in the programmatic imagination of bygone forms of collective virtue (Herzfeld 2005 [1997]). Nostalgia characterized the tone of the encounters between state's officials and the beneficiary population. Such shared nostalgia is the basis of another kind of intimacy, a nation's affection for its lovably unruly citizens. By recalling "an edenic order—a time before time— . . . a time when state intervention was unnecessary for the conduct of a decent social life," both parties implicitly legitimate the state's current intrusion into the nation (147). While Zero Hunger officials knew the region's past was no Eden of unbroken lateral ties, they still dwelled in an imagined present defined by a "damaged reciprocity," a kind of lost "transactional honesty" (149). Imagining that rural people had fallen from grace legitimated a cultural engineering project that officials themselves worried was high-handed. As one agent said, "We need to be careful with this program. We are messing with people's hearts." For their part, Passarinho's inhabitants accepted the legitimacy of these cultural interventions, which is not to say that they always understood them or that they imagined the past in a similar way.

The state's nostalgia resonated with rural beneficiaries' own ambivalent relationship to their recent past, but the beneficiaries imagined the "damaged reciprocity" of yesteryear very differently from the way officials did. While cultivators often lamented their abandonment of mutirão labor arrangements, they remembered mutirão not as an egalitarian practice but rather as one controlled by senior men who led extended families comprised of multiple households. Mutirão labor evoked a past when extended families were unbroken and grown children "respected their fathers." Intimate hierarchical relations with local politicians factored into the cultivators' historical narrative, which was very different from that of the state. For the villagers, the golden age of large patriarchal families was not a time before patronage but rather a time when political exchange had not yet been corrupted by selfish, short-term wants, when people were more humble, less greedy, when fewer drunks and tricksters behaved shamelessly, and when children voted as their fathers ordered, thus strengthening the household's long-term political alliances. Because Zero Hunger incited the cultivators' desire to redeem themselves from their own moral lapses, they engaged its various projects with seriousness and zeal; they wanted to transform themselves. The encounter between state officials and rural cultivators was thus one of shared longing for the past but also one of disjunctive nostalgias. This led the beneficiaries to misunderstand, or to otherwise deviate from, the wishes of the officials, despite the fact the beneficiaries seemed fond of the state agents and seemed to trust them. They claimed time and again, "This government is better than any other. These people really know how to explain things to us." These are the contradictions I seek to illuminate in this chapter.

The Structure of the Productive Project

For the sake of a clear presentation, I have selected one Zero Hunger project to demonstrate the dynamics of induced nostalgia as it unfolded. The Productive Project was essentially a collective livestock-rearing initiative that benefited three village associations and their member households. State officials would meet with the participating association to determine what kind of livestock production its members could best handle. The households would then raise project livestock in special project facilities built on their lands and feed them from their privately owned fields. Each family could consume whatever it wanted of its own project-generated livestock, but if it wished to sell livestock, it would need to join with other families in the association to sell in bulk. The association was supposed to retain 20 percent of the sale price to maintain collectively owned machinery (forage grinder, gas motor, etc.) or to provide for other community needs as it determined through "open and democratic discussion" in the association meetings. The project also included funds earmarked for a year's worth of technical assistance. The project thus had three phases: infrastructure construction, initial livestock rearing with store-bought feed, and the transition to farm-produced forage as feed. The state dispersed a total of 60,000 reais (between $US20,000 and $US30,000) to the association over a twelve-month period in three separate allocations and sent officials to the participating villages to monitor the success of each association's progress before releasing the second- and third-phase allocations.

The Productive Project's status as an official Zero Hunger component was ambiguous, but because this was true of so many small-scale "local" initiatives, it makes for a representative case study. Similar Productive Projects had preexisted Zero Hunger by nearly a decade in northeast Brazil. The model was typical of earlier World Bank "community-driven development" programs that the bank had created during the 1990s in collaboration with state governments across the region (Costa, Kottak, and Prado 1997). In Piauí, the state government's Bureau of Planning had already been borrowing World Bank funds for livestock development projects under the Fighting Rural Poverty Program. When Governor Wellington Dias proclaimed these preexisting projects to be part of Zero Hunger in 2003, the bureau teamed up with the Zero Hunger Coordenadoria and channeled forty projects to villages in the state's most impoverished municipalities. Three such projects went to villages in Passarinho.

Governor Dias and his Zero Hunger Coordenadoria made three modifications to the model of the Productive Projects that the World Bank had developed. First, Dias himself insisted that the state's Technical Assistance and Rural Extension Company (EMATER) be awarded the contracts for the projects' technical assistance component in order to revitalize the Piauí government's failing development arm. Second, whereas the World Bank required the benefited community to repay the costs of the project after five years, the Dias government assumed this debt. The association would never need to pay back any project funds. However, at the end of five years, the villagers would be required to show the state government that their association's bank account had accumulated funds equal to the amount of the project cost (60,000 reais). Presumably, this requirement would encourage the villagers to be fiscally responsible without running the risk of putting the associations into in further debt (as had happened during the 1990s). Third, the Dias government committed to paying the portion of the project costs that had been historically assigned to the municipal governments (approximately 15 percent of the total). When I asked one official from the Bureau of Planning why the state was paying the mayors' matching funds he answered, "Most of these municipalities are broke or in debt. Besides, we don't want any mayors bothering the people saying, 'We paid for this, so you owe us.'"

While state-level agents within both the bureau and the Coordenadoria emphasized that the Productive Projects, rather than the cash grants (Food Card and then Bolsa Família), were the "heart of Zero Hunger," high-ranking officials in the federal government seemed unconcerned with them. In an interview in 2005, Food Security Minister José Graziano da Silva told me that World Bank officials had originally pushed for the Productive Projects to serve as the primary policy component of the Zero Hunger program. But "we in the Ministry of Food Security were against this model," because "it would have been too sparsely distributed [geographically]." In other words, the ministry could not spend 60,000 reais on every northeastern village, nor did state governments have sufficient technical experts available to assist all villages with such projects. Spending 60,000 reais in a year for roughly thirty families meant allotting an average of 2,000 reais per family and entailed considerable administrative costs. Graziano must have compared this cost to that of the monthly cash grants (Food Card and later Bolsa Família) that gave 120 reais per month to all poor households (about 1,440 reais per year per family). Not only were cash grants more than 25 percent cheaper, they also benefited poor people immediately. To function properly, cash grants only required the beneficiary to collect money from a special automatic bank machine operated by town shopkeepers. By contrast, small-scale development projects like this one required complex coordinated action and thus were subject to greater risk of failure. Moreover, even if implemented flawlessly, the projects entailed about a year's delay before the beneficiaries could sell, or even eat, their yields. While Graziano endorsed these initiatives as positive "local" contributions to Zero Hunger, he did not dedicate substantial sums of federal government money to spread such projects throughout the northeastern countryside, much less Brazil as a whole.

The federal government's refusal to expand such projects exposed an ideological rift between itself and the frontline Zero Hunger officials (especially, but not exclusively, those at the state level), who saw projects like these as the antidote to assistencialismo. The frontline agents' commitment to the Productive Projects in Piauí reflected both a practical compromise and a political fantasy. It was a compromise insofar as small-scale development projects were less politically contentious than the sort of large-scale land reform demanded by the Landless Workers' Movement and others on the far left. (The Lula government had already decided not to implement a large land reform policy.) At the same time, these same officials spoke with great idealism about the potential for such projects to transform the beneficiaries' basic livelihoods and community relations.

State officials believed that by recovering (resgatando) the rural tradition of mutirão labor, Zero Hunger would foster sentiments of trust, affection, and sympathy among rural households. This would ideally spark the community to life as a self-animated, entrepreneurial cooperative. While some government officials seemed to harbor the neoliberal hope that cooperation would generate wealth that would "last you longer than the cash grants," others hoped the poor would learn to unite and exercise their force of numbers to demand state resources in the name of their community. In the state officials' view, the traditional communities that participated in the Productive Project could reveal democratic capitalism's possible achievements when placed in the hands of free people who labored alongside one another.

Unveiling the Heart of Zero Hunger

When the state officials and I arrived at the village of Caixa de Água, forty kilometers from Passarinho's town hub, we went into a small, brick chapel that served as the association headquarters. It was June 2003. Zero Hunger was still in its initial phase. None of others in the caravan had ever set foot in this village. (I had been there on only one prior occasion.) About thirty villagers were sitting in the chapel pews when we entered around noon. The four agents sat at the front of the room facing the membership, and after settling in, asked the group, "What do you need to make your lives easier?" The villagers smiled and nodded but none responded. Filipe, the representative from Piauí's Zero Hunger Coordenadoria, addressed the villagers.

> We're here because President Lula has made it his mission to eliminate hunger in Brazil. But to do this he doesn't want just to give you a fish; he wants to teach you to fish. We know that many of you receive the cash from Lula's Food Card, and that is good. That's a help. But that card only lasts for nine months. And even if Lula said it would last forever, what happens when the next government comes and takes it away from you? What will you do then? We want to give you something that nobody, no politician, can take away from you. Only God. But don't worry, because God wants you to have it. [He laughed.] We want to give you something that will not be a gift [*presente*] the way the mayor and councilmen give you but a participation-thing. It is something for you to do in mutirão the way your parents did. What we want to know is: What kind of project would this community need in order to survive on its own?

Filipe thus set up an opposition between the ephemeral gifts given by politicians and the enduring "participation-thing." The cultivators, of course, were no strangers to a line of thinking that equates short-term gifts with self-defeating amorality and long-term gifts with virtuous productivity. Yet the goods (cement, fencing wire, roofing, emergency medical assistance, municipal jobs, etc.) that cultivators associated with long-term exchanges were the very goods that the state agents associated with ephemeral clientelist transactions. Here Filipe raised the threshold for "long-term" assistance ("to last forever") and altered the benefited unit of assistance (from the household to the village association).

For the state, long-term assistance is not a gift but an entitlement, a right. But Filipe had trouble translating this concept into terms he believed the cultivators would understand, so he invoked God (albeit jokingly) as a value-distributing agent (see Bornstein 2005). I found myself wondering what such a statement would do to the cultivators' understanding of the project. Perhaps it would relieve them of their sense of obligation to Filipe and the other agents, but at what cost? To recall David Graeber's (2011: 83) argument, "Kings, like gods, can't really enter into relations of exchange with their subjects, since no parity is possible." That is to say that within a truly hierarchical relation people cannot discharge their obligations because they have no currency of any value to their superior. All they have to give is their obedience. Filipe unintentionally turned God into a metaphor for the state. He told the villagers that they could not repay the development project by, for instance, voting for his brother-in-law or for the local Workers' Party candidate. While he wanted his words to divest them of their sense of obligation to repay his "gift," he unwittingly made himself and the other state officials into beings of absolute superiority. In the universe Filipe evoked, the cultivators could only discharge their obligation to the state by acting morally, and he framed moral conduct in nostalgic terms, as work done in "mutirão the way your parents did." What made his reference to the past nostalgic was its depiction of a world defined by self-sacrifice rather than expedient compromise.

Because the villagers who attended this association meeting indeed understood their generation to have fallen from a state of grace (a period when children respected their parents and labored—and voted—at their command), Filipe's words surely touched an emotional chord in them. "It's true," one man told me after the meeting. "We have strayed (*desviar*) from the path of our parents. We have to face the challenge of working together." As the villagers received the message through their cultural filter, they felt moved to put aside their distaste for the patriarchal domination of collective labor and to engage in interhousehold cooperation.

The villagers actively listened while Filipe spoke. They nodded and smiled at key points in his speech and back-channeled affirmative utterances ("Uh-huh" and "That's how it is"), a kind of call-and-response. But as Filipe drew to a close with a question ("What kind of project would this community need in order to survive on its own?"), the villagers seemed to freeze. His explicit question required them to switch postures—from the deferential, affirming role they strategically embodied in their courtship of local elites to an analytic posture that demanded rational public deliberation. Filipe had called on the association members to come forward as individuals with substantive answers, opinions they would need to defend according to impersonal criteria. The recently formed association venue had not been consolidated as a space in which people spoke in this manner. Thus, as Filipe finished his question, the cultivators shifted their gaze downward and giggled nervously. He even tried to rephrase his final question several times, and other members of the team did the same. With his pitch rising, he continued:

FELIPE: Look, we're saying that you won't have to ask for money anymore. You'll spend your own money. [One woman applauded and then stopped quickly.] Food Card is just palliative. Courageous men and women, what could this community do if it had 50,000 reais? [He smiled and pointed at me.] Tell this American over here what you could do if you had such a sum of money.

WOMAN: [softly] I'd like to raise chickens to sell and eat eggs. I can't work in a garden. I have too many children in my house to leave.

MAN: [softly] I would like to raise cattle.

MAN 2: We have nothing to sell at the marketplace because we have no land here. I'd like to raise pigs.

FILIPE: Yes, this is important. Some have more and some have less. Look here, you know those among you who go hungry. I know you know who they are. These people must be prioritized no matter what we do. Now what would be good for everybody as a community? [silence] What could you do given your life conditions? [silence] You need to debate this among yourselves. It's not for us, the government, to decide. [He locked eyes with a village woman.] This project is for the wives, too, not just the husbands. You, Senhora, do you have land? [The woman looked down and giggled sheepishly.]

WOMAN: [mumbling] I plant on the lands of others. [silence]

This last comment caused a sudden change in mood in the meeting. People shifted in their seats and glanced around nervously. The woman who offered the remark did not say another word. Whereas the prior comments of her fellow villagers had all emphasized a world of equal poverty among neighbors, she had laid bare the inequality among households that compelled the villagers to hold their community together through management of envy and evil eye toxicity. The comment was doubly unfortunate: She had both highlighted her own vulnerability to envy, and broken solidarity with her fellows by revealing to powerful outsiders the presence of evil within the community.

After a seemingly eternal silence, João, the president of the association, offered an apology to Filipe and to the rest of the government team.

JOÃO: It's because we're not used to questions.

VILLAGE MAN: Yes, it's because we don't know anything here.

By 1:00 P.M., the temperature rose to over 100 degrees Fahrenheit inside the chapel. The team of government officials grew restless, looking at their watches and stepping outside in pairs to talk and smoke cigarettes.

Finally, Moisés, an agronomist from the Bureau of Planning, stood up and addressed the assembly. He said he was going to let go of the exercise. He said that the villagers could choose from among four kinds of cultivation projects: sheep, bees, fruit, or chicken. When the villagers made no suggestions, he asked, "Am I wrong to say that not everyone in the village has enough land to raise sheep?" When nobody responded he said, "And am I wrong to assume that nobody here has any experience with bee-keeping?" He went on in this way until he concluded (with the villagers' silent approval) that this community could best be served by a chicken-raising project. He cajoled the association members into formalizing the matter with a vote and the team thanked the association and departed for the town center. I later learned that the matter had been decided in a similar way with the other two participating villages in Passarinho. And so it was that two village associations would raise chickens and a third would raise sheep.

Later that day as they mused over a few beers, Filipe, Moisés, and the other state agents tried to explain to themselves (and to me) why the villagers were so silent during the meeting. Perhaps recalling João's comment about "not knowing anything," Filipe told me the cultivators were a people who "lacked self-esteem" because they had no formal schooling and lived in subordination to local patrons who only valued them (gave them stuff) on the eve of elections. The officials worried that this lack of open discussion in association meetings would prevent the villagers from collectively assessing their community resources—the distribution of arable lands among families, differential rainfall across fields, current livestock holdings, and other material questions that would be relevant to a participatory planning session like this one.

The state agents, as readers of Enlightenment social science, associated transparent public speech with an egalitarian sensibility. Accordingly, democratic discourse entails that people question why they should follow any rule, promote any leader, or continue any custom. People must rationally assess the validity of any and all propositions. In other words, in a true public sphere, one proposition is never favored over others merely because it comes from a person of power or a favored kinsman. "No force except that of better argument is exercised . . . and all motives except that of the cooperative search for truth are excluded" (Habermas 1975: 107–8). The state officials hoped that this kind of public speech would engender egalitarian intimacy among the villagers, in addition to increasing their capacity for moral judgment and self-examination (Warren 1995: 167).

These were the essential qualities of a self-advocating egalitarian community that could demand resources from local elites or fill out grant applications for the World Bank, the Food and Agriculture Organization, or some other development agency. For this reason, the state agents understood rational deliberation within the association as a kind of counterpolitics to the submissive conversational postures the agents attributed to patronage.

Moisés expressed this thought to me later that night as we mused over a few beers, saying, "They don't say a word in the meeting, but you watch. They'll go gossiping in one another's houses about this project later on and the ass-kissers [*puxa sacos*] among them will ask their patrons what to do with it." His comment contrasts the talk of democratic public sphere with two other kinds of speech. The first, gossip, is egalitarian, but it's destructive of interhousehold trust and intimacy. Gossip is secretive, private, biased, off-record, and clannish. As he articulates the image of gossip in his mind, he segues into a description of "ass-kissing" talk, that is, appeals for elite guidance. In his stream-of-consciousness, the two are associated because he imagines them both to be private speech acts by which people betray their fellows. Moisés forecloses the possibility of intimate hierarchical encounters based on mutual vulnerability. He implicitly restricts intimacy to an experience shared by *structural* equals. For him, the trust inherent in transparent, public speech testifies to, and allows for, this egalitarian intimacy to emerge among a group of villagers.

Yet for the villagers, explicit, descriptive, and dispassionate debate felt alien and threatening. Explicit discussion of one's life conditions, even one's intentions, could easily reveal the fault lines dividing the rival households of their face-to-face communities. Villagers' routine talk within their association meetings may have touched on the ongoing challenges that defined all of their lives, but it did so in ways that did not stimulate anxieties about competition. In their regular meetings, association speech would not move from one person to the next, but rather everyone seemed to "have the floor" at once. In a kind of murmur, people made statements about how their fields lacked sufficient rainfall to grow their beans and corn. They would overlap one another's voices to create a kind of symphonic expression of a general village problem. In this "drought murmur," an individual did not assert that his or her fields had received less rain than another's, just as nobody claimed to "plant on the fields of others." God, who heard all talk, would "set the winds against" such a person, sending to their house or crops the evil air that was contaminated by all the envy of the entire village. Thus compliance with the collective management aspect of the Productive Project entailed adapting their customary genres of talk to the new task of public deliberation (Ansell 2009).

As daunting as this discursive task seemed to them, the beneficiaries did identify with the nostalgic narrative that motivated such collective talk. This was because before the agents ever arrived in Passarinho's rural zone, association talk already expressed the villagers' own nostalgic imagination. With overlapping voices, villagers would say, "We no longer respect our parents" and "We need to get back to God." This kind of Christian self-admonition made the villagers susceptible to the agents' characterization of their lives as increasingly individualistic. Yet accounts varied as to what aspect of the golden age villagers believed they had abandoned. Some people lamented that they had stopped going to church services or that they drank too much liquor and chased women. Some offered that they had broken from the tradition of voting as their fathers commanded. Regardless, villagers' feelings about these ruptures with their parents were complicated. While some expressed shame and said that God was punishing them with drought for being disobedient, others seemed defiant, happy to have thrown off their fathers' authority. Even those who gave credence to the idea that they should redeem their history of mutirão through the Productive Project did not want to grant the association (especially its president) any patriarchal authority.

In general, the forms of interhousehold cooperation (verbal and physical) required by the project, coupled with the prohibition of seeking aid from town politicians, created a series of barriers to the villagers' successful realization of the project's potential gains. I examine these challenges below, not so much to highlight the failings of the Productive Project with respect to the augmentation of rural wealth—indeed, the villagers were better off for having had it—but to examine the outcome of the state agents' effort to dismantle hierarchical intimacy through the stimulation of camaraderie among equals.

The Villagers Can't Seem to Make the Project Work

The Productive Projects posed serious difficulties to the villagers, and this resulted in the projects' partial failure. The projects did not jump-start collective enterprises, but at the end of the day, participating families had more livestock than before and village associations gained some inalienable property. The difficulties that the villagers faced when implementing these Productive Projects were threefold: First, villagers tended to conceal (physically and discursively) certain visually impressive forms of wealth (what I called "ocular wealth" in chapter 2) and so to the extent that they categorized Productive Project resources in this way, the villagers would face problems managing the resources collectively. Second, the villagers' memories of the past, while prone to nostalgia, filled them with ambivalence that slowed the collective building of project infrastructure. Third, the villagers' common sense suggested to them that local elites could help facilitate the technical advancement of the Productive Project, and moreover, elite assistance did not seem to threaten the lateral solidarity of their village association. (This last issue gave rise not to material problems but to the state officials' sense of failure.)

THE CONCEALMENT OF PRODUCTIVE PROJECT WEALTH

Early in the Productive Project's implementation the association presidents deviated from the rules outlined by the state officials. The presidents were supposed to invite all village families to join the association and participate in the project, but they tended not to invite extremely poor families. João, association president in Caixa de Água, initially told me that he had not invited the family of Adenísio and his wife, Elena, to join the Project because Adenísio was considered by some a *desmantelado* (broken-down drunk). But when I told him that I had never seen Adenísio drink, João simply repeated, "Adenísio could not make the project work." When I pressed him further by noting the good condition of Adenísio's tiny cornfield, João finally spoke ill of his neighbor, saying that Adenísio "covets the things of others." He went on to remind me of the many times that Elena had "shown up at his door at the dinner hour" waiting for an invitation to eat. "I too feel bad for him, Aaron. But he's dangerous. He has a good heart but his eyes are dangerous." João believed that Adenísio and Elena's hunger would cause them to emit destructive evil that would endanger other people's project livestock (cf. Elyachar 2005: 158). Adenísio's family (and two others in this village) became casualties of the triage that João had to do on behalf of the other villagers.

João was the only president who spoke to me about this subject, so I don't know if the other two thought about their exclusion of poor families from the Productive Project in these same terms. Still, the specter of evil eye danger probably loomed over all three associations. The poorest villagers were those believed to disrupt the fragile system of interhousehold sociability that depended on polite distance and self-reliance. Village sociability also hinged on the collective denial of hunger-driven envy in polite collective conversation. Not only could people like Adenísio and Elena not join the project, the very fact of their exclusion could not be uttered in the association.

The fraught character of Productive Project resources also contributed to a second implementation challenge, one that embarrassed the state agents. Several families from all three villages who had initially agreed to participate in the project soon withdrew after it became clear that project resources would be used as planned rather than "falling into their pockets" (as cash). Members of these families told me that they had initially joined the project believing that their association presidents would liquidate the project funds and distribute them evenly instead of buying project materials. When this did not happen, they wanted out.

Rural people's preference for cash was partly motivated by their fear that they lacked the croplands necessary to produce feed for the project livestock. Believing that they would fail to sustain their chickens or goats, they thought it better to withdraw than to risk visible failure, which could make them susceptible to suspicions of envy that could potentially marginalize them. I suggested to several such families that they sharecrop the lands of other families in the years to come to sustain their chickens, and for the time being, request that the association provide them with added feed rations for their project livestock. Most all of them had already considered and rejected this or similar options because they were concerned that public discussion of the project would force them to reveal their scarce landholdings at the association meetings. One participant did actually undertake such a sharecropping arrangement but simply declined to discuss it in the association. It remained a well-known yet never acknowledged fact.

Concerns about envy also contributed to the slow construction of each family's chicken coops and sheep sties. When building materials were delivered to each participating household of all three villages in December 2003, no household took steps to erect its coop or sty for many months. The participating families were supposed to form work groups to undertake this construction, but the formation of these groups and the initiation of labor were problematic. Let me address the problem of initiating the labor first and then return to the matter of the work groups in the next section.

No family wished to be the first to build its sty, fearing that this action would convey the impression that it "wanted more than what belonged to it." In the association meetings, the presidents would cajole their members to take action, but none of the three presidents had built his own coop or sty. When I asked João about this, his response indicated his nervousness that his position as president already suggested that he was a man of ambition who coveted "more than what was his." If he built his coop before the others, this action would only reinforce that impression. Such ambition is met with collective suspicion (God "sends the winds against" both types) because, like envy, ambition introduces evil into the general community space. Once the construction of the coops and sties began, families proceeded at a slow but even pace in setting them up. No family wanted to be the first or the last to have its built.

Once the structures were built and the livestock arrived, the villagers' general unwillingness to discuss the coops, sties, chickens, or sheep during the association meetings created two additional difficulties. In the villages that worked with chickens, widespread problems (predatory eagles, inappropriate forage, etc.) killed scores of chickens before many families became aware of these threats. As it turns out, eagles were not able to prey on the chicks in coops covered with mesh wire. The association could have used some of its funds to buy wire for all participants, but this simple solution did not become common knowledge for months. In the meetings, the families reported simply, "My chickens are dying. They're laying no eggs." Such remarks could be heard even from the few families that had avoided this fate by using the wire. Rather than specify their situation, they simply added their voices to the collective, polyphonic commiseration that seemed to be a spin-off of regular "drought murmur."

The villagers' refusal to discuss project wealth in association meetings also kept participating families from coordinating the bulk sale of their livestock through the association. Instead, sales were made sporadically and privately by individual families. The state agents had hoped that the associations would eventually operate like rural cooperatives, selling collectively and retaining a portion of the sale price so that it could act a unit of collective consumption. As Moisés told the villagers during one of his project visits, "You can then do whatever you want with this money. It's yours. You just need to decide on it democratically, through open talk. You can buy Christmas presents for your children. You can buy a gas generator. You can even redistribute it as cash to all families or you can pay for another family's entry into the project. It's yours!" Comments like these suggest that Moisés saw the association's ownership of wealth as a mode of enriching horizontal solidarity through democratic speech. Given that association members had little difficulty discussing cash wealth (e.g., members' dues) in public—recall that purse wealth is not susceptible to evil eye danger—he was probably correct.

Yet, the association never gained such monetary resources because families did not want to reveal to one another the quantity of animals they were ready to sell any more than they wished to reveal the deaths of those animals. One project participant, Esmeralda, explained to me this logic: "Aaron, I don't tell anyone about my chickens, not even the others in the project. Some people say the big eye [*olho grande*] is an illusion, but I confess that I believe. We never know who has bad blood, do we? I close up when people ask me about them. Because they gossip, 'Esmeralda has good luck,' and then who knows. If I had another cow horn [an evil eye amulet], I'd put it on my coop." Esmeralda's words succinctly affirm the project's value for the villagers while negating the idealized modes of lateral solidarity that the state agents thought the project would engender. Like others who lined their chicken coops with cow horns, Esmeralda's experience of collective action hinged on not expressive talk but a shared responsibility to keep the village safe from spiritual danger. As a result, the collectively owned association bank account never accumulated the funds needed to prove to the state that it could pay back its debt. The state and the World Bank were left with the impression that the Productive Project was a total failure, even though some people's very real suffering was ameliorated.

REMEMBRANCE OF MUTIRÃO AND THE DAYS OF CHAPEL WORSHIP

Turning to the problem of collective labor, it was clear that the work groups that the association presidents had organized (under the guidance of state officials) were not materializing to build the project infrastructure. Even after the participating families began inching their way toward the construction of their coops and sties, they chose to hire local masons to do this work rather than using the mutirão work groups. This result was more upsetting for the state officials than for the villagers themselves; indeed, the experience of trying and failing to stimulate these groups exposed a rift between two imaginations of the past: the state agents' and the villagers'.

The villagers remembered no time when warm, egalitarian ties provided them with their livelihood and offset the need to solicit aid from the local political elite. That fantasy belonged to the state agents. However, villagers did feel nostalgia for a past in which siblings and siblings-in-law from separate households cooperated with (and rivaled) one another in collective manioc- and sugarcane-processing labor under the direction of a patriarchal figure. Village adults were prone to express remorse for their failure to maintain the chapels that their parents had built and worshiped in during the 1970s and 1980s, the heyday of liberationist Christianity. Perhaps because their association meetings took place in these same dilapidated Catholic chapels, participation in the association did carry an aura of redemption. As one friend told me during a particularly heated moment, "Why do you think they go to the chapel for association meetings? Here we respect our parents, Aaron. Not like you who leave your mother alone far away after your father has died." The comment cut into me, but it revealed the rub. The associations were tied to the memories of revered forebears. If the association members became family to one another in the meetings, then they did so as siblings, and this raised the specter of a guiding father. But villagers did not want a paternalistic association president to designate the members of their work groups.

Instead of forming work groups to erect the coops and sties, each family (when it eventually overcame its reluctance to engage in the project) hired masons to do the job. When I asked why, people often told me that they were not accustomed to working with the people the association president had assigned to their work group. When the state officials heard about this, they asked me (and others) why the president did not simply utilize existing mutirão groups rather than creating new groups out of whole cloth. The answer was that this tactic was only possible for those households who had successful cooperative relations with others, either as groups who engaged in collective labor or as networks comprised of two-way, day-trading relations. For at least half of the households in these three villages, no such relations existed. The three association presidents wanted all their groups to function well, and so they added (unwanted) people to existing labor groups and in some case pulled out people "who know how to work" and redistributed them.

Given that the task involved construction work, the presidents faced an added constraint in designing the work groups; they needed men with some experience in masonry to assist each group. The presidents tried to design groups that included at least one local mason, but masons were few. Moreover, masonry was typically a skill passed from father to son or between brothers or in-laws. Thus, even though one village contained enough masons to supply each of the five work groups, these masons belonged to only one or two families. Their unwillingness to work collectively with other groups did not so much reflect their rivalry with these others as it did the economics of mason labor. A mason's day wages were nearly twice as high as those for normal farm labor. If the masons were to work without pay in exchange for other people's labor, they wanted to receive a mason's wages in return. Otherwise, the exchange would feel unfair. When the association presidents tried to prevail on the masons to cooperate, they generated a backlash. One president, who refused to push the masons to participate, explained, "I don't want them thinking I'm trying to play papa to the association, so I leave them alone." His concern was well-founded. In another village, a group of several village men (including one mason) commented in passing: "Who does he think he is telling us to work with one guy and he tells my brother-in-law to work with another?" The problem was clearly not limited to the masons alone. In general, the idea of a president who directed multihousehold cooperation evoked the specter of a father's command over his adult children, a proposition that was all the more distasteful because the president was an age-mate who had no rightful claim to filial obedience. Ironically, the Productive Project's evocation of the villagers' memories of the past pushed them away from the mutirão and toward the purchase of specialized mason labor with cash. This is ultimately how most coops were eventually built: each family paid a mason and the husband, son, or both would work as the mason's helper. After the structure's walls and pillars were in place, the husband would rely on his sons and his day-trading partner to lay the shingle roofing, a skill that all rural men have.

Yet it would be wrong to assume that the state officials' language of nostalgia only triggered the worst of villagers' memories. By framing the Productive Project as an activity that affirmed bygone social relationships, the officials did induce villagers to speak publicly about the past in ways that helped the poorest families to argue for their inclusion within the project. Moreover, this talk opened the discursive space of the association meetings in ways that broadened participation and made project wealth an acceptable topic of conversation.

Villagers like Adenísio and Elena are a case in point. This couple felt lingering resentment toward João, the association president, for excluding them from the projects. They rarely attended association meetings and were often silent when they did. On one occasion they did attend and Elena made her resentment clear to her neighbors. The topic being discussed at the time pertained to the ongoing failure of the workgroups. João had recently received a visit from Moisés that prompted him to cajole the work groups into action. When he commented that Moisés wanted the association members to work as their parents did, Elena responded angrily noting that, "Isadora [her great aunt] was the mother of Josevaldo, the mother of Sérgio [both project participants]. But nobody asked me to join the project!" The comment went unanswered, but when I later asked other nonparticipating villagers what they thought of it, they affirmed Elena's claim to inclusion. "It's true," one man told me. "We all come from the same parents. We should all be part of the association."

Other grievances and requests framed as genealogical claims to equity periodically resurfaced during the association meetings and in private talk outside them. In another village, an unpleasant incident occurred when a young couple, José and Leilah, wanted to join the Productive Project. The couple had told me that they deserved to enter the project because "Papa helped built the chapel but Mário [that association's president] forgot that. He [Papa] is old now but we can raise chickens and he can have some of the eggs. Isn't that fair?" I suspect that the couple made this argument to Mário in private, because he raised the point during the subsequent association meeting. The meeting was already tense because an older couple had resolved to drop out of the project, claiming that Mário had been meddling in their household affairs. When Mário said that the older couple would have to dismantle its coop and give the materials to José and Leilah, the older woman scolded Leilah, saying that she should be ashamed for "talking about our things." Mário interjected that development was "for whoever ran after it." Then he initiated a vote to decide the general issue of whether a withdrawing family should be required to return project materials to the association for reallocation to new participants. During the brief discussion, Leilah argued that she and her husband had a right to the join the project and take the withdrawing couple's materials because her father had helped to build the chapel (by then the association's physical headquarters). (The vote went her way, though the elder couple remained in the project.)

This minor drama pitted the ethic of concealing wealth against the ethic of honoring an older man's past contributions to the local Catholic community. The vote cast in favor of Leilah and José worked against the tendency to classify development project property as ocular wealth: development wealth belonged not to the families but to the association. Families had exclusive use-rights over this wealth while they participated in the Productive Project, but they could not convert it into alienable private property, that is, they could not sell it. The association membership reinforced itself as a collective body by confirming the rights that this body held against its individual members. At the same time, the event also had implications for the communicative space of the association meetings. While the older woman's rebuke of Leilah for "talking of our things" suggested that project wealth was tantamount to cattle, crops, or other ocular wealth, Mário's interjection served to recast the chicken coops as a different form of wealth, such as cash, which was safe to discuss.

The nostalgia that the state officials induced in the villagers thus had mixed results. The failure of the work groups suggested that the state could not resuscitate traditional forms of shared labor. The fact that the villagers did not engage in collective sale of the livestock indicates that the state could not transform the association into a discursive venue for open, self-expressive debate. At the same time, the Productive Project did cause the villagers to call into question their everyday practices of concealing wealth disparities and ostracizing the poorest people from shared labor arrangements. Moreover, the two conflicts I have discussed (one with Elena and the other with Leilah) expanded the field of topics that villagers could discuss in the association. These incidents alone conferred added power on their associations by affirming their capacity to redistribute project wealth away from individual families. Indeed, while these processes played out somewhat unevenly across the three villages that benefited from the Productive Project in Passarinho, members of all three associations claimed that the project, while difficult, was improving their "unity" (*unidade*).

PROJECT PARTICIPATION AND INTIMATE HIERARCHY

The final difficulty that merits mention here relates to the involvement of local politicians in the Productive Projects. The state officials hoped that strengthening the village associations through the Productive Projects would prompt the rural poor to forgo vertical exchanges with local elites in favor of egalitarian mutualism. The state officials assumed that hierarchical and egalitarian reciprocities were inversely proportionate to one another, such that the more the association had of one, the less they needed the other. Yet the villagers did not think about their exchange relationships in these terms, and so they solicited various forms of Productive Project aid from Passarinho's mayor, vice mayor, and several members of the town council.

Early in the project, the association presidents used their alliances with local councilmen to obtain free delivery of the building materials. When the state officials discovered this practice they grew despondent. After lecturing one president (Mário) on the dangers of becoming indebted to politicians, Filipe lamented to me that "they don't remember anything we tell them. But that's how it is with the people of the interior. You make a bit of progress and then it reverses." When I spoke to Mário afterward, he said he did not understand why Filipe scolded him.

> When they [the town activists] helped us found our association, they told us: "Keep politics out." Because when politics comes into the association, it's one person pulling in one direction and another person pulling in another and it all falls apart So I said to the association, "People, I'm friends with Gustavo [a councilman] for many years and he has a truck and he said if we just pay for fuel he'll deliver without charging. I'm not saying you should vote for him if you don't like him, but this is a good deal. Can we do this, or are you going to revolt?" And they understood. And we did this. And he may have gained some votes but nobody felt, you know, obligated to vote for him.

Mário's comments do not indicate that he thought dealings with politicians were totally safe: they could potentially disrupt association harmony, but Mário thought there was a way to handle that possibility. Accepting Gustavo's aid was fine so long as he made it clear to Gustavo that this aid would earn him no firm electoral commitments and that the association reserved the right to invite other (rival) politicians to help as well. Mário's actions (and those of the other presidents) afforded Gustavo (and others) an opportunity for mild political courtship on the condition that, as Mário reported saying to Gustavo, "Don't get jealous if we ask other councilmen to help us, too." For Gustavo, this was a good deal. He reported this, "This is my chance to show the people that I know how to work. They may vote for my adversary now, but they'll see that the lies he tells about me are not true. That I respect them and that I can leave them satisfied."

Gustavo's favors may have been persuasive, but they did not oblige the villagers to vote for him—a distinction that the state agents did not recognize. Such gifts to the association were essentially overtures of courtship. They did not directly elicit a countergift (i.e., a vote) so much as they lay the groundwork for creating future intimate hierarchical reciprocities. Such services to an association were token demonstrations of the type of "work" these councilmen would do for those who allied with them. As such, the councilmen understood that they had no right to prevent the association from obtaining favors from their rivals, and they did not expect that all association members would vote in a uniform way. In fact, Mário was quite clear that if a president solicited aid from only one municipal faction, he or she would face internal dissent.

Under these circumstances, to quarrel over such a visit out of loyalty to one's (rival) patron would indicate "disunity" in the association. In fact, for the villagers, their ability to solicit a politician's help without contracting electoral debt was the ultimate expression of group cooperation. Welcoming these councilmen into their meetings, the villagers increased their collective prestige in the eyes of the political class, and they altered the criteria by which individual families made electoral decisions. For the villagers, the extension of courtesy, even open-mindedness, toward otherwise rival politicians signified a "forward-thinking" posture and a critical attitude toward the loyalties of yesteryear in which "we never cared about what they did for the community." The association's tolerance of politicians' favors could be read as a mode of democratization to the extent that it made the association meeting a space in which people held in abeyance their personal alliances long enough to entertain rivals.

The tragedy of such practices lay in the fact that the state officials viewed all such courtship as a symptom of co-optation whereby the politician would buy off the votes of the association members, control the decisions made in the association, and somehow undermine the Productive Project in the process. The officials entertained a fantasy in which the village association, once strengthened by the material cooperation induced by the Productive Project, would transform into a revolutionary entity. For the officials, a truly "united association" would seek to "reclaim [reivindicar] resources" that the local government owed them as citizens rather than engaging in political reciprocity (see Holston 2008).

Disjunctive Nostalgias

The state agents who brought the Productive Projects to Passarinho under the rubric of Zero Hunger sought to inspire a social and political transformation of village life through the introduction of cooperative economic organizations. Like much of what is called "participatory development," the Productive Projects linked ideas of collective labor to the formation of horizontal political solidarities that contrasted with vertical patron-client buy-offs. They sought to build these political solidarities out of the cooperative labor arrangements that would lead to more sheep, chickens, and eggs. But the egalitarian rapport that defined the interactions among village households did not conform to the state agents' fantasies of communitarian democracy. Their public discourse revolved around rituals of collective sympathy and commiseration rooted in the management of envy and evil, not descriptive self-revelation and explicit deliberation. When the state agents told the beneficiaries to work together in mutirão as their parents once had, they stimulated a historical memory very different from that of the officials themselves. Villagers came to believe, perhaps more strongly than they had before, that they had deviated from the righteous ways of their parents through their declining church attendance, increased use of cash, electoral autonomy (from fathers), and abandonment of paternally controlled labor. As these encounters reoccurred across multiple Zero Hunger projects, the villagers in Passarinho and other places became convinced that their participation in Zero Hunger would offer them a path toward moral redemption, even if the nature of that path was never really clear to them.

CHAPTER SIX

Programmatic Pilgrimage

On an unusually cold night in early May 2004, I stood next to my friend
Augusto by the old church in the municipality adjacent to Passarinho. We
were waiting there for a chartered bus to pick us up and take us on a ten-
hour ride to Teresina. Standing around us were roughly two dozen other
people—mostly young, mostly men, mostly dark-skinned—all shivering in
the evening's chill and trying to stay in good cheer. The others, who clung
to their makeshift sacks full of rolled clothes and toothbrushes, all hailed
from villages in Passarinho or its surrounding municipalities. Augusto, a
respected, pension-collecting senior, came from the village of Serafim; he
was its association president.

Once our group got to Teresina, these village representatives would
participate in a three-day intensive workshop meant to prepare them for
the Quilombola Project, one of Zero Hunger's "local initiatives" that prioritized the *remanescentes das comunidades quilombolas* ("remainders" [de-
scendants] of fugitive slave communities). But none of the people waiting
that night knew what sort of resources this project would afford their communities, or why they had to travel to Teresina to learn about all this. In
fact, none of these people had ever heard the terms *quilombo* or *quilombola*
prior to receiving a visit from an activist from the regional Movimento
Negro ("Black Movement").

Augusto pulled me aside, "Aaron, these are good people from the government. This is a very good government that knows how to do things
correctly, but I'm not sure what they're thinking with this Quilombola
thing. There may come a time when we need your help." It had taken me
some time to gain Augusto's trust. After my initial scouting research in
2003, I had sent a request—via my assistant, Jorge—to the three association presidents I had met, asking them to sign letters of support for my
research grant applications. Augusto was the only one who had refused.
Jorge explained to me: "Our people don't read well. They have sometimes

been tricked out of their land by government agencies and lawyers—well-educated people like you." Augusto's refusal came at some risk to him—which made me wonder if I was right to request those signatures to begin with. He had weighed the possibility that I might carry a grudge, that I might devote my attention (and whatever material benefits my attention might bring) to the other villages whose presidents did sign. I admired his caution, and when I returned during my main field stint, I visited him repeatedly and ran errands for him—anything to feel worthy in the eyes of a discerning father figure. I once raced to Serafim at sunset to give him an association tax document because I'd told him it would be in his hands before dinner. He later told Jorge, "That boy is crazy," and Jorge explained, "You've conquered his heart."

Yet what Augusto was asking of me in that moment remained unclear. Did he think the government had made a mistake in identifying the village of Serafim as a quilombo? If so, was he requesting that I use my anthropological credentials to convince the government that Serafim was, in fact, comprised of descendants of fugitive slaves? Or was this less about credentials and more about patronage, that is, was Augusto asking me to use my influence to ensure that Serafim would receive project benefits even if nobody ever believed it really was a bona fide quilombo? Maybe I should have asked for clarity on these matters, but I was too cold, too tired of asking taxing questions, and too lazy to pull out my journal to record the conversation. I told him I would help in any way I could, and he was satisfied.

As it turned out, Augusto never needed my help, because the state officials and regional activists who organized the training session in Teresina were under no illusions regarding the history and social memory of the region's "*negro* communities." The purpose of this training session was to induct community leaders into the quilombola identity category, to teach them about both the history of African slavery that they had "forgotten" and the present reality of racism in Brazil that they suffered every day. Material resources would surely flow to these communities once they assumed this identity, but more important to both the state officials and the regional activists was a transformation in their subjectivity (see Fry 2005). During the long, chartered bus-rides to the capital city, officials encouraged village representatives to imagine a race- and class-based connection to the *negro* inhabitants of the municipalities they were passing along the road.[1] Once in Teresina, they challenged the beneficiaries to demonstrate combativeness, indignation, and a demanding attitude toward the state officials themselves. In this way, the state inducted Passarinho's dark-skinned rural poor into a rite of passage, a "programmatic pilgrimage" meant to reorient their basic attitudes toward one another and toward authority.

The strategic usage of pilgrimage as a social engineering technique, like "induced nostalgia," was based on the state officials' own experiences of meaningful, solidarity-enhancing travel from the capital city to the backlands. It was also strongly resonant with Catholic folk practices throughout the region whereby common people historically engaged in pilgrimage and other millenarian movements when they believed their patrons had become morally or spiritually bankrupt (Pessar 2004). Piauí's Coordenadoria drew into Zero Hunger's administration not only state officials from various other bureaus but also activists from the Movimento Quilombola, an offshoot of the Movimento Negro headquartered in a small city adjacent to Passarinho. They worked together to instill in the beneficiaries a shared racial solidarity and an indignant rejection of both racism and political exploitation (read patronage) by making pilgrimages of the beneficiaries' experiences as well.

Yet while the state and its allied activists linked the assault on patronage to a state-led stimulation of quilombola identity, Passarinho's Afro-Brazilian villagers did not absorb all parts of this complex message equally. The technique of programmatic pilgrimage and the social program that it infused led villagers to refashion the terms of their intimate hierarchical relations but not to reject intimate hierarchy entirely. With regard to race, officials and activists helped to forge an essential ethnic identity where previously there had only been an awareness of racial discrimination. That essential identity turned out to be more *negro* than quilombola.

The Quilombola Project and the Problem of Quilombola Identity

The Quilombola Project involved a partnership among the federal Ministry of Food Security (MESA), Piauí's Zero Hunger Coordenadoria, Piauí's Technical Assistance and Rural Extension Company (EMATER), the U.N. Food and Agriculture Organization (FAO), and the Quilombola Movement in southeast Piauí. In the context of this project, the activists from the Quilombola Movement operated as extensions of the state, a novel and uncomfortable role for them but also one that brought some power and resources (travel grants, meals, phone cards, etc.). Their job was to identify the beneficiary villages within Passarinho and the other participating

municipalities adjacent to it and to convince their inhabitants to participate in the project. EMATER would then host village representatives (later
dubbed "community leaders") at its training facility in Teresina, where
various state officials (Zero Hunger, the Quilombola activists, EMATER)
would work with the representatives to diagnose the needs of the communities and plan specific initiatives that responded to those needs. The FAO
would then channel money to MESA and EMATER, which would spend
this money on the projects. EMATER would provide technical support for
those initiatives, and Zero Hunger Coordenadoria officials would facilitate
participatory dialogue among the parties. Everybody involved felt they
were in uncharted waters; in fact, not all the officials involved knew what
a quilombo was or believed that the villages in question were, in fact, bona
fide quilombos.

Historically, the noun *quilombola* refers to a fugitive slave who joined
with others to form a rural community (quilombo) of their own, sometimes fighting off the incursions of slave owners empowered by the racist
colonial, and later the imperial, state. (Confusingly, *quilombola* is also an
adjective, e.g., *negros quilombolas*). During Brazil's more than three centuries of slavery, there were hundreds, if not thousands of such communities; the most famous was Palmares, located in what is now the northeastern state of Alagoas. Palmares had more than 30,000 inhabitants and
survived for over 100 years (1580–1710) before the governor's hired guns
eventually overthrew its king, Zumbi. Brazil's contemporary Black Movement views Palmares, Zumbi, and the quilombola in general as icons of
Afro-Brazilian resistance against racism. In 1988, the Palmares Cultural
Foundation emerged as a government entity (attached to the Ministry of
Culture) dedicated to ensuring Afro-Brazilians full citizenship and cultural
rights. The Palmares Cultural Foundation had lobbied for Lula to include
language in Zero Hunger that prioritized quilombola communities along
with several other "vulnerable populations."[2] Passarinho's Quilombola
Movement activists maintained strong ties to the foundation, and they
successfully lobbied the Piauí state government to push for the FAO to
steer its resources toward the region's quilombola communities in accordance with Zero Hunger's federal priorities.

The quilombola concept is mired in confusion and controversy in Brazil. Jan French (2009: 94) notes that during Brazil's redemocratization period, struggles for the codification of Afro-Brazilian rights in the new constitution resulted in a small "quilombo clause" (Article 68) that allowed
the state to grant communal lands to surviving quilombos. The model for

these grants came from indigenous rights organizations that had long militated for cultural recognition and collective, inalienable lands. But despite these formal similarities, there were key differences in the way the nation imagined these two populations. José Maurício Andion Arruti (1997: 10) elaborates how in "their imagined ideal forms [Indians] correspond to isolation, while [rural blacks] correspond to interaction; Indians correspond to purity, while blacks correspond to contamination." In other words, the exotic splendor with which the general population regards indigenous peoples does not extend to rural black communities; the latter are marked not for preservation but for assimilation, an imperative that has led to racist anxieties that *negro* blood and culture would contaminate the population. The identification of surviving quilombos is thus bound up in the general assertion of the cultural value of *negro* ethnicity, especially given the complexity of Brazilian racial identity.

Given the fluidity of Brazilian racial identity, the question of what constitutes a modern "quilombo" becomes doubly complicated. Prior to 1994, a contemporary (postslavery) quilombo was a rural community whose living residents had "actually descended from living communities of fugitive slaves" (Jan French 2009: 95). Yet, "the Brazil of today does not contain the types of quilombola societies—with evident historical continuity from the rebellious communities of the slave era, and with profound historical consciousness and self-independent political organization—that still thrive in other parts of the Americas (Jamaica, Surinam . . .)" (Price 1999: 8). The origins of Brazil's quilombos, as David Price discerns from reviewing the ethnographic literature, are quite varied: "Some were formed from slaves (or ex-slaves) after the collapse of a ranch or plantation in the decades prior to Abolition, some took root on lands donated to ex-slaves by land-owners (*senhores*), some were bought by free slaves" (9). To adjust to this reality, the designers of Article 68 used the term *remanescentes dos quilombolas*, paralleling the legal verbiage pertaining to indigenous communities. The term emerges "to resolve the difficult problem of continuity and discontinuity with the historical past, for which descent does not seem to provide a sufficient connection" (Arruti 1997: 21; also see Almeida et al. 2010). The term *remanescente* presumes some form of cultural loss without implying that such loss forfeits authentic identity. Thus the stereotypic features of slave-era quilombola communities, such as collective land ownership, African spirit worship, or the material artifacts of slavery (e.g., manacles) are not necessarily found in today's "quilombos."

In 1994, the Brazilian Anthropological Association (ABA) relaxed the

criteria for designating a living group of people "quilombolas" by defining *remanescente* in a way that did not require direct descent from fugitive
slaves, or even a uniquely African cultural survival.[3] As such, the quilombola identity shed its "strictly historical significance" (Jan French 2009:
93). Quilombola identity now rests on presently shared experiences—
shared land management, shared discrimination, a shared project for the
future—and on the self-identification of the community through practices
of "affiliation and exclusion" vis-à-vis other populations. This definition
theoretically enables any rural black community to claim quilombo status,
and in 2003, Lula issued a formal decree (4887: Article 2) making collective self-identification (*autoatribuição*) the legal criterion for state recognition of quilombo status (see Mitchell 2013).

My own involvement in Passarinho's Quilombola Project began in
2005. I was in Teresina attending the Second National Conference on Food
Security when I was approached by Maria, the leader of the Quilombola
Movement in the southeastern region of Piauí. She told me that the FAO
and federal and state governments were partnering to bring $90,000 to
the "quilombola communities" of southeast Piauí, and to three villages in
Passarinho: Caixa de Água, Serafim, and Escondido. It came as no surprise
to me that two of the villages that participated in the Productive Project
were also identified by the Movimento Quilombola as quilombos (Caixa
de Água and Serafim). They had been chosen for the Productive Projects
because they were the poorest, and the poorest villages tended to be those
whose inhabitants had the most prominent African physical characteristics. Maria was well acquainted with several people from Serafim (including Augusto) but none from Caixa de Água. Knowing that I had lived in
Caixa de Água, she asked if I would "make the bridge" to bring her into the
village. I assented and later spoke with João (the association president)
to facilitate a future meeting between representatives of the Quilombo
Movement and the villagers.

Two weeks later, Maria arrived in Caixa de Água. She addressed the
thirty or so villagers gathered there:

> We've all heard the story of how the little white Princess Isabel
> freed the black slaves so many years ago [through the Golden Law
> of 1888], but do you think your *negro* ancestors simply walked off the
> fields of the white masters and started their own farms? No, they had
> nowhere to go, so they had to keep working. They still took the whip.
> The beauty of *negro* women was still exploited. They continued living

under an abominably racist and exploitative capitalist system. They were still slaves. So no matter when this village of yours was founded it was founded by escaped slaves. You are escaped slaves. Will you assume your identity as quilombolas? Will you fight for your rights?

Maria's speech was brilliant and smooth. I watched in awe as she stretched the definition of slavery from that of a national legal labor regime, to informal oppression in the immediate aftermath of Abolition, and finally to a description of race-relations under capitalism (also see O'Dwyer 2007). I don't think the villagers present were familiar with the term *capitalismo* or with the history of Brazilian slavery, but she spoke to experiences and memories that were very real to them. As she spoke of racial inequality, several villagers nodded in response, "Yes, yes." When Maria asked the villagers how Caixa de Água was founded, the middle-aged Josevaldo told her that his great uncle Raimundo had "run away" from a farm where he was whipped and settled on the outskirts of the municipality. Raimundo's daughter, Isadora, gave birth to eight boys who imported wives from surrounding villages, and thus the village was born. Few others from Caixa de Água had ever heard the tale. Maria lit up as he told it, and she turned to me. While on most occasions Maria took pleasure in degrading anthropologists in my presence (for thinking they had the authority to arbitrate questions of identity), on this occasion, she asked me publicly what I thought about the prospect of the village "fighting for its rights as a quilombo." I responded, "I think this village has everything it needs to press this claim."

Still, Maria was fighting an uphill battle. Three barriers impeded villagers' adoption of the quilombola identity. First, since their historical memory of slavery was totally absent, the concept of the quilombo was also alien (also see Arruti 2002: 238; cited in Jan French 2009: 97, 99). Second, villagers in Caixa de Água typically resisted the racial designator *negro*, referring to themselves as moreno (a person of mixed black and white features), or some other term indicating brownness. Moreover, people who called themselves *negro* at one moment might refer to themselves as moreno at another. Anthropologists have long noted that many Brazilians cherish their freedom to shift back and forth across various racial classifications depending on the situation at hand (Fry 2005: 175). Some have even celebrated the freedom afforded by this flexible system. Sean Mitchell (2013) takes issue with this claim. He argues that, for many potential quilombolas, the problem is not that as Brazilians they are prone to resist "ambiguity-erasing terms," of which *negro* happens to be one, but that "they are being called upon to identify with 'black' rather than 'white,' where 'black' is a color designation associated with slavery, from which most Brazilians have tried actively to distance themselves as individuals." While it is not technically necessary for quilombolas to refer to themselves as *negros* (as opposed to an intermediate racial category like moreno or pardo), solidarity with the struggles of their African ancestors (as opposed to the domination of their white ancestors) is implicit in quilombola identity, and a de facto priority of the Black Movement. Third, most rural communities were based on private property and labor, not communal land ownership (cf. Guilherme do Valle 2010). Thus, the mobilization of Afro-Brazilian villages in the sertão required that activists teach rural people the history of African slavery in Brazil, convince them to embrace the *negro* identity, and encourage them to "rediscover" (*resgatar*, literally "to redeem") the "shared values" of community labor and Afro-derived custom.

The night of Maria's visit I witnessed a telling debate between Josevaldo and his cousin, Celina, pertaining to Maria's message:

CELINA: She says we were slaves like the *negro* Africans. But, Josevaldo, we are not *negros*. We are not *negros*. We are *morenos*.
JOSEVALDO: It's true, Celina. It's true. In truth [*na verdade*] we're *morenos*. But, in reality [*na realidade*], we're *negros*.

Josevaldo's response to Celina bears out a point that few scholars of Brazil acknowledge: Brazilians have multiple discourses for talking about race. As Robin Sheriff (2001: 30–31) brilliantly identifies, Brazilians use their elaborate color vocabulary "to describe" individuals' appearances, but not "to classify" them into racial groups. Afro-Brazilian racial classification, she argues, is actually binary. Thus, she finds people in a Rio favela who say, "I am *parda* [brown], but I am of the black race" (43). The interaction above suggests that a similar double-system existed in Passarinho. Celina used the middle term (*moreno*) to lay claim to a physical appearance that was not *negro*. Josevaldo acknowledged that, but affirmed that she was nonetheless *negro* in an ethnoracial sense. But alongside graded differences of color, Passarinho's inhabitants saw a parallel and starker "reality." Activists like Maria considered this to be the only true reality and all intermediate color terms to be symptoms of the denial of racism, the words of false-consciousness and internalized racism. This dual sensibility made Maria's words ring true when she addressed the villagers as *negros*.

The people of Caixa de Água, like the people of Serafim, knew that

Passarinho's white population considered them inferior. In fact, many in Caixa de Água had turned against Passarinho's incumbent mayor, Rodrigo, during his final term, because word had reached them of a comment he had made to one of his aides: "If you put all those black drunkards [from Caixa de Água] into a sack and set it on fire, your only loss would be the sack and the match." "These words hurt us," one woman told me, her eyes sad and pleading, her hands over her heart in a gesture of woundedness. The performance of her own pain and that of her fellows affirmed her full sentimental capacities, and thus her full humanity. Like Shakespeare's Shylock, if pricked, she would bleed. Yet on another occasion, this same woman threw into doubt the very humanity of *negro* blood: "My skin is this color, but my blood is white," she said, assuring me of her upstanding character. It was precisely this internalized racism that Maria, the other Quilombola activists, and the Zero Hunger Coordenadoria officials tried to undo through the process of pilgrimage.

Stretching the Boundaries of Horizontal Solidarity

As I waited next to Augusto for the bus that night, I watched the group of villagers standing around us get to know one another in the usual way, by situating each other within mutually familiar kinship, friendship, and regional matrices. But the mood felt anxious. They knew that once they got to Teresina, they would participate in a three-day intensive workshop meant to prepare them for the Quilombola Project. They commented that they knew nothing about what sort of resources this project would afford their communities, nor why they had to travel to Teresina to learn about all this. The bus's arrival was delayed, and the villagers began to air their uncertainty about the project. Soon they talked of returning to their homes. A few turned to me for explanation, but I knew no more than they did. Augusto stepped in with a quiet voice: "Look, in my opinion we should hear the proposal of the government. Let's see what we can bring back to our communities." The others heeded Augusto's words and waited in near silence until the bus showed up twenty minutes later, with two of the Quilombo Movement activists and one person from the Zero Hunger Coordenadoria already aboard. The group entered and began the jostling and uncomfortable ten-hour ride to Teresina.

As I was falling asleep, I heard the state officials and movement activists talking to some of the village representatives about the social geography across which the bus was traveling. One Coordenadoria representative spoke of the small landholdings and poor labor conditions of all Afro-Brazilians who were descended from a shared history. At one point he recounted his personal version of Piauí's colonization, "The Portuguese took all of this land from the Indians who were here, and they killed or enslaved the Indians. There were no municipalities. Here it was all one big ranch. Then they put your grandfathers and grandmothers to work. Now we have municipalities and mayors but look, it's the same thing. Do you know what they plant? Corn and beans. They work in the hot sun just the way you do." As the official spoke, he pointed to the small dirt roads leading off from the paved highway into the vast underbrush, roads that presumably ended in villages. His talk emphasized the ubiquity of agricultural toil across the landscape, which he contrasted to the recent emergence of municipal boundaries and their local potentates ("mayors"). His talk depicted a scenario in which the passengers' solidarity with the imagined inhabitants of the landscape was real and natural. This solidarity was grounded in shared, objective labor practice, which had remained more or less the same (according to him) throughout several hundred years of regional history. This narrative of the past differed from those I discussed in chapter 5, narratives that evoked a preclientelist golden age. Still, while hardly nostalgic, the officials' words suggested that the horizontal solidarity among cultivators during slavery was stronger because they had not yet been fragmented by "municipalities and mayors." In other words, mayors comprised a more artificial aspect of the cultivators' social reality than their fellow black cultivators. As such, in traversing the state's many municipal boundaries, the villagers were effectively transgressing the hierarchical relations that quarantined each municipality.

The bus talk of the state officials and Quilombola representatives evoked a community comprised of all rural *negros* who possessed certain common features: shared subjection to racial discrimination by whites, small lands with poor soil, a shared memory of slavery, and an attitude of revolutionary defiance. As the bus passed through the town of "Criação," one activist from the movement explained, "Here we have already identified three quilombola communities. Only two accepted the challenge. The third has not found the courage to fight for its freedom. They're afraid of the mayor." As in the other agents' speech, this excerpt posits an antagonism between the mayoralty and the cultivators; only the latter are now racially marked. Her words equate the struggles of slave-era quilombolas with the present-day mobilization of dark-skinned communities that assumed the identity of "descendants of quilombolas." This narrative built on the messages that the Quilombola Movement representative delivered to the association members during the initial visit to the villages: "No, you're still slaves living in this racist system of capitalism." Her talk on the bus portrayed the beneficiaries' participation in the Quilombola Project as tantamount to resistance of the ongoing racist-capitalist system. She equated this contemporary resistance with the defensive violence practiced by their putative quilombola ancestors.

As we gazed out the windows onto a series of passing bus stops and billboards, the community leaders responded to these narratives. While they did not articulate any historical discourse about African slavery, or use the term *quilombo* on their own accord, they did talk about the difficulties that all small farmers faced in their fields. At one point the representative of Caixa de Água village said, "Wherever he goes, the *negro* suffers discrimination [*leva prejuízo*]." The comment was no mere passing phrase. He proclaimed it loudly and emotively, and other villagers on the bus affirmed his words with expressions like "And how!" and "It's just like that!" This was the first phase of a programmatic pilgrimage, one that seemed relatively successful in stirring up new bonds of solidarity.

As I mentioned in chapter 4, pilgrimage rituals work because they strip people of their social status and hold them in an indeterminate (liminal) phase during which they are exposed to esoteric knowledge that transforms them (Turner 1967). Pilgrimage creates a visceral experience of transcendent and euphoric oneness ("communitas") among those traveling together. The esoteric knowledge pilgrims encounter provides a compelling experience of a power that is outside of the pilgrim's everyday territory. The "central representations of transcendent power in pilgrimage correspond to a kind of sociological distancing . . . from immediate social context" (Sangren 1993: 571; also see Herzfeld 2005 [1997]: 161). This enables both new ways of imagining one's relationship to strangers and a critical perspective on the norms and authorities of everyday life. As pilgrims move away from familiar spaces, they draw closer to the transcendent power that trumps their everyday forms of authority.

As rites of passage go, the pilgrimage is one of the more arduous. The physical hardship of the journey helps make it spiritually transformative, especially when pain, disorientation, and endurance are overtly thematized. The exhausting dimension of pilgrimage often operates as a metaphor for the weakening of old identities, and it helps to emphasize raw (presymbolic) experience as the appropriate mode of knowing the self (Daniel 1984: 238). Suffering and disorientation block linguistic rationalization and suspend cultural logics, rules and categories, leaving only visceral communitas, absolute oneness. Put simply, a pilgrimage is "an exercise in a new way of knowing one's self in the world" (ibid.: 242).

Neither the state officials nor the beneficiaries discussed these programmatic pilgrimages in an overtly spiritual way, but the journeys nonetheless acquired a sacred feeling because they introduced a new, effervescent power that provided villagers with a new philosophical outlook on their everyday lives. A mystical mutuality awakened among them, which we might grasp, as Emile Durkheim told us long ago, as a projection of the power of their newfound group solidarity. The activists and state officials further sanctified the bond among the village representatives by deploying talk that aligned the mundane bus-ride and training seminar unfolding in 2004 with the legendary acts of slave resistance undertaken in ancestral time. It is through such alignments of present and past personas ("nomic calibration" is the technical term) that pilgrims everywhere come to see their actions as allegories for the actions of mythical heroes (Eisenlohr 2004; also see Silverstein 1993). Like the technique of induced nostalgia, programmatic pilgrimage afforded activists and state officials the means to tap into, and reshape, social memory. The heroism ascribed to these slave-era quilombolas energized the community representatives, giving them courage to transform themselves and their worlds.

Fostering Indignation: Participation at the EMATER Training Center

Once the buses arrived at the EMATER training center on Teresina's outskirts, the community representatives were assigned rooms for their three-day stay. The facility had nearly enough units to lodge them individually, but the EMATER project supervisor, a long-bearded, light-skinned fellow who dressed in store-bought African and Indian prints, thought the cultivators should room with their peers from other villages.

During the all-day training sessions, the community leaders sat in a large classroom and listened to numerous speeches that described the Quilombola Project and the transformative role it was to play in their lives. State officials initiated most of these sessions with kinetic ice-breaking exercises (dinâmicas) designed to further bond the village leaders with one another. Some of the ice-breaking games confused the villagers, who were uncertain what purpose they served. In one instance, a young woman from EMATER pushed two village men together into a hug, something that rural men rarely do with other men unless they are in the midst of revelry. The two men complied but were mortified, and they stayed far away from each other for the remainder of the week.

After the ice-breaking games, the state officials showed the villagers diagrams that described all the affiliated organizations that were participating in the Quilombola Project in any manner. These diagrams placed the beneficiary communities in the center, the Zero Hunger Coordenadoria on top, the FAO to one side, the Quilombola Movement to the other, the municipal Rural Workers' Union below, and the mayor's office far to the side. They emphasized that the resources for the project did not come from any government or even from the FAO; rather, as one Coordenadoria agent said, "These are your resources that you've already given the state through your taxes. The Lula government is just returning this money to you in the form of social programs. You don't owe anybody anything for it, not Lula, not us, not the mayors, not the Quilombola Movement, not anybody. So you need to tell us what you want us to do with your money. What kind of resources do you need? You must reclaim [*reivindicar*] it from us." This sort of comment contained two central ideas that state officials reiterated throughout the event. The first was that the exchange relationship between citizens and their leaders was one in which leaders were in perpetual debt to their citizens. In other words, no government resource given to one of Zero Hunger's beneficiaries should be considered an initial gift that elicited a countergift. No local politician could legitimately claim that he or she had played a part in bringing a policy gift to a municipal resident, nor—and this is key—should the PT-controlled federal or state governments be treated as generous patrons. (This, of course, does not imply that the beneficiaries actually internalized this message.)

The officials' symbolic alignment of race-based resistance with a rejection of patronage made sense in light of prevailing assumptions about authentic quilombola land use. Quilombola villages are often assumed to own land collectively (even if informally), and, in fact, when the Brazilian state "regularizes" lands (i.e., appropriates and redistributes public or private lands) in response to quilombola petitions, it allots them to communities as collective, inalienable property. (These "regularizations" increased substantially under President Lula.)[4] Collective land use symbolizes not only community solidarity (for activists) but also the absence of a patron-landlord. Price (1999: 15–16) observes that Brazilian ethnographers (who often write reports to the state in support of quilombola land claims) sometimes attest to a community's authentic quilombola identity by reporting that its members "always worked free" and "never had a boss." Even if these community members own and work land privately, this alleged independence from a boss affirms the dignified image of a defiant quilombola, an essentialized identity at odds with the presumed deference to patrons among the general population.

The second point that reverberated throughout the planning session pertained to the demanding attitude that the state officials tried to inculcate in the villagers. On several occasions the officials tested the villagers, asking them to stand up one at a time and tell the government why they had come. The village representatives nearly always responded proudly that they were there to see what they could "bring back to [their] community." This answer frustrated the state officials for several reasons, and they let the villagers know it. First, as the officials saw it, the language of "bringing something back" reflected a passive engagement with the state officials, an attitude of gratefully receiving rather than actively demanding what one was entitled to. Second, the villagers' references to "my community" suggested a kind of navel-gazing village parochialism. The officials wanted the villagers to feel solidarity with their peers from neighboring villages and neighboring municipalities. The officials told them that all of the quilombola villagers from the entire municipality needed to "show up together" (*chegar juntos*) in the offices of their mayors to reclaim (*reivindicar*) resources. There was a broader, national cause at stake in this program, that of *negro* solidarity throughout rural Brazil. However, the very scale of the project's interventions was presumed to be "the village." After all, it was the village that had received a visit from a quilombola activist, who asked villagers to identify "their community" as a quilombo and to "fight for their community." Finally, the officials were bothered by the villagers' hope that the Quilombola Project would transfer money or farm inputs to their villages. But material resources were by no means a certainty in this project. Agents from the Zero Hunger Coordenadoria also wanted project money to fund training courses that would teach the villagers to market their quilombola ethnicity in some fashion, for example, training them to cook a "traditional" African meal, or to learn the Afro-Brazilian martial art capoeira. Many of the quilombola representatives wanted the project to include funds for demarcating village lands in the hope of augmenting their tiny, privately owned fields with collective lands expropriated from their wealthy, lighter-skinned neighbors. These less concrete projects aimed to transform political and racial subjectivity rather than merely satisfy immediate economic needs.

On more than one occasion, EMATER personnel asked me to assist the project in the "recovery" (*resgatar*) of the villagers' African culture. I was not very helpful to them. I approached quilombola identity in much the way José Maurício Andion Arruti (1997: 25) describes, not in terms of cultural "similarities . . . inscribed on bodies and in customs (and) whose explanation resides in the past, but in [terms of] a positive and declarative [*propositiva*] attitude through which demands and a common project are produced, that is, whose reason for being is tied to the future." At some level, a similar, tacit understanding of ethnicity underscored the thinking of quilombola activists, who were not deterred from mobilizing rural black villages merely because these communities lacked a clear-cut set of African customs distinguishing them from other (whiter) villages. That said, activists and officials alike still considered a community's "recovery" of its African customs to be a sign of its commitment to a future defined by quilombola identity. Unfortunately, I was no encyclopedia of African customs—this led some officials to question my professional competence—and I felt uncomfortable convincing my friends from the villages to adopt such alien cultural fragments.

As the training seminar progressed, the village representatives ceased to worry about their communities' cultural qualifications as quilombos, but they did suspect that they were being evaluated to see if they met some other standard. Listening to them talk among themselves in their dorms, it was clear that the nature of this standard remained a mystery to them. Was it about having enough men of working age to farm or raise animals? Was it about having a community unblemished by adultery, envy, or internal feuding? Was it about having money in their association's bank account? Was it about having enough *negro* people or having only *negro* people? (Virtually all of these villages had at least one white family.) These questions went unanswered. The villagers were therefore initially cautious and vague when they described their demographic, historical, topographic, and economic details in the classroom forum. As the villagers tried to feel their way through these events with polite and thoughtful etiquette, the officials bemoaned their graciousness. Instead, they tried to coax the villagers into adopting a more indignant attitude: "You need to demand what you want from us!"

Inside their quarters, the village representatives grew anxious. They sensed that they were frustrating the state officials, but they did not know what the officials wanted. They had heard state officials calling on them to make demands on the government, but a literal interpretation of this exhortation seemed out of the question. It was unthinkable that the officials wanted them to behave in such a rude and ungrateful way. What the villagers wanted to know was what stake the state officials had in their actions. This was especially vexing given that there seemed to be no way for them to give anything back to the officials. So the villagers polled one another privately to find out if any of them had been approached by an official to vote for a particular deputy or something of this sort. The answer was no. They all knew they would need to return to their villages and explain what had happened; they were afraid their neighbors would blame them for not bringing back any material resources.

Convinced that the officials' lack of clarity regarding the project benefits could not be an accident, a few villagers resolved that the planning session was in fact a protracted test. The government agents were evaluating the worthiness of the community representatives (see Collins 2008a and 2008b). But how? One explanation was that the community representatives were being judged on their sheer determination to serve their fellow villagers back at home. "Just keep saying that you want to do good for your community," one man counseled his friend. "That's what they want to hear. Just show your faith to these people. They'll let go of this game [abrir mão] and tell you in the end."

During the following day's planning session, the state officials organized the villagers into breakout groups, mixing participants from different villages together in classrooms and asking each of them to talk about the economic details of their villages. At the session I attended, the villagers were extremely reluctant to speak explicitly about the distribution of wealth, poverty, hunger, cattle, land, or water resources in their villages. They said things like, "We could all use a little help from the government." The state officials took to lecturing them in general about certain patterns of economic stratification that they had observed in similar villages over the years. "Is it like this?" they would ask. They got only tentative nods in response.

In contrast to the reluctance that villagers exhibited in the formal classroom sessions, on coffee and lunch breaks, these same people would occasionally call the state officials over to a corner and engage in private conversations. Because I had built a friendship with Augusto, I asked him what he had said to the official he had summoned for a private chat. He launched into an elaborate description of his village, Serafim, implying that he had aired out the village's dirty laundry to the official: land concentration in the hands of a nasty man who sought to usurp Augusto's presidency, watering holes that had dried up as a result of "some evil" that had befallen their owners, three families living in hunger, disabled children poorly cared for by their parents, and so on. "He needs to know this stuff," Augusto said, "but it's only for private talk." Providing such information afforded Augusto dignity in the encounter; he was giving a higher-status person something the latter needed. Later he explained in greater depth that the state officials "need to know what villages have self-respecting people who can make a project work and what villages have a bunch of no-good *negros*. If you were them, wouldn't you want to know whom to invest in?" The model that Augusto was using to interact with the state officials came directly from his life experiences negotiating political exchanges with municipal politicians. He was willing to make himself privately vulnerable to the state by revealing the embarrassing details of his village, while still affirming that his neighbors could work together as a united front.

The villagers' interpretation of the seminar as a moral test guided their subsequent engagements with the state officials. They remained steadfastly polite as the project officials repeatedly cajoled them to "yell for their rights." They nodded indulgently when their graciousness was criticized. One village man insisted, to the apparent confusion of some officials, that "we are here for you, always ready to work." The phrase indicated to me (and to the officials, no doubt) an expression of intimate alliance, a loyal readiness to put one's full energies to the service of another's cause, not unlike the way electors assured their allied politicians that they would campaign vociferously for them to ensure their electoral victory. Through the gaze of this villager, the state officials, for all their condemnation of patronage, appeared as benevolent patrons themselves. I am reminded of John Collins's (2008a: 250) insight that "patronage sometimes plays a role that goes beyond reproducing inequality and includes de-fetishizing the basis of such inequality." If we take "de-fetishize" to mean simply withdrawal of investment in an image, then this man's profession of loyalty negated the charade of equality in the training workshop; he opted instead to act with full appreciation of the institutional hierarchy that defined his relationship to the officials . . . and then from there to work against that hierarchy by assuring them that his força would be at their disposal when they needed it; he would help them at their moment of vulnerability when they had to report back to their bosses.

After two days, the officials gave up on eliciting the performances of indignation from the villagers and instead set themselves to controlling their side of the interaction. What followed was a series of institutional promises for project support, all prefaced by a speech from an EMATER agent establishing the cultivators as the deserving and rightful recipients of the promises. He proclaimed, "These promises will be made in front of you guys [the cultivators], not in front of us. We are the technical people [*técnicos*]." One after another, the institutional representatives who spoke of their agencies' roles in the Quilombola Project repeated that the cultivators had "rights," that the government was fulfilling its obligation to the people, giving back "the people's money." Over and over, the state officials repeated that the project materials in each village belonged not to the government but to the community, that the fulfillment of project requirements constituted an obligation not to the government but to one's neighbors. Then one official drew the exercise back to its implications for local politics: "Now that you see there is work to be done at the community level, you have to ask, 'What can our partners do for us?' The community has partners. EMATER is a partner. . . . Zero Hunger Coordenadoria is a partner. . . . And the municipal government is a partner. The municipal government is a partner because it knows the problems each community faces and it is the most local level of democracy. Now how many of you think that you could walk into the mayor's office and ask for more technical support and have the mayor say, 'Okay, I'll give it to you'?" Nobody responded to the question. The agent went on to talk about the utility of collective action. He said that if the community association president went to the mayor and was turned down, then the entire directory (vice president, treasurer, etc.) needed to go with him again. If refused, they needed to join with the presidents of the other associations in the project and go to the mayor's office, and "If you don't [all] fit, then stand outside the building and yell for him to recognize your rights."

On the third and final day of the planning session, the official conducted a closing exercise designed to solicit criticisms from the villagers regarding the planning session itself and their shift in attitude toward greater solidarity (*companheirismo*). The village leaders gathered in the classroom and sat silently as the government representatives urged them to "use their voice" to "tell us where we went wrong." If the beneficiaries decided to join in a chorus of complaints about the planning process, they would effect the ultimate "nomic calibration," aligning their present actions with their future militancy, demonstrating that they would one day complain to and make demands of their local mayors.

But only one community leader spoke up after a while and said that he was grateful for the lecture (*palestra*), that the government had done nothing wrong, that he had come to see what he could bring back to his community, and that he was satisfied. As he finished, he received a pat on the back from Augusto who sat behind him. The government representatives looked uneasy. Everything the young man had said was wrong in their eyes: He was supposed to protest some aspect of the event, an act that would testify to his acquired ability to stand up to authority. He was supposed to speak of himself not as the representative of a single village but of a whole class of small cultivators no longer willing to rest in a cemetery of unfulfilled patron promises. He was supposed to valorize not the material benefits of the project but the "knowledge" (*conhecimento*) of his rights that democratic participation in the project fostered. And he was not supposed to be grateful, because the project was not supposed to be a gift to initiate a return gift. The officials' intended inculcation of "rights talk" didn't seem to be working. They kept trying to solicit complaints and grievances from the community leaders, retaking the scene "from the top" until finally Augusto said, "I think we are all satisfied, because, when in the past has a black man from the field had the chance to come to the city and listen to these lectures? I and the other leaders from the quilombola communities and the other communities are just saying that. So the only point I'll raise [*fazer questão*], and it's not really a complaint just a comment, is that three days is a lot of time for a *negro* to be away from his field." The EMATER agent leading the closing exercise thanked Augusto for his "critique" and assured him that they would try to keep the evaluations shorter next time.

These closing exercises were designed as culminating rituals for the village participants, and the state officials hoped that they would be the pinnacle of the administrative pilgrimages at issue in this chapter. Like most rites of passage, the villagers had been sequestered, held in limbo, and tested. They were made the focus of attention in grand events presided over by powerful authorities who commanded esoteric knowledge. However, they didn't always respond in the intended way. Some of the state officials I spoke to later considered the exercise and even the entire event a failure. The villagers said they felt like they had not lived up to expectations, but they didn't know why, and they weren't sure what to tell their neighbors when they returned.

Before the community representatives boarded the bus to go home, the state officials told them that they had discussed the question of benefits among themselves the night before and come to a conclusion about what the project would entail. They said that each community would receive both an experimental agricultural initiative and a participatory culture-enhancing initiative. The EMATER agronomists wanted to experiment with several low-cost, rain-capturing, and fertilization techniques, and so they would fund one such initiative on one person's farm in each village. More important, the women of each community would form a special group within the village to market herbal remedies (*remédios caseiros*) for everyday maladies. This would, in theory, "revitalize quilombola culture" (implying that their local knowledge of medicinal plant life could be attributed to the savvy survivalism of escaped African slaves).

A few hours later, the group boarded the bus for the journey home. Some grumbled that the event had been a waste of time (because they were unhappy with the resources), but others were glad that their steadfast morality had paid off. Some even expressed admiration for the state officials; they reasoned that the government was right to ensure that its scarce resources were being spent on the virtuous, and they commended themselves for proving the good character of their communities. Yet a few expressed concern that, because the project's material benefits were relatively small, their neighbors and fellow association members would assume that they had failed to impress "the government people."

The Impact of the Quilombola Project on the Villages

Neither of the two benefits associated with the Quilombola Project brought much economic improvement to the *negro* communities of Passarinho, but one of the two initiatives did facilitate new egalitarian relations within villages and innovations in political alliances.

Basically, EMATER's experimental attempts at low-cost soil fertilization amounted to nothing. The EMATER agents hoped that the "dead cover" technique would be adopted by other villagers who saw how well they worked on the fields of their neighbors. But no such "multiplication effect" ever occurred; these experiments simply benefited the individual farms where they were tested. Thereafter, few villagers maintained any relationship with the EMATER agents.

However, the herbal remedy project had the effect of shifting the balance of gender power in women's favor. In Passarinho's villages, Caixa de Água and Serafim, about a dozen women formed a kind of cooperative economic arrangement. They were to share their knowledge of local remedies with one another, forage together for medicinal herbs and plants, process these herbs into a liquid, and bottle the concoction with labels provided by the project funds. The women were each supposed to sell as many bottles as they could, splitting the proceeds equally among them. While the production part of the project went fine, the women of both villages soon began to quarrel over the division of the proceeds. In Caixa de Água, two women claimed that they sold many more bottles than the others, and thus that they should receive more money than the others. Several women who were unable to sell any bottles dropped out of the project, fearing that the others would accuse them of destroying the project. They were the poorer women, unfortunately. Those who were already better off (economically and socially) than the others profited from the project because they were able to pay junior sisters and in-laws to work in their homes so they could travel to town to sell the bottles. Moreover, these successful women were all members of one extended family that had strong connections to a town councilman and to middle-class townspeople who belonged to their church congregations (both evangelical and Catholic). They were surely able to use these relationships to facilitate their marketing efforts. In any case, each of these women sold her bottles individually and kept the profits.

In 2005, one of the women from the herbal remedy project successfully ran for president of Caixa de Água's village association, defeating my friend João. Once she began her term, the association dynamic shifted. The women who sold home remedies became a far more vocal presence, and other village women seemed inspired to participate more actively than before. João claimed their victory was the result of a conspiracy against him. Indeed, the new association leadership had alleged that he had embezzled funds from the Productive Project discussed in chapter 5. Moreover, João's fellow villagers had become aware that he had impregnated his sister-in-law. It was one thing for a man to have a discrete affair with a woman far from home; it was quite another for his liaisons to corrupt his household and family: "How can this man represent our association?" one man asked. "He's lowering our morality. The association is seen by all. It must be clean. Clean!" The association members had never given up the idea that the state's assessment of their moral character played a role in their receipt of resources.

In general, the women of the two villages denominated as "quilombos" built a lasting relationship to the state by maintaining intimate ties to Maria and others in the regional Quilombola Movement. The quilombola activists (mostly women themselves) sought them out and encouraged them to participate in, and to bring others to, various race-based demonstrations happening in the region. In Caixa de Água, the village's women proved far more capable of remembering and reciting the history of African slavery in Brazil and of proclaiming the villagers' rights to resources based on that history of disenfranchisement. The movement's recognition of the solidarity of these "women quilombolas" led it to funnel resources to Caixa de Água: the movement built a special headquarters for quilombola and regular association meetings. By the time I left Passarinho, the women who had participated in these projects had begun to speak to state officials on behalf of their households. When state officials approached village households, women would offer comments in response to questions while standing next to their husbands, and they sought out state officials for private conversations during the latter's visits to their village. One village man explained to me, "This project is more for the women. They have rights, too." Women tended to speak in support of village youth and elders, who were often charged with running errands for the association, or with representing it in various programmatic venues. An alliance, or at least a pattern of verbal support, seemed to occur among youth, the elderly, and women—all previously disempowered categories. The town politicians still tended to solicit alliances from male family heads. Senior women, however, were developing stronger relationships to state-level politicians, including the Coordenadoria officials, EMATER agents, and, of course, the regional Quilombola Movement activists (who are popularly identified with the state government). Households' intimate political relationships thus grew more complex in these villages as families strived to expand their vertical connections to include activists and state officials.

The Project's Effects:
Ethnic Identification and Patronage

By turning the travels of this participatory Zero Hunger project into a pilgrimage, state officials sought to inculcate in the beneficiaries an enhanced sense of racial solidarity that would inspire them to assume a more demanding, rights-asserting posture vis-à-vis local authorities. Their efforts were partially successful. During their bus voyage across the countryside, village participants came to identify with the larger rural population of Afro-Brazilian cultivators who labored, much like themselves, on the poorest and most marginal lands. While they never fully internalized the historical account of quilombola resistance to slavery, the villagers did come to see themselves as part of the *negro* race that "always suffers discrimination." This was no small accomplishment, given the prior unwillingness of many beneficiaries to be identified as *negro*.

The state officials, however, were not fully satisfied with this effect, because the village representatives spoke of their agenda to help their communities, rather than the wider community of all *negros* throughout Brazil. I would argue that this expression did not reflect the villagers' failure to identify with other *negros*; rather, it reflected the fact that the beneficiaries had historically been mobilized at the village level, both by liberationist priests and association organizers. The villagers had presumed, and were correct, that the village (at least its women) was the benefiting unit of the Quilombola Project. Thus, the project's activities elicited a level of horizontal cooperation that was narrower than state officials and Quilombola activists actually wanted.

With regard to the state's objective of dismantling local political intimacies, the programmatic pilgrimage did not distance the beneficiaries from municipal political elites, or from the norm of establishing intimate alliances with superiors. In fact, the project probably gave the benefited villagers more negotiating leverage within their local political alliances. The project also introduced a whole new set of political benefactors, that is, the state officials and especially the Quilombola Movement activists. In their intimate talk with the activists, the beneficiaries revealed the embarrassing problems of community life, and I imagine that activists revealed the limitations of their own successes with regard to the mobilization of other black communities. The project did not undermine patronage so much as it gave people a stronger, more diverse, and more dignified place within intimate hierarchies.

Coda: Auctioning Rival Intimacies

In 2005, the village of Caixa de Água held a fundraising auction outside a newly built Catholic chapel. The Quilombola Movement leaders were there and, prior to the start of the auction, they made speeches claiming that some of the funds used to build the church had been secured because the villagers had finally assumed their identity as quilombolas. (This was not true; I had donated the funds to build the chapel in order to provide a public forum for community discourse, but I had given Maria permission to "do politics on top of" the chapel.) They spoke of the Quilombola Project and praised the PT state and federal governments for finally taking quilombola communities seriously within the Zero Hunger program. In attendance at this auction event was the new mayor, Henrique, who felt slighted that his name went unmentioned as an ally of the community. Henrique had been willing to assist the PT federal and state governments with the implementation of the Zero Hunger and Bolsa Família programs, but his own political allies at the state level were opposed to the PT governments, and so Henrique's relations with Zero Hunger's officials were tense at the moment. Feeling challenged by the Quilombola Movement, he insisted that its leader bid against him "on behalf of the government" for a cooked chicken. Maria protested: "My força doesn't come from money but from the people." She nonetheless entered the bidding, and the wealthier Henrique won the chicken and distributed its pieces to the villagers gathered there. He then outbid her on a sweet cake that "I could tell she wanted, so I gave it to her with a big smile to show that it was all in good fun [brincadeira]." It was precisely through such symbolic action that Henrique could both one-up the Quilombola Movement and portray himself as its political benefactor. The logic of his practice was not to defeat an enemy but to subordinate an upstart, to put her in her place.

As political theater, these preauction speeches and bidding competitions between (state and federal) "government" and municipal politicians dramatized the fact that the Quilombola Project, like several other Zero Hunger initiatives, had turned the PT-governed state into an alternative source of support for the villagers. The mayor had the advantage in this competitive engagement, not only because he had more money than the quilombola activists did—which was certainly critical in this auction setting—but also because he was glad to play the political game that the auction exemplified, rather than trying to disabuse beneficiaries of their commitment to that game. The auction format provided politicians with an opportunity to give away moral gifts in order to "help the villages" and to "help the association."

It is unclear how the relationship between the Quilombola Movement and Passarinho's benefited villages will evolve. Perhaps if the movement is able to broker federal lands for the villages' benefit, villagers will cease to care who wins them chickens at community auctions; they will place their eggs in the Quilombola basket. Until then, they will look to local politicians who, after all, control much of the wage labor in the town and perform favors—sometimes emergency favors—without ensnaring people in red tape. On a return visit to Passarinho in 2012, however, I noted that the villagers of both Caixa de Água and Serafim had changed the title of their community associations to include the word *quilombola* and that Passarinho's politicians, when speaking of these villages, acknowledged publicly that "we need to prioritize the quilombola communities with the benefits that come from the government."

CHAPTER SEVEN

Marginalizing the Mayor

Passarinho's inhabitants told me of an event that occurred in February 2003, about a year before I took up long-term residence in the municipality. The story goes that one day a helicopter landed unannounced on the town soccer field—a first for Passarinho. Out of it stepped none other than Eduardo Suplicy, the famous PT senator from São Paulo, who stood before a bewildered crowd. He told the people gathered there that he had come to speak to their mayor about "ending hunger." Rodrigo, the erstwhile mayor, arrived on the scene and announced that he only had fifteen minutes to give the senator. Suplicy then launched into a condescending tirade. He began to list the many benefits that Zero Hunger would bring to Passarinho, following each with the refrain, "But Mr. Mayor can't hear this because he only has fifteen minutes." Rodrigo apparently stood mute for a moment and then stormed off.

People both allied and opposed to Rodrigo told me similar versions of this story, but they used it to convey different messages. Those opposed to the mayor narrated the event as a comedy with their mayor as a clownish half-villain whose brutish stupidity was his main offense. Here was the great Eduardo Suplicy making time in his busy schedule to come to Passarinho and talk about all of the interesting programs that the state and federal governments would bring to their backwater town. But the illiterate, narrow-minded mayor would not give him the time of day. Rodrigo's response was a municipal embarrassment; if the mayor represented all of Passarinho's inhabitants, he made them all look like a bunch of rude caipiras. Those who narrated the story this way were not necessarily defenders of the PT (at any level of government.) Indeed, Rodrigo had many local adversaries who wanted nothing to do with the PT. While most of them knew that Suplicy was a PT leader, in this story he figured primarily as a nonpartisan icon of modernity. By contrast, Rodrigo's allies made Suplicy out to be a bully: This fast-talking, insincere city-slicker flew in, flaunted his power and success, and then demanded to see the most important man in town as if the mayor's schedule were irrelevant. Then, when the mayor showed up and advised him of his time constraints, the statesmen debased him by running circles of sarcasm around this sincere, plainspoken farmer. In such versions, Rodrigo's choice to walk away signaled the victory of small-town values over the shallow pomposity of the city. Their mayor had stood up to a more powerful outsider, and done them proud.

Both versions of the story hinged on interpretations of political etiquette and its breach. Had Suplicy picked a fight by behaving in a high-handed and superior manner, or had Rodrigo received his guest ungraciously by failing to extend him the respect that a man of Suplicy's stature deserved? The safest answer is "both," but the pro-Rodrigo version is corroborated by the fact that Zero Hunger officials, during their prior sojourns in Passarinho, had already debased the mayor as a way of undermining the clientelistic basis of his power.

The marginalization of the mayor is the final technique for dismantling patronage that I explore in this book. This technique is twofold. It entailed both public spectacles by which state officials humiliated the person of the mayor (treating him as a symbol of patronage exploitation) and the administrative bypass of the mayor's office in the selection of Zero Hunger's beneficiaries. Here I examine this twofold technique in Zero Hunger's most famous, expensive, and geographically widespread initiative, the Food Card (Cartão Alimentação). I look at how Passarinho's mayor and other townspeople responded to the state officials by generating their own counterspectacles, which asserted various forms of autonomy in opposition to the state's violations of local norms. I then turn to the municipal Management Committee (Comitê Gestor) that the state created to select the Food Card's beneficiaries. I explore the committee's challenges, successes, and failures in light of the seasonal intensification of municipal factionalism and the inherently difficult task of identifying Passarinho's "hungriest citizens." My account leads me to explain the PT's electoral defeat in the municipal elections of 2004, as well as the significance of the transition from the Food Card to the Bolsa Família cash grant.

Humiliation in Context

Returning to the conflicting interpretations of the helicopter incident, I suggest that the question of political etiquette can be approached by recalling the traditional system of coronelismo (the "politics of the colonels") that organized rural power relations in much of Brazil.[1] This system structured the relationship between local and central authorities during the First Republic (1889–1930), and left a long-lasting influence on these relationships. It entailed the submission of the municipal bosses (whose landholdings had already diminished during the Second Empire) to state and federal authorities. The local boss (the "colonel"),[2] who increasingly held the formal office of mayor, implemented the policies that state governors and their allied legislators dictated without complaint and delivered municipal votes to these higher-ups. For their part, these more central authorities allowed the local boss full authority over the local distribution of state resources. Leal (1977 [1948]: 17) writes, "the very state functionaries who serve in the area are chosen in accordance with his wishes . . . [so the state would not] . . . threaten the prestige of the political boss of the municipality." A pattern of "reciprocal legitimation" defined the relationship between state or federal and municipal authorities such that the centralization of power actually reinforced the mayor's monopoly on local resources (Bursztyn 1984: 12).

This manner of relating to higher-ups endured despite regime changes, but during the 1970s the military dictatorship effected what Marcelo Bursztyn (1984: 104) calls a "concentrating" process, whereby an increasingly diverse set of federal development agencies began engaging independently with the municipal political economy. Mayors lost control over the state-level appointment of municipal representatives (ibid.: 106). The municipal chapters of the Rural Workers' Union gained autonomy and increasingly identified with the political Left (Pereira 1997: 151–54). New sectors of organized civil society (most notably the liberationist priests) arose outside the mayor's grasp, and often critiqued politicians' neglect of the poor. Village development associations proliferated during the 1990s in conjunction with more decentralized World Bank funding for community development projects (Costa, Kottak, and Prado 1997). An elected municipal council (FUMAC) emerged that determined which villages would receive what World Bank projects. These new actors did not necessarily oppose a seated mayor (though they often did), but they created other channels for brokering resources from government and private entities (Bursztyn 1984: 162–68; Pereira 1997: 125–26; Carvalho 1997; Woodard 2005: 99–101). Some mayors continued to see themselves as the sole legitimate municipal authority. "The only association around here is me," Rodrigo once proclaimed. But they nonetheless have had to reckon with the loss of their monopoly over this brokering function.

Despite the emergence of these new political brokers, mayoral power was revitalized by certain reforms associated with postdictatorship Brazil. The democratic Constitution of 1988 decentralized primary education and health services to the municipal governments, giving them large funding blocks to run these services. The number of municipal jobs that the mayor could fill increased from about 25 to 120 during the 1990s, giving him (the mayor was nearly always male) a powerful electoral currency. Similarly, the mayor could control the flow of the federal cash grants, mainly Bolsa Escola (School Grant) and Auxílio Gás (Gas Assistance) from Lula's predecessor, President Cardoso. This granted mayors increased autonomy from state officers insofar as they now controlled some public resources independent of those alliances; but they still relied on those higher-ups for infrastructure (roads, dams, electricity, water resources) and so they continued to deliver votes to their benefactors in the hope that the latter would send these projects their way.[3]

Coronelismo also implied a kind of theater: the state and federal officials helped the mayor sustain the myth of his generosity through public performances that suggested that he was the source of the goods that the poor received, or at least that without his intervention, those goods would never have found their way to the municipality. Coronelismo "depended, in no small part, on the state's attentions [atenções estaduais], whether in the form of infrastructural works or in the division of federal economic policies" (Faoro 1957: 646). Giving attention entailed performances, publicly promoted visits by legislators and bureau directors to the municipality. Even the appointment of the mayor's preferred locals for state positions was construed as a performance of confidence in his person (ibid.: 630). I saw such spectacles repeatedly in conjunction with various projects having nothing to do with Zero Hunger. State deputies and bureau directors would show up to commemorate the building of roads or the opening of a preschool. During these public ceremonies state authorities called the mayor to the stage with them, praised him, repeated his name over and over, shook his hand, and announced to the crowd that he was a man of "good heart" who had "helped the people" of the municipality.

Consider Suplicy's behavior toward Rodrigo in light of these customary spectacles. On the one hand, Suplicy could be said to have honored the etiquette of coronelismo by asking to speak to Rodrigo as soon as he landed. On the other hand, he (allegedly) did not call ahead of time to announce his arrival. Rodrigo had no way to prepare his own part in the drama. Rodrigo had long been affiliated with the PMDB, the catch-all centrist party that normally opposed the PT in Piauí and throughout much of the Northeast. Recall that in 2002, a faction of Piauí's PMDB had split away to support Wellington Dias (of the PT) for governor. In this context, Rodrigo could have read Suplicy's arrival as a gesture of friendship, but he was suspicious. Still, the state-level alliance between the PT and PMDB was precarious. It was unlikely that any PMDB politicians encouraged their municipal allies to endorse the PT at any level. Thus, Rodrigo regarded Suplicy with a jaundiced eye.

For its part, the new PT state government had already given Rodrigo reason to distrust it. In March 2003, Governor Dias showed up with journalists to inaugurate a housing project that officially fell under Zero Hunger's aegis. Aware that the media's cameras were on him, Dias improvised a ritual that he probably thought would play well with Teresina's middle class. He told the townspeople gathered to raise their right hands and swear an oath: "I will assume the commitment to get myself out of poverty" (Ribeiro 2003). The oath—photographed for the Piauí newspapers—would perhaps persuade the urban middle class that Zero Hunger was not assistencialismo, that it did not promote laziness and endless state expenditure on the poor, or deepen the poor's subordination to elites. Rodrigo was nowhere to be seen in the photos. The photo of the townspeople taking the oath appeared in a special issue of the regional newspaper *Meio Norte*, next to an interview with Governor Dias titled, "Wellington Dias Believes Zero Hunger Will Make History in Brazil: The Governor Compares the Changes That Will Occur with Zero Hunger to the Liberation of the Slaves."

The Lula and Dias governments faced acute media pressure in Passarinho. With the 2004 municipal elections on the horizon, many in the PT governments (state and federal) believed that the election would serve as a referendum on Zero Hunger. If the local PT chapters in the pilot towns could not get their mayoral candidates elected despite all the resources that President Lula and Governor Dias had poured into these small towns, it might cause great embarrassment to the PT administration (or so the PT feared). Inviting Rodrigo to copreside over the oath could have opened the door for him to co-opt Zero Hunger, in other words, to claim to Passarinho's inhabitants that he had successfully brokered its benefits. That could cost the PT's local chapter, Rodrigo's longtime rival, the election in 2004.

Rodrigo and his allies were generally aware of the PT's electoral concerns, and Rodrigo resented the PT administrations' effort to "climb on top of me." One of his key allies commented, "Why do we need such an

FIGURE 8 Passarinho townspeople swearing an oath to lift themselves out of poverty before Governor Dias. From *Meio Norte*, March 30, 2003.

oath? This is not right." The real grievance lay not with the content of the oath but with Rodrigo's exclusion from its ritual performance. Denied his right to share the stage, to stand next to Dias and copreside over the affair, Rodrigo grew more rigid in his hostility toward the PT.

In truth, the most pungent of the state's humiliating exercises had already occurred, and it was intimately linked to the creation of an institution that bypassed the mayor in the distribution of the Food Card. In mid-January, a team of Piauí's Zero Hunger Coordenadoria agents, joined by the famous PT Catholic theologian Frei Betto, drove into Passarinho to found the Management Committee, which would select the beneficiaries of the Food Card and monitor their purchases (see chapter 1). Once in Passarinho, they began to question the townspeople about how the extant Cardoso cash grants were being distributed. In effect, they invited local criticism of the mayor's role in the allocation of these cash grants.

Technically, all of Cardoso's grants were allocated by formal criteria that the local civic commissions (each grant had its own) applied to each household (poverty level, coresident school-age children, etc.). They were scarce resources. The School Grant program, for instance, which had the broadest coverage, benefited only 216 families in Passarinho, roughly one-fifth of the municipality's population (Coordenadoria 2004: 16). The mayor had exercised his right to appoint all the members of these commissions, and his office was also responsible for keeping each household's relevant data on file in an automated system called the Single Registry (Cadastro Único). In theory, a computer centralized in the federal government accessed this information and automatically sent money to the families that met the requirements. In practice, Cardoso's Single Registry was quite plural; each federal program seemed to have its own list at both the municipal level and the national level. Moreover, the application of the grants' formal criteria in the municipal selection process was highly problematic.

The Coordenadoria team's field report recorded the following set of comments from Passarinho's townspeople:

COMMENT 1: The Registry for the Income Grant has problems: those who need it are not on it; some have it without needing it.

COMMENT 2: Our local commissions do not operate in practice. The power remains centralized in the mayor.

COMMENT 3: Civil Society [the commissions] is guilty because it accepts suggestions from "people who are not committed" [*descomprometidas*].

COMMENT 4: The mayor's Registry shows only the families that are benefited by the grants. It should also list the families that have not benefited. (Coordenadoria 2003a)

Taken together, these comments suggested that mayors and other elites who were "not committed" (to the social justice efforts embodied by the grants) systematically manipulated the civil commissions into allocating the Cardoso grants based on political allegiance to the mayor rather than the objective needs of the poor. Like all documents that inform an ethnohistory, this one is hardly above suspicion of bias. PT officials and activists in Brazil's food security movement began critiquing the clientelist manipulation of the Cardoso grants long before Zero Hunger's inception (see Maluf, Menezes, and Valente 1996; Campanhola and Graziano da Silva 2000; and Graziano da Silva, Belik, et al. 2002). The team thus was probably on the lookout for local allegations of patronage interference when it asked the townspeople about the Cardoso grants. Moreover, the event in which it solicited this information took place in the local Rural Workers' Union (which doubled as the local PT headquarters). The presence of these well-scrubbed strangers, especially the famous Frei Betto, would have drawn quite a crowd. Thus, not only did the Coordenadoria team set up a dialogue with local interlocutors who were likely to be from the opposition, it mounted a spectacle of distrustful scrutiny. At one level, it was a didactic spectacle insofar as it modeled the kind of "social control" that citizens should exercise over their public authority. At another level, it was partisan muscle-flexing. Because of its setting, the performance implicitly linked the allure of Zero Hunger resources to oppositional politics, and to the PT specifically. While I never saw any state official explicitly drum up votes for the PT (at any level), the very framing of events like these made that argument for them.

That said, there were real problems with the Cardoso grants that derived from intimate hierarchical exchanges at the municipal level. While I try not to judge political intimacies in Passarinho, the combination of long-term, intimate exchange and the decentralization of grant-distribution power resulted in an injustice. The problem was not simply that mayors awarded scarce grants only to their own electors. (In a place as poor as Passarinho one can usually find enough poor families allied with the mayor so that, if this were the only problem, the mayor could still have allocated all the grants to legitimately needy families.) The main injustice was that mayors had an incentive to allocate scarce cash grants to families that were better off economically. Cash grants were a currency of long-term, intimate exchange relationships in Passarinho, not short-term buy-offs. As such, they generally flowed toward "electors with multiple votes," that is, large, relatively well-off families with strong cooperative labor ties in the villages. For mayors, solidifying their ongoing relationship with these families by enrolling them in a cash grant was a better electoral investment than giving the same grant to a small, desperate, socially isolated family. It did not surprise me to learn that middle-class families residing in the town hub (shop owners, truck drivers, fare venders, etc.) had been receiving Cardoso's Income Grant and School Grant programs. These long-term allies of the mayor also wielded influence over others' votes.

The team's main act of disrespect to Rodrigo occurred later during this visit, just following the discussions at the union headquarters. The team called an open-air assembly of the townspeople in which they would vote (by show-of-hands) to elect members of the Zero Hunger Management Committee. The mayor would not be able to appoint the people who allocated the Food Card, and his absence from the assembly made the election of the committee members seem like a collective rebuke of his prior monopoly of the Cardoso grants' commissions. While the mayor's power was hardly absolute in Passarinho, the convocation of a large gathering and plebiscite on a matter of public concern without his blessing was an aggressive violation of coronelismo etiquette.

It is highly doubtful that the Coordenadoria team knew this, but Rodrigo imputed to the team a deliberate disrespect. Another field report written three days later recorded the mayor's response to this assembly as conveyed by his lawyer.

> That night, [the mayor's attorney] invited the team to a meeting in the mayor's office. . . . He said, "The mayor was never invited to discuss the assembly." "Everything was happening from the top down . . . transparency is in the constitution and is one of the PT's calling cards," argued the lawyer. He said that he did not receive a formal invitation to the event. (Coordenadoria 2003b)

Two aspects of the lawyer's rebuke merit mention. First, the mayor, once again, objected not to the convocation of a popular assembly per se but rather to his exclusion from that public ritual. This is not to say that Rodrigo would have been happy to give up his power over the distribution of cash cards, but he might not have felt so defensive had he been included as a symbolic authority in the assembly. Second, the lawyer voiced his objection to the officials' actions by mobilizing rhetoric associated with the Brazilian Left: critiques of "top-down" politics and calls for greater "transparency." He did not defend the mayor's purported patronage based on the local ethics of intimate exchange. The lawyer, aware of his audience, artfully deployed an ethic of participatory democracy in which the state officials appeared to threaten the autonomy of local communities. Talk of local autonomy proved a key idiom through which local people voiced their reaction to the perceived humiliation of their mayor.

Counterspectacles of Localism

This local pride or, better, localist defiance of the state and federal governments became clearer to me one afternoon in November 2004, as I was waiting with a Zero Hunger Coordenadoria official on the highway shoulder for the bus that would take us to Teresina. I struck up chat with a middle-aged, well off–looking man from town who asked me, "You are the guy from Zero Hunger who lives with that bunch of blacks [*negrada*]?" As I started to reply, he cut me off with a mocking tone, "There are three things a man does only once in his life: be born, die, and vote for the PT. This Zero Hunger is worth nothing. They come with this little cash nonsense. Do you know that our mayor [Rodrigo] has been trying to get the government to build a road from [the town hub] into [a large village]? Do you know that our water reservoir has been muddy for two years? He has a history of care for this place. A good government listens to the people who have history . . ." and we went on in this vein for several minutes.

This was one of those instances when I felt compelled to defend Zero Hunger, both because I found these accusations inaccurate[4] and because I wanted to prove myself to the Coordenadoria official standing next to me. I tried to retort, but my words failed, and he kept cutting me off as his rant escalated. There were others standing around, and I grew aware that he was playing to the crowd, using me as a proxy for the PT governments. As he walked away, he chuckled, "I put the gringo *petista* [PT supporter] in my pocket." My friend from the Coordenadoria was the first to console me: "I get this all the time; welcome to the team." Indeed, this man had already made me, a gringo, a member of "the team." My membership on the team fit with his main point; the Zero Hunger program was a cosmopolitan externality.

By contrast, Rodrigo embodied the locality itself through his historically deep exchanges with its families. Here the idiom of locality and history (*história*) assumed a nonpartisan guise. Rodrigo emerged as a figure linked to familiar places and problems, someone who knew the terrain and who had suffered its deprivations alongside other residents. Like other performance genres in the sertão, the praise of local leaders was "a domain for memory and what is defined as true social (as opposed to political) history—a place where the past, not as grand events, but rather as daily affairs, is inculcated through mingled acts . . . of remembering" (Dent 2009: 97–98). Accordingly, Rodrigo stood for intimate justice, gifts and favors given based on detailed knowledge of individual character, family circumstances, and alliance legacy. Rodrigo's own "history" (*história*) had sedimented over the years, compiling emotionally evocative acts of "helping the people."

In Passarinho, to say that a politician has "history" is to affirm his or her politician's moral embeddedness in a series of long-term exchanges that require etiquette to be maintained. Key to this etiquette is a politician's memory, the "memory of past electoral feats, but also his own capacity to store in the memory who is who in the game, in the electoral gamble. . . .

At issue are [a politician's] guesses based on variables that are difficult to control because they are supported by impressions, information, reputations, and, therefore, memories" (Villela 2012: 13). By suggesting that the government lacked history, my aggressive interlocutor was denying it the very tool, memory, by which it could engage in moral resource distribution. He was making a claim to local autonomy that distinguished the logic of municipal exchanges from that of impersonal state distribution. As I stood there on the road blushing, it occurred to me that I had become the victim of this man's memory of Rodrigo's humiliation at the hands of the state. This was payback. He needed to humiliate me (the state's proxy). After he walked off, another Passarinho resident offered added consolation, "Don't get heated up; he votes for the Liberal Front Party," the Partido Frente Liberal, then Brazil's largest right-wing party (renamed Democratas in 2007). Rarely did people in Passarinho allude to such left-right political divides, distinctions that operated only at higher levels. Thus, this consoling utterance aimed to reverse the depoliticizing logic of my aggressor's localism by situating his comments in the very external arenas to which he had consigned the PT (and me). My defender's counterallegation of partisan bias undermined the other's claim to speak for local history and memory, while at the same time affirming the value of municipal autonomy.

The idiom of local autonomy channeled various objections to Zero Hunger, mostly from Rodrigo's supporters. A friend from town recounted public comments that Rodrigo's would-be successor, Miguel, made in early 2003 during a public meeting with the Zero Hunger officials: "Miguel said that here in Passarinho we didn't need this Zero Hunger program because we all had the means to support ourselves and that everyone had fields and livestock and that nobody went hungry and I remember that he even said that here we have not sunk so low as to plant marijuana." Miguel's putative comments built on the association between hunger and immoral personhood: hunger breeds envy and criminality. Classifying Passarinho as Brazil's "hungriest municipality," the PT government had committed a moral affront against its citizenry. This line of discourse caught fire in Passarinho as everyday citizens turned their porches into amphitheaters, insisting that their municipality had become Zero Hunger's pilot town because "the government did not know our home" (*Não conhece nosso lugar*). The verb *conhecer* refers to a familiar way of knowing (i.e., being acquainted with a person or a place, rather than knowing [*saber*] a fact).

Within the context of intimate politics, to know (*conhecer*) another implies "a moral relation that can only occur between persons" who appropriately engage the local circuits of exchange (Chaves 2003: 56). The state's technical, objective knowledge of Passarinho's destitution (gleaned from IBGE 2000, in which Passarinho had the nation's lowest Human Development Index rating) put it at odds with the local knowledge, in which Passarinho was a dignified place where people basically overcame life's challenges.

Even Henrique, the opposition candidate, inveighed against Zero Hunger's violation of local ways of doing things. Sitting on a chair outside his sister-in-law's house, he launched into a critique with a voice loud enough for onlookers to stop and listen: "It is good that the PT has brought resources to Passarinho, but they should have done it differently. They should have called all of our leadership together—Rodrigo, me, all of us—and had us show them who were the poorest people." Henrique's remarks did not challenge the depiction of Passarinho as destitute or hungry, but they criticized the state's imposition of its own knowledge forms over local memory, history—in short, the intimate modes of knowing. For Henrique, the knowledge of the municipal "leadership," accumulated through years of intimate (and nonintimate) exchange, is needed to sort out Passarinho's normal poor from its truly destitute. He was glad the state wanted to keep factional politics out of the Food Card, but the way to do this was not to exclude politicians but to involve politicians from all sides and factions. This strategy would, as it turns out, also occur to the members of the Management Committee.

In sum, in their own improvised theaters, Passarinho's inhabitants mounted a series of counterspectacles that voiced their indignation at their mayor's humiliation. These counterspectacles ranged across participation frames, from official commentary to the state press to the roadside tirades to which I fell victim. They exhibited a variety of tones and stances toward Zero Hunger, but nearly all of them asserted the importance of a local, historically deep knowledge of people and places that the Zero Hunger officials lacked. This was not a knee-jerk xenophobia but rather a response to the state's violation of the informal protocols for engaging local authority. The local population neither embraced nor rejected Zero Hunger in its entirety; rather, through these theaters of evaluation, Passarinho's inhabitants held the state at arm's length, and spurred themselves to articulate their knowledge of poverty and hunger, a knowledge derived from intuition, intimacy, memory, and deep historical coexistence.

Bypassing the Mayor:
The Management Committee

In addition to mounting these spectacles of humiliation, Zero Hunger officials bypassed the mayor by creating the Management Committee, to which the mayor could appoint only one member. The express intent of this maneuver was both to prevent the mayor from turning the Food Card into a clientelist currency and to monitor the beneficiaries' compliance with the card's spending restrictions. The Ministry of Food Security set up management committees not only in Zero Hunger's two pilot towns, but in all of the 2,285 municipalities that were participating in the Food Card initiative by the end of 2003. The ten seats on each committee were filled according to a formula: three seats would be appointed by government representatives (two by state government officials, such as directors of the state-run high schools, and one by the mayor). The open assembly elected the remaining seven members, each of whom was to represent "organized civil society." Official Zero Hunger rhetoric celebrated the "two-thirds" predominance of "civil society" over "public authority" on these committees. Thus, the administrative structure of the Food Card embodied the belief that patronage interference was somehow restricted to those who held public office, even though state officials knew (at another cognitive level) that personalized political exchange was a widespread cultural phenomenon.

The two most prominent members of Passarinho's Management Committee were Belinha, the leader of both the Rural Workers' Union and the PT's local chapter (she technically represented the Rural Union), and Benedito, the college-educated agronomist and aide to Henrique who represented his native village's development association. Both were elected by the assembly. The other members elected included a young woman who also represented the Rural Workers' Union (Belinha's junior ally), a man who represented his village association, a middle-aged woman who owned a small grocery store in town and who represented the Catholic Church, a young municipal employee who entered data via computer into the Single Registry (for the Cardoso programs), and a man who was a municipal health agent and who represented the Assembly of God Church. Two brothers who ran the public high school represented the state government and were thus able to appoint themselves. The mayor appointed Passarinho's secretary of health (his daughter). In early 2003, three of the committee members identified with "the mayor's side" and seven belonged to "the opposition." The seven in the opposition were subdivided into two smaller factions; four of them looked to the wealthy rancher, Henrique, as their primary benefactor (and thus to Benedito on the committee), and the remainder followed Belinha.

Despite the factional differences that existed within the Management Committee membership, its meetings were cordial, at least for the first few months of 2003. The committee members knew the potential for *politicagem* ("dirty politics" or "factional politicking") to set them at each other's throats. Most of them did not want to be involved in partisan rancor, and they openly discussed with one another the need to "keep politics out of the selection process." Generally, they came up with effective practices for doing so, and they needed to because the Food Card was originally a scarce resource, just as the Cardoso grants had been. By the end of 2003, the MESA had made 500 Food Cards available for distribution among Passarinho's roughly 1,000 households, but these arrived in smaller allotments with no guarantee that more people could be enrolled in the future. The first allotment (in February 2003) contained 200 grants; thus, the committee had to select the poorest fifth of Passarinho's population.

To select the beneficiaries, the committee divided itself into subgroups comprised of members of different factional allegiances. These groups traveled together to several nodal points in the rural zone to assess poverty levels among the cultivator families. (Word reached the families through the local radio station, which people regularly used to pass messages to villages where there were no telephones.) When they arrived at these nodal locales, the villagers initially lined up in front of the committee members who were "from their side." In their interviews with me in 2004, all committee members claimed that they publicly announced to the prospective beneficiaries, "Do not approach us for favors," "Politics has nothing to do with this," and other statements to this effect.

The committee's maintenance of factional neutrality bumped up against the beneficiary population's default models of engaging factional allies when seeking municipal resources. In late 2004, I watched an awkward interaction unfold between the young, computer-literate municipal employee on the committee and an older village man who had come into town because his Food Card had stopped payment (for what I believe were technical reasons unrelated to local politics). With his magnetic card in hand, the old man leaned in close to the youth who was asking him household demographic questions from the Single Registry questionnaire. He responded to these questions rather expediently, as if they were of secondary concern. He seemed focused on something else, and he kept tapping the younger man's wrist with his card, asking in hushed tones, "You see?" and "Do you understand?" The card tap, his tone, his unwavering eye contact—these were keying devices meant to indicate that his talk should be regarded as innuendo, perhaps to indicate that he was part of an inside circle of the mayor's allies (Bauman 1984: 15–25). (My presence at this encounter may have contributed to the man's felt need to use such a code.) Later, another committee member indicated to me that the rural beneficiary's behavior in this encounter was typical of the cultivators but not of more educated townspeople like himself: "Just because I support the mayor does not mean that I can help him get the benefit. These people of the fields don't hear us when we tell them that it doesn't work that way anymore. It's a new system." The committee members' struggle to convince the beneficiary population that the committee was not playing politics probably augmented their solidarity with one another. It gave them a language for acknowledging their factional differences that simultaneously affirmed their collective transcendence of politicagem (in contrast to the less-educated, disparaged beneficiary population).

Once the committee collected data on each rural household's economic circumstances, its members discussed the family's eligibility. The formal guidelines for selecting the beneficiaries had already been determined by Piauí's Coordenadoria (in conjunction with the Ministry of Food Security). The committee was to grant priority access to families with incomes lower than ninety reais per month per person, to families with a large numbers of coresident individuals, to families with pregnant or nursing women, to families that had lost their most recent crop harvest, and to families with disabled members.[5] Passarinho's committee members imposed on themselves the burden of a unanimous, rather than majority, vote. Every faction on the committee feared that a simple majority would harden alliances on the committee, and that a minority faction would then hurl allegations of politicagem at the majority. The members also feared such allegations from outside the committee, particularly from political candidates who might have alleged "persecution" (marcação)[6] if none of their supporters received the grant. Similarly, they were wary of would-be beneficiaries alleging that people from "the other side" received more than one grant while they received none. To deal with this threat, the committee created an added guideline for itself: it would not give priority to any family that was currently receiving one of the Cardoso grants. Finally, to ensure that politicagem could not be alleged, the committee meetings added another informal criterion to the selection process. "We made it a point to award the grant to people from all sides,"[7] as one member said. For the committee members, there was no contradiction between enrolling needy families and maintaining roughly equal representation of factional alliances. All factions contained plenty of clearly eligible families.

Thus, while the committee members agreed with the state officials' belief that local political culture impeded fair grant distribution, they understood the problems of their own political culture very differently. Whereas the state officials focused on the problem of domineering patrons who would co-opt the grant, the committee members understood politics as a game that everyone played, rich and poor. Their primary critique of that game was its disruption of community harmony, not its reproduction of social inequality.

The committee members also faced challenges in this enrollment process that had little to do with factional politics. First, the Zero Hunger officials gave them very little time to complete this work. As I noted earlier, the 500 Food Cards were allotted episodically over a period of six months (as the Ministry of Food Security gained access to more funds). For each allotment, the state Coordenadoria agents gave the committee one week to select the beneficiaries. The rush created anxiety among all the committee members, who feared that they would be unable to deliberate properly on each family's eligibility. Second, the committee received no resources from the state or federal governments. Its members, all working people, received no stipends and the committee had no budget for transportation, Internet, phone, space rental, or energy costs. In Passarinho, this was not a crippling problem because the Rural Workers' Union allowed the committee to use its headquarters and computer. According to the Coordenadoria members in Teresina, however, management committees in other municipalities relied wholly on the mayors for these resources, and in some cases the mayors withheld them in protest.

One of the biggest problems with the selection process lay in the reporting of poverty and hunger by the resident population. Virtually all rural families (the majority of the municipality's population) reported their monthly cash income as "zero," even though many earned some money through informal crop sales.[8] Committee members navigated around these data problems by tapping into intimate knowledge and intuitive ways of distinguishing everyday struggles from extreme poverty, such as hearing that a person "is alone and never goes to the open market," or seeing that a woman "was skinny and sick-looking," or learning that "this man works alone all the time; he has nobody." The committee's activities situated it along the divide between the state's way of seeing poverty and the local modes of recognition with which its members were familiar. The committee routinely translated the technical guidelines for poverty into morally inflected narratives of deprivation. After all, they had checklists and questionnaires to reckon with. Upon deciding to award a grant to the woman who had shown up at a neighbor's door for food, they had to recode this justification in the language provided by the state, checking off a box labeled "crop loss" on their form.

While the committee members generally endorsed the selection criteria, they sometimes experienced it as a hindrance to ethical resource distribution. A man on the committee told me of a case in which "the paperwork told us nothing useful about . . . Senhor X, and he had no wife and no children so he wouldn't have been prioritized, but I knew he was hungry. [The committee member started to cry.] I've seen him ask people for food. He was a good man, Aaron. I told the committee. . . . They did not argue. Aaron, no heart can stand [to see?] hunger [*Não tem coração que aguente a fome*]. When someone on the committee said they knew of someone who was truly going hungry, we enrolled them." The committee member's emotional outpouring during our interview moved and puzzled me: I don't know if it was the sight of Senhor X's hunger and indignant begging that brought him to tears, or the prospect of the hungry man's falling through the cracks of the formal selection criteria. Regardless, this member told me he begged his colleagues (including his factional adversaries) to tolerate his patron-like intervention on behalf of Senhor X. He claimed personal knowledge of circumstances that the formal data-collection instruments had missed, and implored his fellow committee members to bend the rules in the service of the good, and to take him at his word that this wasn't just some vote-getting scheme. It is not clear to me how much such intimate knowledge informed the Management Committee's decision-making; I suspect relatively little. Yet I know that local politicians who did not attend the committee's sessions sometimes relayed to the members that a particular family the politician knew was "going needy" (*passando necessidade*). So long as their source was reported to, and confirmable by, the rest of the committee, these reports were factored into the committee's judgment. Indeed, committee members acknowledged that "our politicians walk these roads more than anyone else. They know everybody's situation." In short, knowledge of individuals' and families' hunger became intimate knowledge insofar as the hungry confessed their need in the context of intimate hierarchical relations.

At another level, talk about hunger in the committee meetings made the members vulnerable to one another. While collective talk about hungry persons was usually a matter of malicious gossip, committee members seemed to qualify such talk with affirmations of hungry people's decency. Together, committee members from all factions violated local custom; they spoke of a specific person's hunger, enacting a kind of moral gossip that they would not want others to overhear. A shared tone of pity endowed their bureaucratic allocations of funds with a sense of moral and spiritual transcendence that nullified the factional differences among them.

Committee members were keenly aware that they were being scrutinized for their partisanship, but they saw no absolute contradiction between listening to local leaders and "keeping politics out of their decisions." It was a slippery issue, but one they could manage. The committee had become a kind of liminal cultural setting located betwixt and between the state and the municipal inhabitants. The committee became a site where two different political cultures (the intimate and the impartial) were interwoven and negotiated, one in which factional warfare was suspended and political warriors were able to lay down their swords, if only temporarily.

A trickier problem was the beneficiaries' sense of the stigma against hunger, which caused some of them not to show up during the initial enrollment sessions. Families that were poor but not starving could solicit the grant without fearing the stigma of literal hunger because their village reputations affirmed that they were not desperate, and therefore dangerous, people. But families whose reputations hung by a thread feared that showing up would affirm their neighbors' suspicions that they were indeed hungry. The cultivators who did show up to declare their need for the Food Card were aware of this problem and were bothered by it. And they did something about it.

In June 2003, Passarinho received additional Food Cards from the Ministry of Food Security. The allotment occurred during my first scouting trip, and I accompanied Benedito to one of the nodal points. A dozen or so men had gathered there in response to a radio announcement from the committee asking families not enrolled in the Food Card to report to the locale. After taking down their demographic information one by one, Benedito asked, "Is there anyone who lives in your midst who is going needy but who is not here today?" The group fell silent. Then one man said in hushed tones, "Antônio is father of a family. [He] works well, but he is a little out of touch [*desatualizado*]. He probably meets the conditions. . . . Down the line I know he'll thank you for helping him." The phrase "down the line he'll thank you" is sometimes used as a euphemism to mean "vote for you or your candidate come election time." Thus, the speaker may have been turning the grant allocation into an intimate hierarchical exchange. But cultivators don't make promises on behalf of other cultivators who are not their coresident dependents. The man was primarily trying to save the face of his neighbor, Antônio, first by euphemizing his hunger ("out of touch") and then by asserting Antônio's dignity by confirming that he was a man worthy of long-term reciprocal exchanges that served his family's interest. On a related point, some beneficiaries claimed that they received the Food Card because of their savvy political alliances, even though follow-up research indicated that no such favoritism occurred. Such comments served as smokescreens by which people deflected attention away from their actual neediness, and from the fact that they received benefits because their needs did not go unnoticed. In the eyes of the state, these words would signal programmatic corruption and incite further auditing. To the committee members who intuitively knew how to read such displays, such claims of patronage did not cause alarm. They would not give rise to accusations of factional favoritism, because they would not be taken literally.

In sum, the Management Committee faced myriad challenges pertaining to factional divisions, deadlines, lack of resources, and local practices of dissimulation. Its members had to improvise solutions with peers they regarded as political adversaries. Their solutions reflected their shared commitment to keep factional politics from tainting the grant-allocation process, and their ability to interweave intimate knowledge and considerations of factional allegiance with a formal beneficiary selection process that sought to prioritize the hungry. The Management Committee thus emerged as a politically independent, and highly effective, entity not because its civil society members stood outside the local political game but because, despite their embeddedness within that game, the many challenges forced them into a zone of improvisation in which useful insights about merit and fairness, whoever they came from, were welcomed by all.

The Political Season and the
Collapse of the Management Committee

As the political season matured from mid-2003 through the following year's election in October, it eventually undermined all cooperation in the Management Committee. One reason the committee members had been able to avoid factional rancor was that the relationships among the three factions were malleable and shifting, subject to new favors, expressions of trust and overtures of intimacy—all typical of everyday time. The possibility of refashioning alliances was accentuated by the fact that Belinha, Henrique, and the mayor's would-be successor, Miguel, were all full siblings. But the political season in northeast Brazil nearly always reorganizes plural factions into two large, warring camps. Once these camps were formed, the battle lines became rigid; they formalized as electoral coalitions.

As it happened, that year in Passarinho, the PT's state-level directory shaped the formation of Passarinho's electoral coalitions. In Piauí, Governor Dias needed the support of the PMDB's many state deputies, so the PT leadership in Piauí made a series of concessions to the PMDB that affected the election in Passarinho. Piauí's PT directory gave PMDB officials state government posts and, after April 2004, decided to pressure municipal PT chapters to ally with municipal PMDB politicians in the upcoming elections. (This would also result in municipal electoral gains for the PT.) When the state-level PT officials learned from Belinha that Henrique had a strong base of support, they pushed Belinha to ally with him—but only on the condition that he run for vice mayor with his sister as the lead candidate. Henrique refused. The PT's state-level leaders tried to launch Belinha as an independent candidate, but when they realized that she did not have sufficient support to beat Henrique, they arranged an alliance between her and the erstwhile mayor's would-be successor, Miguel (PMDB). Belinha initially resisted the alliance but eventually acquiesced and endorsed the candidacy of one of the PT's other local leaders for vice mayor on Miguel's ticket. She then dropped out of the mayoral race and ran for the town council (as was the plan).

I attended the municipal PT meeting in Passarinho at which state-level PT officials convinced the small group of local party members to enter an electoral coalition with their longtime adversary, Rodrigo's faction (the local PMDB plus its allied small parties). A few of the eighty or so PT members in Passarinho, most of them townspeople, protested the move, but the majority voted for the alliance, holding their noses. Belinha had convinced them to do so before the meeting had even begun, though a few members defected from her side and joined Henrique.

The irony of 2004 was that even though Zero Hunger's state officials had marginalized the mayor, the PT itself ended up allying with his faction in the municipal elections. This drove a wedge between Benedito and Belinha that, by May 2003, translated into open arguments and accusations during the meetings of the Management Committee.

The inherently combative character of this staunchly bifactional arrangement was compounded by the diffuse paranoia that set in over the entire municipal population as the political period matured. More and more, Passarinho's inhabitants narrated their grievances with the cash grants as accusations of political persecution by "the other side." And there was no shortage of cash card grievances in 2004 because the federal government was in the midst of "migrating" Food Card beneficiaries to the new Bolsa Família program. The migration process was riddled with technical snafus that resulted in the suspension of the grant to beneficiary families.[9] To my knowledge, most of these occurrences were "innocent," but the aggrieved beneficiaries explained them to me by saying that either Benedito or Belinha (depending on their factional affiliation) had conspired to persecute them by cutting their benefits. And they pursued their grievances with their allied committee member, who, by this time, was surely promoting these factional narratives of blame and persecution (marcação).

Most members of the Management Committee did not want to work in a context of virulent factional bickering and accusation, and so they simply stopped showing up to the meetings. The committee, which had begun to disband in June 2003, was utterly defunct by early 2004. My contacts in Piauí's Coordenadoria told me of similar stories happening in municipalities throughout the Northeast. The committee members, for all their effort, could not withstand the bifurcation of the municipality that occurred during the political season. They found themselves caught up in a world of deep factional division, narratives of persecution, and practices of accusation. This violent reorganization of local social relations compounded the mayoral hostility that crippled many of the more resource-dependent committees throughout the Northeast.

The federal government's solution to this problem was to return control of the Single Registry to the mayor's office once it completely phased in Bolsa Família in 2005. While the new minister (Patrus Ananias) paid lip service to the committees' ongoing role of "social control," this reform effectively deprived them of any power in the beneficiary selection process.

Many of my friends in the Coordenadoria who had organized these management committees were infuriated. "Patrus threw away two years of social mobilization in the sertão," one official told me. Several suspected that this reform was part of a secret pact with the PMDB, another condition of its agreement to ally with the PT in municipal elections and give it legislative support. If so, one could argue then that the PT government, in an effort to build its municipal electoral base in the sertão, abandoned its marginalization of the mayors.

Yet the failures of so many management committees across the Northeast suggests that these entities drew so much local hostility from the mayors that they could never have been viable. Did the PT's breach of coronelismo etiquette cause their hostility? Given that many of the public spectacles I described here may have been accentuated by Passarinho's special status as a pilot town, I cannot say if other small-town mayors felt similar disrespect. I suspect that the mere creation of elected management committees, which usurped yet another brokering function from the mayor, elicited resentment across the northeastern interior. Thus, the federal government's decision to discontinue it was, I think, reasonable. Graziano and the MESA had miscalculated the risk of inciting the wrath of the conservative mayors, underestimating the mayors' power to subvert the Zero Hunger management committees. As the administration phased out Zero Hunger's Food Card and transitioned to Bolsa Família, it had to create a new beneficiary selection process that would be both viable and that would not allow the new cash grant to become an electoral currency. Thus, when he annulled the committees, Minister Ananias did not simply restore the old way of doing things; he forced each mayor to appoint one Bolsa Família "manager" whom the federal government could subject to training and scrutiny. Instead of bypassing the municipal executive, Lula's new cash grant tried to increase the mayor's accountability.

Another feature of Bolsa Família protected it from mayoral interference. Bolsa Família, unlike all the prior grants (including the Food Grant program), had no predetermined, finite number of beneficiaries per municipality. It created a de facto entitlement system, eventually relaxing the poverty criteria so that "moderately poor" people, not just the "extremely poor," could receive benefits (Lindert et al. 2007). Small, impoverished municipalities like Passarinho were flooded with these grants, so much so that local people no longer reckoned them as political currency. This is probably because no local politician could legitimately withhold them from an eligible family, and thus no politician could use them to any great electoral advantage (see Ansell and Mitchell 2011). If the shift to Bolsa Família signaled the federal government's abandonment of its assault on municipal patronage, it indicated Brasília's continued effort to ensure that its key federal resource remained outside those municipal patronage circuits.

Losing the Passarinho Election

In Passarinho, the PMDB/PT ticket lost the election to Henrique (who by then had affiliated with a small, vaguely right-wing party). Belinha did get herself elected to town council, though she died shortly thereafter in a bus accident. The PT's failure to win the mayoralty was somewhat embarrassing for the Lula and Dias administrations, but the media reported little on the loss in the two pilot towns. President Lula had already shifted his focus from Zero Hunger to Bolsa Família by late 2004, so the pilot towns were already "yesterday's news" by election time. It is nevertheless useful to consider why the local PT lost the election given the considerable resources that the state and federal governments spent on Passarinho's inhabitants. There would be no mystery to solve if the mayor had been able to co-opt cash resources and distribute them to his own electoral advantage. But Passarinho's inhabitants knew that Food Card was a federal grant issued by the PT administration. In fact, like most poor northeastern Brazilians, they rewarded the PT with their votes at higher levels of government: President Lula and Governor Dias were both reelected in 2006, and political scientists agree that this victory was largely due to the widespread satisfaction with Bolsa Família (Hunter 2007; Fleischer 2008). (Over 80 percent of Passarinho's citizens voted to reelect Dias and nearly 88 percent voted to reelect Lula.) But why couldn't the PT reap some electoral reward for its investment at the local level as well?

The answers to this question help to illuminate the unanticipated problems that the PT faced once the Zero Hunger officials marginalized the mayor. In the first place, the multifactional character of the Management Committee meant that the local PT (Belinha) could not monopolize credit for enrolling people in the Food Card any more than the mayor could. In other words, the price the PT paid for Zero Hunger's democratization of local grant distribution was to forfeit its own use of Zero Hunger as a municipal electoral currency. Of course, Passarinho's residents might have nonetheless rewarded Belinha and the PT's would-be vice mayor just for being identified with the governing party that benefited them. Given the popularity of the PT at higher levels, it would certainly make sense to put the party in power locally if one assumed that higher-ups favored their local allies when channeling resources down to the municipal level.

Yet by humiliating the mayor, the PT had unwittingly defined itself in opposition to the values of personal history and familiar modes of recognizing poverty, and thus became an affront to municipal sensibilities. Whatever gains the local PT made by riding the coattails of the Zero Hunger program were offset by the fact that the program represented an alien mode of knowledge out of synch with local ways of doing things that worked well, and that worked well precisely because they were not reducible to coercive stereotypes of "patronage." Intimate hierarchy, because it emerged from relations of vulnerable information-sharing, was useful to the selection process.

I would argue therefore that the humiliation of Passarinho's mayor generally backfired on the Zero Hunger officials. It spoon-fed Rodrigo an easy narrative of local pride through which he could portray the government's actions as an assault on local values of intimacy, history, and rural simplicity, and not merely as an assault on himself. If the humiliation of its mayor taught Passarinho's citizens anything, it was that a good government, however helpful, should keep out of the everyday spaces of local decision-making. In that sense, Zero Hunger reinforced the idea that people should keep their criteria for electing municipal officials separate from the criteria guiding their choice of state and federal executives. This was hardly the lesson that state officials wanted them to learn; the officials wanted to cleanse the municipality of its messy intimacies, and, more cynically, to shore up the PT's electoral base in small northeastern municipalities.

By bypassing the mayoralty through the Management Committee, Zero Hunger may have also further propelled the ongoing transformation of coronelismo, creating another local broker for federal resources that did not answer to the mayor. This new broker stood neither for intimate hierarchy nor for insurgent democracy (Holston 2008) but rather for the effort to achieve objective fairness within the context of local political ethics and etiquette. Thus, the marginalization of the mayor did not undermine intimate hierarchy in Passarinho, but it did offer people an opportunity to critically reflect on these relations and to interweave them with other ways of distributing resources. If the state's experiment with the committees ultimately proved that intimate hierarchy and fair-minded resource distribution were compatible, it was the town residents who found the means to do this, not the state.

Intimacy and Democracy

I have argued that state officials tried to impress on the beneficiaries of Zero Hunger and Bolsa Família that there was a better way to do politics than "patronage" (what I've called "intimate hierarchy"). In doing so, I may have committed an injustice to these officials by implying that they were insensitive to the nuances of municipal political culture, and that their perspective on this matter remained unchanged despite their own intimate encounters with program beneficiaries. In fact, their encounters with the beneficiaries prompted state officials to reflect on their preexisting ideas about patronage in the sertão and in their own lives. I learned this lesson by bungling an opportunity to discuss some of the general challenges that the Zero Hunger Coordenadoria was facing in 2005 (around the time the government was phasing in Bolsa Família). I was out drinking with the Coordenadoria's interim director one night in Teresina when I tried to ingratiate myself by parroting what I assumed was her stereotype of northeastern mayors. I said something like, "These illiterate, clientelistic mayors are the biggest drag on Zero Hunger that the program faces." She took issue with my prejudicial remark, "Aaron, these mayors may be illiterate, but they do their best to help the people with what they have, with what they know. It's not their fault that they're illiterate." The interim director had spent several years working with homeless children in Teresina and was herself a natural ethnographer—very good at tuning in to the way different people navigated their life-worlds. As we spoke further, she confirmed that many of her associates did harbor this stereotype of municipal mayors, but she suggested that they were nonetheless learning to appreciate the earnestness and problem-solving potential of intimate exchange. Many state officials came to question the intimate obligations that informed their own professional practice. As one EMATER agent (who worked closely with the Quilombola Project) confessed, "Every time I meet with the rural cultivators [*produtores*], I ask myself, 'Am I practicing clientelismo? Am I being *assistencialista*?' We in the government have to be very careful ourselves."

These conversations recall Roberto Schwarz's (1992: 23) claim that "under a thousand forms and names, favour formed and flavoured the whole of national life" in Brazil. While at some moments, state officials (and Passarinho's townspeople) may have scapegoated the cultivators of the sertão, treating them as the embodiment of a political culture that they themselves were anxious to disown, their actual encounters with Passarinho's cultivators brought them face to face with the complexities of clientelismo, troubling any such simplistic condemnation. The officials' respect for the people of the backlands allowed them to temper and revise their critiques of patronage in their policy encounters. The state officials were not missionaries devoted to a singular democratic deity, even if they often voiced the belief that social justice and political emancipation entailed the inevitable sacrifice of intimate hierarchy.

The cultivators, for their part, profited from the new modes of critical reflection that the officials inspired, even if the officials' assault on patronage complicated some of the concrete challenges they faced in the implementation of Zero Hunger and Bolsa Família. The officials' assault on patronage elicited their own critiques of local political culture that partially overlapped with those voiced by the officials. For instance, while Passarinho's cultivators still do not consider hierarchical and egalitarian relations to be antithetical, much less mutually exclusive, they now recognize a distinction between those politicians who honor their horizontal associations and those who would monopolize their loyalties (e.g., "The only association around here is me"). Moreover, they have become increasingly wary of politicians who persecute adversary voters and of voters who allow friendships and family to be torn apart during the political period. The ethics of intimate politics are thus transforming; intimacy remains a desired mode of alliance but not a legitimate cause for enmity.

These transformations are the product of a range of sociohistorical factors, state policy being only one of them. Still, social policy is a powerful vehicle for reengineering political culture because it forces officials and beneficiaries alike to see how named ideological abstractions ("liberal democracy" or "patronage") are implicated in the concrete and practical dilemmas that pertain to people's livelihoods (e.g., how to form work groups to build chicken coops). Social policy, because it provokes a story of social ills and hopes for improvement, also channels myriad fantasies of rescue, redemption, and personal conversion. Social policy, for this reason, is good to think with. Zero Hunger and Bolsa Família intersected with the emotionally laden thoughts of Passarinho's cultivators and townspeople in ways that indeed "mess[ed] with people's hearts." Let me review its effects on these communities by recalling the three culture-changing techniques that I ascribe to the state officials and the specific social programs I addressed in the last three chapters.

Induced nostalgia, a technique I discussed in relation to the Productive Project (chapter 5), was designed to align villagers' sense of duty to their parents and grandparents with a nostalgic golden age of virtuous reciprocity among equals, conjuring the image of a time before morally compromising hierarchical exchange was necessary. (Of course, the state officials knew at an analytical level that intimate hierarchy had existed for centuries in the sertão.) In deploying nostalgic talk, the state officials inadvertently evoked the villagers' historical memory of a time when powerful fathers controlled adult children's labor and votes. The villagers came to think about their participation in the Productive Project as a mode of reconciliation with this oppressive, yet morally firm, patriarchal past. This reconciliation with the past opened up the discursive space of the village association to statements that exposed interhousehold inequality. A few of the most deeply impoverished villagers were able to cite their descent from honored elders to leverage their inclusion in the cooperative Productive Project. Kinship talk in the association meetings made people's particular social identities relevant to their utterances in a "public sphere" and compelled collective acknowledgement of their vulnerability. To the extent that such frank discussions of kinship enter the association meetings, the discursive space of the village community comes to resemble not a classical public sphere (à la Habermas) where formal equals deliberate dispassionately but a place where people acknowledge the dimensions of inequality, antagonism, and rivalry that circumscribe all decision-making and shape their orientations toward a debate (see Mouffe 1993).

While the state officials failed to induce in the villagers a feeling of nostalgia for a golden age before patronage exchange, they did reinforce this commitment to a moral system (under threat from various factors) that condemned commodified (short-term) vote-buying and sought to build moral, long-term relations of reciprocity. The village development association began to transform into a new unit of moral exchange, in part as an analogue of the patriarchal family (though many villagers were critical of this tendency because they did not want to subordinate themselves to association presidents). Contrary to what state officials advised, association members did not exclude local politicians from their efforts to implement the Productive Projects; in fact, they asked local councilmen for favors that would help them to resolve some of their Productive Project's logistical challenges. Recalling the state officials' warnings against allying the association with local politicians, beneficiaries were careful to inform those councilmen that they were offering no votes in exchange for these favors, only the opportunity for the councilmen to present themselves to association members in a favorable light. The politicians' incentive to accrue voters was channeled into the well-being of the project in a way that did not commodify, or even commit, the association members' votes.

The programmatic pilgrimages I discussed in the context of the Quilombola Project (chapter 6) aimed to inspire egalitarian solidarity among Afro-Brazilian villagers and to incite them to defy authority. The pilgrimage-like bus rides and training sessions in Teresina explicated the racism that these villagers experienced in their daily lives. By bringing racial issues to the surface of conversation, state officials spurred villagers to identify with a broader swath of the region's rural underclass. As the project unfolded, village women emerged as its primary beneficiaries, and although their cooperative enterprise (home remedies) failed at the collective level, several women profited individually. Moreover, these women gained power in the village association (one was elected president) and became their households' primary interlocutors with the regional Quilombola Movement and other state officials. As women developed these new, upward lines of communication, they eroded the long-standing male privilege of representing the household to the outside world. Presuming that the household remains a significant unit of political exchange, one can imagine new strategic electoral discussions between husbands and wives that may result in more egalitarian marriages. Ironically, the nature of the new vertical alliances between quilombola villages and state officials (and regional Quilombola Movement activists) assumed elements of intimate hierarchy insofar as village women revealed to state officials, among other things, the deficiencies of the villagers' historical memory (e.g., of African slavery) and the resulting lack of mastery of the Afro-derived cultural practices that affirmed their authentic quilombola identity. For their part, activists in the Quilombola Movement and allied state officials revealed to the villagers their own vulnerability, that is, the ongoing difficulties of enlisting affiliates among a mixed-race population that was slow to accept the category *negro* as an identity in which one would take pride.

It is also worth recalling João's loss of his association presidency in connection with this project. Intimate hierarchical relations with state officials and activists in no way precluded association members from punishing João for his embezzlement of project funds. It was not just João's "eating" project monies or impregnating his sister-in-law that caused the association to vote him out. It was the fact that he had done these things at a moment when the village was operating under the judgmental eye of the state. It was in relation to this perceived audience that João's actions undermined the association's dignity.

The Quilombola Project generally had a more lasting positive impact on its beneficiary communities than the Productive Project, even if its material benefits were modest. Of course, the Quilombola Project was also based on something of a fiction, in other words, the idea that its beneficiary villages were culturally distinct in their Africanness or in their historical memory of slavery. Yet this fiction was productive for the benefited villagers, because it resonated with their lived experience of racism and race-based poverty. The quilombola identity, like the *negro* identity, became a pragmatic reality that coexisted alongside a more commonplace discourse of racial mixture and comingled history. As one villager described it, "It is true. It's true. We're morenos. But in reality, we're *negros*." As a result, the benefited communities balanced both an instrumentalist approach to their quilombola identity (i.e., a strategic ethnic identification oriented toward material gain) with an emotional investment in building toward a fuller embodiment of quilombola subjectivity. These quilombola communities have gained leverage in their dealings with municipal politicians who seem to recognize that various federal and state development programs call for these communities to receive priority when scarce projects are meted out. Moreover, the very fact that these communities have considerable access to state officials and to local activists who engage higher-level institutions (e.g., the Palmares Cultural Foundation) has had the ironic effect of making the municipality's most impoverished communities into potential brokers who can provide local politicians with access to state officials. In this way, the Quilombola Project gave its beneficiary communities added leverage within intimate hierarchical relationships rather than undermining those relationships.

The technique of mayoral marginalization that I traced through the Food Card and later the Bolsa Família programs (chapter 7) also met with partial success. As an effort to alienate the vilified mayor from the population, it backfired, provoking common people's sympathetic identification with the mayor as a figure representing local autonomy and the intimate forms of knowledge, history, and memory that organized moral political exchange. Yet the resilience of intimate loyalties did not preclude the emergence of egalitarian cooperation across political factions on the Zero Hunger Management Committee. The townspeople (and some villagers) who served as "civil society representatives" on the Management Committee may have perceived faction warfare as a general threat to their practical ability to collaborate with one another, but they found ways to circumvent that threat. They employed a consensus system, projected nonpartisan messages to Food Card's would-be beneficiaries, informally ensured that all factions were represented among Zero Hunger's beneficiaries, and utilized intimate knowledge (from politicians and others) of family poverty to make determinations about the neediness of would-be beneficiaries. The committee's success in selecting the neediest beneficiaries depended on its members' recognition that intimate hierarchy was both a danger and an asset to the selection process. Eventually, the cyclical maturation of the political season exacerbated tensions and paranoia to such an extent that the Management Committee could no longer function. (Clearly, cash grants and other state projects should never be meted out during the municipal political season in Brazil.) All its troubles aside, the committee's brief existence testified to the possibility that cooperative modes of civil governance and equitable resource distribution might be compatible with some aspects of intimate hierarchy.

The Food Card and later Bolsa Família were, by far, the PT administration's most successful measures for fighting poverty and hunger. There is strong consensus among those who have evaluated the impact of these programs that they (especially Bolsa Família) significantly reduced the prevalence of extreme poverty and increased economic equality (Lindert et al. 2007; Soares, Perez Ribas, and Guerrero Osário 2010). Anecdotally, I can report that dozens of Passarinho's families have increased their food intake since the program began. On my subsequent visits in 2010 and 2012, I noticed that many previously emaciated people (e.g., Adenísio and his family) came to look normal in my eyes. With regard to its ongoing effect on municipal politics, Bolsa Família's administrative structure did not entail bypassing (much less humiliating) the mayors. Instead of utilizing a civil society–dominated committee to select the beneficiaries, this task went to a mayor-appointed "manager of Bolsa Família" who received federal training and monitoring. This was the condition the federal government placed on the mayors in order for their municipalities to receive Bolsa Família. Not only did this reform represent a withdrawal of the state's assault on local intimate hierarchy; it arguably created the conditions for intimate hierarchy to factor into the enforcement of the beneficiaries' grant conditions in a positive way. Consider that, in practice, a beneficiary's violations of the grant conditions (e.g., keeping a child out of school to work in the fields) is rebuked by the manager, a mayoral appointee. To defy the manager is to risk losing one's status within the mayor's intimate network. Thus, in practice, relatively few families are ever cut from the Bolsa Família program for violating the grant conditions, because the municipal manager has extraprogrammatic leverage over them to enforce compliance.

These various modes of combining intimate and liberal political ethics emerged in the context of a highly plural reaction to the Zero Hunger state officials. Some people in Passarinho assimilated the officials' critiques of patronage into their local grievances with the status quo: divisive factionalism and amoral vote-buying. Some people ventriloquized the state's critique of patronage, collapsing the distinction between vote-buying and long-term exchange as the officials did. It's probably fair to say that, in general, the Lula administration's effort to dismantle patronage prompted Passarinho's citizens to use their political intelligence to integrate those aspects of liberal democracy that accorded with their sense of what was practical and moral. I cannot predict the fate of such hybrid forms, but I hope that they will not simply crumble under the weight of liberal democracy. If nothing else, intimate hierarchy offers a standpoint of critique from which one can see the flaws and limitations of liberal democracy as we know it.

Let me conclude with a final story from the field.

One day, while I was talking to Augustinho, I caught him in a curious slip of the tongue, a malapropism actually, though at the time I thought it was a conscious play on words. Augustinho was trying to find a ride to the town notary, whom he needed to authorize some official documents related to the Quilombola Project. This and other project requirements were wearing on him and in a moment of frustration he uttered a version of the well-known phrase *É uma burocracia danada* ("It's a damn bureaucracy"). People typically utter this little curse when they've been ensnared in a mess of protocol, paperwork, and mind-numbing procedures that slow down their problem solving. But what Augustinho actually said was, "*É uma democracia danada*." I laughed, thinking he had made a joke. He seemed confused. Equating democracy with bureaucratic tedium, Augustinho's understanding of democracy had little to do with elections or human rights or equality before the law or uncorrupted voting. It had little to do with the ideals that motivated the Zero Hunger officials. He was up against the mundane features of large-scale democratic governance, remote institutions that did not sympathize with his particular circumstances.

Democracy's remoteness from Augustinho's life was due not to his geographic distance from the capital city but to liberal democracy's impersonal character. Liberalism doesn't preclude personal friendships between officeholders and citizens, but it does work to define the precise limits of officeholders' authority so that their institutional power does not define their full relationship to citizens. As president of a village association (in Serafim), Augustinho had to manage the implementation of public policies that hit the ground in very personal communities. On one occasion, an interfamilial quarrel (stemming, as I recall, from a romantic jealousy) led several households to threaten to break away and found another association. Augustinho wanted one of the state-contracted technical agents associated with the Productive Project to talk to these families and urge them to "remain united." He hoped the agent might even mediate the quarrel, which Augustinho thought was silly to begin with. Augustinho had easy geographic access to the agent, whose office was in the neighboring city, but the agent told him that this "private dispute" was not his business and that conflict mediation lay outside his responsibilities. Augustinho felt disheartened. As it turns out, the faction did not break away, but its members refused to participate in collective actions associated with several Zero Hunger projects, disparaging them as a waste of time.

Read through a liberal lens, the association members were at fault for failing to separate a personal quarrel from their shared interest in, and responsibility for, a collective project. Augustinho understood this interpretation; he even chastised his fellow villagers for not living up to this ideal. But he also understood that to "deal with people" (*lidar com gente*) means acknowledging the artificiality of such rigid distinctions between private and public life. That's why he tried to engage the technical agent as an intimate authority who would not let formal protocol stand in his way of solving a concrete problem. The agent declined that invitation, evoking the sanctity of the liberal public-private divide and his duty to exercise only the forms of authority granted to his public office by the state. Thus, at stake in this incident was the curtailment of personal authority as well as the extent of a leader's duty to those loyal to them. Seen from the vantage point of intimate hierarchy, such curtailment of an officeholder's accountability is unacceptable. Good authority figures—technocrats or politicians—respond to whatever needs emerge in the lives of their citizen-allies; they cannot hide behind the limited, contractual obligations of public office. We thus find throughout the world evidence of recently democratized peoples who long to return to a time when leaders could not simply leave for the capital cities, erect walls around their houses, send their children abroad for schooling, and all the while claim to be fulfilling their duty to the people. When applied to places where intimate power is the norm, liberal democratic regimes provoke the complaint that they've "promoted irresolvable conflict in their midst and provided cover for dominant political actors to forgo the responsibilities of authority and to feed themselves at the expense of others" (West 2008: 118).

Such abdication of responsibility does not happen in a functioning system of intimate hierarchy, even if that system is guilty of other ills. Intimate hierarchy is defined as an encounter between unequals in which one confronts the other's particular needs in the context of one's own needs and works to help them regardless of the formal or legal barriers. Mutual sympathy and vulnerability between the partners become the basis of a shared humanity that transcends the structural hierarchy that separates them. These intimacies result in favoritism of resource distribution and undermine equality before the law, but they also socialize the political class to the daily challenges of a region's poor. They forge political duty not from impartial civic virtue but from intersubjective compassion. Intimate politics generates feelings and obligations that know no boundary between the public and the private. As a result, a politician can never escape his or her obligations to an elector's needs; the politician must fulfill them even at his or her own expense and even if that elector might objectively be judged undeserving. From the perspective of liberal democracy, the politician's refusal to hold such personalistic considerations in abeyance is simply unfair. From the vantage point of intimate hierarchy, liberal democracy fetishizes its standardized rubrics of merit, "abandons its non-achievers[,] and gives rise to feelings of impotence" (Gunes-Ayata 1994: 21). Intimacy thus defines the standpoint of critique from which liberal bureaucratic entanglements, broken promises, and absentee politicians become subject to legitimate grievances. Both of these perspectives grasp real and complementary challenges faced by people living in Passarinho and elsewhere. Today, ten years after the Workers' Party government's first forays into the Northeast, both critical perspectives coexist among the region's cultivators and inform the way they apprehend their lives.

Appendix

TABLE 1 Zero Hunger Component Programs Implemented in Passarinho, Piauí, 2003–2004

Program[a]	Number of Beneficiaries	Cost in Brazilian Reais (1 Real = $US .35)	Agency[b]
Cash transfer (Food Card/Bolsa Família)	728	364,000	MESA/Coordenadoria
Productive Development Project	74	204,104	World Bank/Piauí Bureau of Rural Development
Street Market Project	17	1,830	Coordenadoria
Milk Technology Assistance	24	n/a	MESA
Zero Thirst (Cistern Project)	325	310,081	World Bank/Piauí Bureau of Rural Development
Emergency Food Basket	728	n/a	MESA
Nutritional Diagnostic	86	11,684	MESA/UNESCO
Basic Residence[c]	132	211,200	COHAB
Quilombo Project	75	32,265	EMATER/FAO/Movimento Quilombola
Zero Illiteracy	275	91,000	UNICEF
School Garden	n/a	n/a	Coordenadoria
Happy Face of Piauí	n/a	n/a	Coordenadoria
Total	1,814[d]	1,135,164	

Sources: "Cartilha do Programa Fome Zero: Direito de Cidadania Piauí: Primeiros 180 Dias," document prepared by Coordenadoria de Estado de Segurança Alimentar e Nutricional, coordinated by Rosângela Maria Sobrinho Sousa, January 2003; "Projeto de Cooperação Técnica EMATER/FAO. Assessoria/Assistência Técnica e Capacitação em Paiuí Ao Desenvolvimento Sustentável da Agricultura Familiar, No Contexto do Semi-Árido, No Estado do Piauí/Brasil," Secretaria de Desenvolvimento Rural/Instituto de Assistência Técnica e Extensão Rural Version 01/28/2004; "Síntese das Ações Realizadas Pelo Programa Fome Zero em 2003," document prepared by Coordenadoria Estadual de Segurança Alimentar e Erradicação da Fome, coordinated by Simplício Mário de Oliveira, March 2004.

a. The items included here are those for which there is documentation and that I confirmed to have existed through direct observation or reports from Passarinho's citizenry. The cost of these programs is taken directly from the sources and was not confirmed independently.

b. Many of the programs listed were administered and financed by multiple agencies. For each program, the agency shown here is the agency listed first on the program documents.

c. The data given for this project reflect two sources. The "Cartilha do Programa Fome Zero" estimates the unit cost at 1,600 reais per housing unit. I attended an implementation meeting in Passarinho at which officials from the Federal Housing Company (COHAB) stated that 132 housing units would be built in the municipality: 42 in the town and 90 in the rural zone. I confirmed the construction of all 42 in the town center and extrapolated the completion of those in the rural zone based on word of mouth from municipal inhabitants.

d. Many of the same individuals received multiple Zero Hunger program benefits.

TABLE 2 Federal Investments in Zero Hunger Component Policies, 2003–2004

Component Policy	Spent in 2003 in Brazilian Reais (1 Real = $US .35)	Spent in 2004 in Brazilian Reais (1 Real = $US .42)
Cash transfer programs (Food Card, Bolsa Família)	3,356,886	5,627,527,240
School Lunches	954,164,181	1,014,315,489
Cistern construction (potable water for households)	0	63,635,953
Popular restaurants	0	19,716,400
Food banks	0	4,233,080
Distribution of food to specific groups	0	8,130,676
Urban agriculture	0	5,350,000
Healthy food	5,884,808	10,791,985
Support for the Project for the Improvement of the Family Socioeconomic Conditions	143,663,947	88,753,532
PRONAF (Family Agriculture)	63,505,200	93,951,645
Interest financing for Family Agriculture	1,377,293,776	1,925,130,927
Food Acquisition from Family Agriculture	224,168,747	169,611,634
Operationalizing Strategic Stocks for Food Security	0	9,207,898
Professional qualification programs	32,707,002	52,944,312
Solidarity Economy	0	10,708,443
Productive inclusion	18,879,619	15,459,112
Support for the Creation of Productive Enterprise	0	1,498,250
Support for cooperatives of pickers of recyclable materials	0	495,000
Family housing	18,610, 551	60,665,658
Management and capacity building	2,132,095	15,069,098
Total	6,197,896,197	9,204,563,774

Source: "Evolução dos Investimentos no Fome Zero, De 2003 a 2005," table on p. 6 of *Fome Zero: Balanço dos Programas e Ações,* coordinated by Malu Oliveira, Ministério de Desenvolvimento Social e Combate à Fome, Produzida pela Assessoria de Comunicação Social, October 2005.

Notes

INTRODUCTION

1. The right-wing generals who had overthrown the government in 1964 managed a slow restoration of free press, freedom of assembly, and, lastly, direct election of the president. The military government had lost its legitimacy by the late 1970s and was facing enormous pressure from a multiclass alliance. The national bourgeoisie, early on quite supportive of the military coup, turned against the generals after the regime shifted its economic model to benefit international corporations over domestic businesses. The bourgeoisie allied with unions that wanted more freedom to organize across sectors and to strike without the approval of the Ministry of Labor. Journalists and lawyers joined the opposition, decrying the military's use of torture and imprisonment to silence dissidents.

2. All translations from Portuguese sources cited in the book are my own unless otherwise stated.

3. Here I am indebted to my colleague Gregory Morton, who raised precisely this point in a private conversation with David Graeber and me in 2010.

4. This book does not do justice to the impact that Lula's policies had on rural gender relations in the rural Northeast, though I do address the issue a bit in chapter 6. Alessandro e Rego Pinzani and Walquira Domingues Leão Rêgo (2013) argue that Lula's main cash-transfer program, Bolsa Família (Family Stipend), gave poor Brazilian women more control over their family purchases, as well as more freedom to leave their spouses. Lula's social policies also seem to be correlated with women's increased use of contraception.

5. This chapter structure replicates that of Erica Bornstein's ethnography, *The Spirit of Development: Protestant NGOs, Morality, and Economics in Zimbabwe* (2005). I am grateful for her brilliant design.

6. Throughout this book, I refer to Brazilian state policies by their English translations, e.g., Zero Hunger. However, in the case of Programa Bolsa Família, this makes less sense because most of the scholarly literature that has emerged to evaluate this program uses its Portuguese name.

CHAPTER 1

1. James Holston (2008) argues that the imperial and republican phases of Brazilian history were liberal in several regards but not democratic. He usefully defines liberalism as having four properties: (1) a critique of the naturalization of social

hierarchy, (2) an emerging emphasis on self-regulation and the public-private divide within its proposal for social organization, (3) a conception of the individual as the "seat of rights," and (4) an economic theory favoring the self-regulating free market. He notes that democracy "gets entangled with several of these developments, but with a different agenda of citizenship" (318, n.15).

2. Given the literacy requirement for suffrage (only lifted in 1985), I am led to wonder how broad a phenomenon *coronelismo* truly was. Reports from older consultants in Passarinho and conversations with colleagues (e.g., John French) suggest that the restriction was easy to circumvent. For a rural (and illiterate) worker to vote, a man of standing (and wealth) simply had to vouch for the worker at the notary. The more votes a local *coronel* (landowner) could register and deliver to his state-level benefactor, the more resources the latter would channel down to him for discretionary use. Thus, local *coronéis* had enormous incentive to "enfranchise" the local population.

3. Unlike several other Latin American military dictatorships of the era, Brazil's military allowed limited democracy to continue. The ruling party, National Renewal Alliance (Aliança Renovação Nacional—ARENA), and the official opposition party, Brazilian Democratic Movement (Movimento Democrático Brasileiro—MDB), contested legislative positions at the federal, state, and municipal levels of government. The selection of presidents and governors remained the prerogative of the generals. Municipal mayors could be elected with the exception of those in "strategically important" cities (mostly the capitals) chosen by the generals.

4. Under pressure from the liberationist Christian movement, the Vatican eventually replaced its prodictatorship bishops with clergy who supported human rights (Moreira Alves 2001: 286).

5. In 1979, the generals legalized the creation of new political parties with the "Organic Law of Political Parties." This was one of the first steps in a slow process of "opening" the country to democracy, though it can also be seen as an effort to fragment the opposition by encouraging its division into competing parties.

6. Below are a few examples demonstrating the linkage between assistencialismo and clientelismo in critiques of prior food policies and the governments that implemented them.

> Upon reducing food security to one of the items of social action, [prior administrations] restricted it to an assistencialista dimension, within a context of generalized misery and impoverishment in the country. (Maluf, Menezes, and Valente 1996: 71)

> The food interventions of the military dictatorship . . . evinced . . . assistencialismo, paternalism, and political-electoral clientelismo. (Vasconcelos 2005: 445)

> For the first time in this country, the municipal government's monopolistic control over public policies is breaking . . . freely associated anonymous persons, each motivated for different reasons to participate, wanted to destroy the traditional clientelismo of local politics. (A. Gomes, quoted in Takagi 2006: 157)

The challenge (of Zero Hunger) is to break with the logic, and to overcome the identifications, of social policies with assistencialismo and with the fragmenting power of clientelismo (Yasbek 2004: 112).

7. Lula released this televised statement as part of a public critique of President Fernando Henrique Cardoso's redistribution measures. In 2008, the video began to circulate widely on the Internet, when PT adversaries cited it as evidence of Lula's hypocrisy (http://www.youtube.com/watch?v=-oXRjEZ3Mes). The dubious premise of those critiques was that Lula's Bolsa Família program was no different from the "food basket and milk distribution" programs of President Cardoso.

8. In addition to the School Grant (Bolsa Escola), the Cardoso government implemented two other cash grants: the Food Stipend (Bolsa Alimentação) gave every family earning less than one half a minimum wage monthly income fifteen reais per month for every child up to six years old (with a maximum of three children). Fuel Aid (Auxílio Gás) channeled fifteen reais to poor families every two months to purchase canisters of gas for cooking. Finally, Cardoso's Income Stipend (Bolsa Renda) gave benefited families thirty reais per month for one year if they lived in a municipality declared to be in a state of "calamity" as a result of drought. (The federal government declared that Passarinho, and several other municipalities around it, were in a state of calamity in 2002, but by 2003 the temporary grant had run out.)

9. The labeling of these three policy modalities shifted between 2003 and 2006, conforming to philosophical disputes within the federal government regarding what constituted, for instance, "structurally transformative" policy. In 2003 the national leadership of the PT issued a colorful pamphlet to the party's affiliates called *The Zero Hunger Program and the PT*, in which the three modalities are "structural policies," "specific policies," and "local policies." Land reform is nowhere to be found. Instead, "structural policies" include headings like "Income and Job Creation," "Bolsa Escola" (School Grant), "Basic Health Attention," and so on. The classification of the cash grants as "emergency" also changed in 2004 when Bolsa Família replaced Food Card. Unlike Food Card, Bolsa Família was not time-limited, and thus the category *emergências* (which implied a temporary measure) was changed to *assistenciais*. This term sounded dangerously close to *assistencialismo* ("welfare statism"), creating the need to defend Zero Hunger against that charge.

10. The landless workers' movements were infuriated with President Lula, though they remained officially supportive of the PT administration. Many in the movements mocked Zero Hunger and called Lula a traitor for failing to implement land reform. In 2005, eleven thousand landless demonstrators marched on Brasília in opposition to what was strategically phrased as "those forces in the state that impede land reform" (ParanáOnline 2005).

11. The means for linking municipal grocery stores to the federal bank (Caixa Econômica Federal) was the Casa Lotérica, literally a lottery house. Here Brazilians pay their bills and play the lottery numbers. Small municipalities like Passarinho often do not have proper lottery houses; instead they have automatic teller machines called *unidades lotéricas* ("lottery units") installed in local stores. The use of these "lottery units" to distribute cash grants began in 1999, with President

Cardoso's cash programs. Some people in Passarinho complained that some store-owners demanded that the beneficiary spend the cash grant at their store.

12. Patrus Ananias had been a PT mayor of Minas Gerais's capital city, Belo Horizonte, from 1993 to 1993. He was liked in the food security movement because, as mayor, he had experimented with several municipal food and nutrition policies. The administration changed its social policy leader because many people in the national CONSEA had blamed Graziano da Silva for the poor coordination of Zero Hunger's many component initiatives, and for the general public's growing disillusion with Zero Hunger. Moreover, Ananias's appointment coincided with the administration's general shift away from Zero Hunger and toward Family Stipend. At this time, the Special Ministry of Food Security (MESA) was downgraded and placed within a new Ministry of Social Development and the Fight against Hunger (MDSCF). Family Stipend was given top priority.

13. After 2005, Lula created several lesser-known programs that also included supportive services seeking to bolster the safety (and productivity) of the nuclear family by diminishing family violence and sexual abuse and offering psychological counseling and family planning.

14. In my one interview with Graziano da Silva, I mentioned that of the 4.43 billion reais (1 Brazilian real = approximately thirty U.S. cents) spent on Zero Hunger, 3.57 billion were dedicated to Food Card (MDSCF 2005). Graziano replied that I was not taking all the facts into account: Zero Hunger entailed the coordination of many social policies undertaken by other federal ministries. He claimed that if one factored the cost of those policies into Zero Hunger's budget, the Food Card would appear less prominent.

15. Another administrative contrast between Food Card and Bolsa Família was the restriction on the type of purchases that could be made with the card; beneficiaries could only spend their fifty reais on food and hygiene products, and these restrictions would be enforced by ledgers and store receipts that each family would have to show to the Management Committee. These purchasing restrictions created controversy within the food security movement, whose members believed that by telling beneficiaries how they could spend their money, the state was controlling its poor citizens in a way that raised the specter (once again) of assistencialismo (see Anthony Hall 2006). Members of the food movement marshaled studies showing that poor families typically spent much of their cash aid on food, common-sense behavior that made spending restrictions a superfluous, costly, wasteful, and onerous bureaucratic procedure (see "PSDB Critica o Fome Zero do Futuro Governo: Tucanos Avaliam Propostas do Programa Apresentadas como 'Inovadoras' pelo PT e Afirmam que Elas São Inviáveis," *Gazeta de Alagoas*, December 6, 2002, http://www.achanoticias.com.br/noticia.kmf?noticia=618386). These restrictions were never enforced and rarely discussed in Passarinho. When the Food Card was merged into Bolsa Família, Minister Ananias removed both the purchasing restrictions and the time limit for benefits and instead reinstated the conditions (originally from the School Grant) that required children to attend school and children and pregnant women to receive medical consultations (Filho 2007).

16. The data substantiating this paragraph come from the municipality's *Municipal Rural Sustainable Development Plan, 2001–2004*. The plan was prepared by a technocrat who was under contract at the parastate development company EMATER and was paid for his services by Passarinho's municipal government. I cannot cite the report appropriately without revealing the actual name of the municipality I refer to as "Passarinho." It thus does not appear in the bibliography.

17. The Superintendency for the Development of the Northeast (Superintendência do Desenvolvimento do Nordeste—SUDENE) was created in 1959 under the guidance of the celebrated economist Celso Furtado, who argued that the region's poverty and vulnerability to famine was the product of fiscal and monetary policies that greatly favored Brazil's industrial Southeast. During its first few years under Furtado's command, SUDENE implemented a spate of water and transportation infrastructure projects and invested in textile industry, artisanal crafts, fishing, public health, and education. The military coup of 1964 replaced Furtado with more conservative leaders and drained the superintendency's budget, steering the agency toward immediate drought relief. These factors, along with SUDENE's alleged corruption, likely motivated President Cardoso to close it down. Cardoso created a replacement entity, the Agency for the Development of the Northeast (Agência do Desenvolvimento do Nordeste—ADENE), which President Lula later renamed SUDENE in 2007 (see Hirschmann 1963; Francisco de Oliveira 1977; Barros and Magalhães 2009; and Pedroza Júnior, Andrade, and Viera do Bonfim 2011).

18. The Constitution of 1988 increased the federal funds allocated to municipal governments by over 600 percent, allocating to them 22 percent of the federal budget and making them responsible for education services. In 1996, the public health system was municipalized as well (Fry and Kempner 1996).

19. These data come from a study conducted in 2005 by the Fundação Centro de Pesquisas Econômicas e Sociais do Piauí. The study focuses exclusively on the socioeconomic indicators of the municipality I call Passarinho. I am projecting these numbers back to 2003, because the number of municipal jobs remained virtually the same between 2002 and 2005, though population growth during this period suggests that the percentage may have been higher in 2002.

20. The demographic information given in this paragraph come from the Demographic Census of 2000 which is conducted by the Instituto Brasileiro de Geografia e Estatística [Brazilian Institute of Geography and Statistics]. Data pertaining specifically to hunger or malnutrition come from the CESACF Nutritional Diagnostic, sections 5.1.3 and 5.2.1.2.

21. The Zero Hunger program did not include provisions for the electrification of the interior, but in 2005 the Lula government spread the energy grid throughout the rural Northeast with a program called Luz para Todos ("Light for All").

CHAPTER 2

1. L. A. Rebhun's analysis of the evil eye in northeast Brazil situates this belief within a broader set of folk understandings of bodily forces, emotions, and self-control. Many of Rebhun's findings hold true for Passarinho. Indeed, people in

Passarinho claim that the evil eye can result if a person's blood is "bad" (a kind of congenital condition with no moral implication), or if his or her blood is "hot" from anger or exertion (see Rebhun 1994). A more comprehensive analysis of the place of evil eye belief in the sertão would have to engage folk beliefs about the body and the perils to its health.

2. Some of the differences between my account of hunger, labor, and patronage and that of Nancy Scheper-Hughes may derive from the regional disparity between our field sites. She worked in the lush coastal region of the Northeast, where rural labor is more often wage-based; Passarinho is located in the dry interior, the seat of family agriculture.

3. Regarding patronage and hunger, Donald Nelson and Timothy Finan (2009) make a point similar to Scheper-Hughes's. Looking at drought relief policy in the northeastern state of Ceará, they argue that government patronage has become an institutionalized response to drought. This government relief undermines poor farmers' *resilience* to hunger. Here, "resilience" refers to a social system's ability "to absorb disturbances . . . while protecting its capacity for change and adjustment" (305). Accordingly, "systems" can "absorb disturbance" when their "subsystems" (individuals, families, communities) are able to make small-scale, fast-responding changes to resolve urgent problems. Thus, Nelson and Finan suggest that government relief keeps people frozen in place. They look up to the state for support rather than using their creativity to "absorb disturbances" to their food production system. I agree that these exchanges may lead to the reelection of conservative politicians who deny them policy-based resources, though the argument implicates state-municipal patronage relations more than the intimate, vertical alliances within the municipal sphere that are at issue in this book. At the municipal level, vertical alliances often contribute to "resilience," as Nelson and Finan define it (see chapter 3).

4. This respectful use of the first name (instead of "you") does not occur throughout Brazil, or even throughout the sertão. Jorge Mattar Villela informed me that it is not used in his field site in rural Pernambuco and that it is more frequently associated with "continental" (i.e., European) Portuguese. To my knowledge, no linguistic analysis has explained, or even mapped, the geographic distribution of this practice.

5. Marques's code of respectful distance should be read as an aspect of the more general "code of the sertão," which is typically elaborated around acts of masculine honor and capacity for violence.

6. Cash has circulated in Passarinho since its colonization by cattle ranchers in the 1700s, but it became a regular presence in the lives of poor cultivators in the 1930s with the influx of the cotton crop (decimated by boll weevils in the 1980s). The standardization of rural wages in 1963 (Pereira 1997: 33), coupled with the opening of government-subsidized plantations in the nearby city of Petrolina around the same time (Chilcote 1990: 147–53), opened up seasonal wage-earning for young village men. In the early 1990s, the Fernando Collor government enforced the federal dispersal of rural retirement funds equal to a minimum wage (Schwarzer 2000: 73). (The value of these pensions stabilized with the Real Plan

of 1994 [Araújo 2004: 357].) The initiation of welfare stipends under President Cardoso further increased household cash, though the scarcity of these grants also introduced discernible inequalities. The cash grants associated with the Zero Hunger program (mainly "Family Stipend") are more plentiful and thus cover most rural households. None of these cash sources exacerbate, perpetuate, or call attention to intravillage material inequality. Rather, every family with senior citizens earns the same retirement, and men, regardless of their land holdings, have an equal chance of finding work on the plantations in Petrolina.

7. For the vast majority of formally Catholic villagers, God's agency revolves around his capacity to intervene in the distribution of envy-derived evil, but such interventions are only occasional. People protect themselves posting cow horns and other amulets on their fences and houses because God is simply not reliable in this regard. In contrast, the few who have converted to evangelical Christianity claim that Jesus will always protect them from such evil (though many still post the cow horns).

CHAPTER 3

1. State and federal deputies exercise considerable control over regional hospitals in the sertão and often allot to their allied mayors a certain number of beds or health services for them to pass along to their electors.

2. In *Barren Lives*, a classic novel about the drought-ravaged sertão, Graciliano Ramos depicts a humiliating encounter between the cowherd Fabiano and his boss that we might treat as iconic of the relationship between the sertão's rural underclass and the local bosses during the early to mid-twentieth century. At one point in the novel, Fabiano goes to talk to his boss about his debt, which seems larger than Fabiano's wife has calculated:

> He protested and received the usual explanation: the difference represented interest. He refused to accept this answer. There must be some mistake. He was not very bright, that he knew. . . . But his wife had brains. Surely there was some mistake on the boss's paper. The mistake couldn't be found and Fabiano lost his temper. Was he to take a beating like that his whole life long, giving up what belonged to him for nothing? . . . The boss became angry. He refused to hear such insolence. He thought it would be a good thing if the herdsman looked for another job. At this point Fabiano got cold feet and began to back down. All right, all right. There was no need for a fuss. If he had said something wrong, he was sorry, He was ignorant; he had never had any learning. He knew his place; he wasn't the cheeky kind. He was just a half-breed. He wasn't going to get into any arguments with rich people. . . . He was sorry and he wouldn't make a blunder like this again. The boss calmed down and Fabiano backed out of the room, his hat in dragging along the brick floor. (Ramos 1965: 94–95; also quoted at length in Forman 1975: 81–82)

I certainly cannot say that such humiliating encounters no longer occurred in Piauí's sertão during the time of my fieldwork, but the interactions I saw and heard reported deviated from such demeaning events.

3. Here I omit discussion of the issue of the interval between gift and countergift and the practice of strategic delay that has been of great concern to anthropologists (Mauss 1990 [1950]; Bourdieu 1977). These issues are less critical to local distinctions between moral and immoral exchanges for reasons I cannot discuss here.

CHAPTER 4

1. The PMDB was heir to the official opposition party permitted by the military dictatorship, at the time called the Brazilian Democratic Movement. During the dictatorship, a broad cross-section of progressive (and less than progressive) thinkers and activists comprised the party, including many of the PT's founding members. When the dictatorship lifted the restriction on party formation in 1979, many of the brightest, most ideologically committed opponents went into new parties, turning the PMDB into a residual grouping with very little ideological coherence. Because of its great number of elected officials and its centrism, the PMDB has been very successful in patronage-based alliances. Virtually all governors and presidents have needed its legislative support, especially in the Northeast. Margaret Keck writes that by 1988, "the PMDB became the status quo party . . . while maintaining a position in the northeast, and losing the large cities while winning in the interior" (1992: 157). This was certainly true in Passarinho as I discuss at length in chapter 7.

2. A "dead cover" (*cobertura morta*) is a pile of rotting underbrush gathered together and placed over infertile soil. The objective of the technique is to restore nitrates to soil in the absence of chemical fertilizer. It was one of many sustainable development techniques taught to cultivators by projects that officially partnered with Zero Hunger.

3. Rural people typically traverse the unlit highway from the villages to Passarinho's town hub by rickety motorcycles, bicycles, or animal-drawn carts. Many express concerns about bandits or truck drivers who will maliciously run them over.

4. In his classic ethnography of a small town in northeast Brazil (the state of Bahia), Marvin Harris (1956) argued that the distinction between the urban and the rural was not fixed but relative. An "urban ethos" pervades small-town life, such that townspeople see themselves as the local guardians of individualism, secularism, and heterogeneity when compared to the residents of the villages (278). Among the townspeople of "Minas Velhas," there was a "high value placed on civic improvements, such as the town garden; the disapproval of agriculture and menial labor in general; the high value placed on professions . . . the high value placed on education, literacy, fluency of speech, formal speeches, and legal process; the desire to wear 'city clothes' . . . an awe associated with wealth in the form of cash; the love of noise, movement, crowds, and houses close together; the low value placed on knowledge of the countryside; the high value placed on knowledge of the coastal cities; the love of individualism and the low value placed on communal conformity" (280–81). Harris's mention of education and "civic improvements" suggests that even in 1956, small-town residents associated cosmopolitanism with programmatic development. In 2004, similar statements could have been made for the residents of Passarinho (only a few hundred kilometers from Bahia). There the

town middle class took advantage of Zero Hunger's participatory features to align themselves with the principles of education, literacy, professionalism, and democratic modernity (as they understood them).

CHAPTER 6

1. Unlike my usage of other Portuguese terms, I continually italicize the word *negro* when referring to the Brazilian racial category in order to avoid confusion with the (U.S.) English word "negro." While the two terms arguably have similar denotations, they have very different senses. The English "negro" is antiquated in the United States, whereas the Portuguese *negro* is quite current, and is in the process of being critically appropriated into the rhetoric of race-based politics.

2. Zero Hunger's other "vulnerable populations" included urban populations who made a living salvaging items from trash heaps, indigenous communities, encampments of landless rural workers, small sertanejo municipalities subject to drought, such as Passarinho. Other than the current program discussed in this chapter, I am not sure to what degree these formal priorities manifested in policy.

3. The Brazilian Anthropological Association defined contemporary *remanescentes de quilombos* as "groups that developed practices of resistance in the maintenance and reproduction of their ways of life characterized in a determinate place. The identity of these groups is not defined by size and number of members but by the lived experience and the shared values of its common trajectory and of its continuity as a group. They constitute ethnic groups conceptually defined by anthropology as an organizational type that confers belonging through norms and methods employed by indicating affiliation and exclusion" (Barth 1969). As to territoriality, the "occupation of land is not by individual lots, with common use predominating. The utilization of these areas conforms to the seasonality of activities . . . kinship and neighboring ties based on solidarity and reciprocity" (ABA 1994; cited in Jan French 2009: 98).

4. According to the Fundação Cultural Palmares website, prior to Lula's administration, the federal government certified the existence of only eleven *quilombola* communities, all of them in 2000. By the end of 2004 (following Lula's decree making self-identification the criterion for legal recognition), there were ninety-five federally certified *quilombos*. By 2006, the end of Lula's first mandate, there were 404. (These included the three Passarinho communities discussed in this chapter.) As of 2013, there were 1,802 certified quilombos. http://www.palmares.gov.br/quilombola/. Site accessed May 21, 2013.

CHAPTER 7

1. Jorge Mattar Villela, in his analysis of electoral politics in Pernambuco's sertão, uses the term "etiquette," to explore exchange relations in order to avoid the contractualism implicit in "patron-client" reciprocity. As an analytic category, "etiquette" refers to "the evaluative elements that ethically and aesthetically distinguish electors and candidates and indicate for one another what, from whom, and in what way they should receive distributed resources, by one another" (2012: 8). These "evaluative elements" include memory, delay, humility, and fame. My usage

of the term is influenced by Villela's work, though I place more of an emphasis on the performativity and theaters in which gestures of etiquette operate as public signs.

2. In many cases the local boss did not hold the official military title "colonel." The use of the title dates back to the nineteenth century, when Emperor Dom Pedro II issued such titles in the National Guard to the landed elite to secure their loyalty and to acknowledge the legitimacy of the private violence they carried out on their plantations and ranches.

3. During much of the twentieth century, the office of governor enjoyed the allegiance of every municipal boss. As the state executive changed hands, the municipal bosses would realign themselves so as not to be cut out of resource circuits. Raymundo Faoro (1979 [1959]: 631) offers the one mayor's stereotypical explanation: "The government changed, but I didn't change. I remain with the government." Alliances with state bureaucrats and legislators were secondary, and they shifted depending on executive power. But the local boss's die-hard adherence to the governor changed as the deconcentration of state power afforded other resource-distributing agencies (e.g., parastate development companies) more independence from the governor. As party competition intensified after redemocratization, governors awarded command posts in the state bureaucracy to party rivals in order to secure their allegiance in the legislature. The state itself thus became a more fragmented power for the mayors to confront, and mayors had increasing incentive to adhere to benefactors who rivaled the governor. This was the case in Passarinho in 2003, when Rodrigo (PMDB) found himself opposed to the incoming PT governor.

4. In both Passarinho and the other pilot town in Piauí, Zero Hunger officials cooperated with local technical agents to create a multiyear municipal development plan based on the particular needs and resources of these localities. In Passarinho, where the weekly open-air market for local produce had been defunct for nearly a decade, the Coordenadoria got special funds to regenerate it by installing a large covered patio and corral area. In the other pilot town, where potable water was extremely scarce, the special funds built an enormous water tower. Even standardized "local" Zero Hunger projects, such as housing and sanitation, were tailored to the specifics of each municipality where they were implemented.

5. While the criteria for receiving the Food Card pertained the family as a whole, the direct beneficiary of the Food Card grant was the female household head. If a household had no adult women but otherwise qualified, then a man could receive the card. While the issue of actual Food Card usage lies beyond the scope of this analysis, I note that men sometimes gained control of their wives' benefit cards and used them to pay off debts to local venders. However, this practice seemed to recede by 2005, and subsequent trips to Passarinho and interviews with venders and government officials suggest that women, by and large, now control the card. Further research is needed to determine how Bolsa Família has changed the structure of family life. I suspect it has resulted in a reduction in male labor migration, an increase of household proliferation, more independence from seniors who draw pensions, less domestic violence, more equality among spouses, and so on.

6. The term *marcação* can also mean "covering" or "coverage" and is used in reference to the guarding of an opponent in soccer, that is, "man-to-man" defense. I am grateful to John F. Collins for bringing this to my attention.

7. I am not certain whether or how the Management Committee considered the issue of proportionality in regards to factional alliance. I suspect the matter was not addressed with mathematical precision but with an impressionistic sense of what would "look fair" to the region's political class.

8. The questions pertaining to monthly cash income were useful for filtering out families that included a coresident member with formal employment (usually in the municipal government). This was easily discoverable through documentation, so cultivators rarely lied about it. This question also weeded out families with co-resident seniors who drew a federal pension equal to a minimum wage.

9. Suspension occurred, for example, if somebody's identification number was copied incorrectly to the new list of beneficiaries, if a person's identification number appeared on the new list but also remained on the list of one of the three pre-existing grants, or if a daughter who had previously been listed as a coresident member of a benefited household married and applied for independent beneficiary status.

Bibliography

ABA (Associação Brasileira de Antropologia)

1994   "Documento do Grupo de Trabalho sobre Comunidades Negras Rurais."

Adad, Lúcia Maria Said, and Maria da Graça Ferreira

1987   "Tensões no Campo Piauiense." *Carta CEPRO* 12, no. 1: 81–101.

Agrawal, Arun

2005   *Environmentality: Technologies of Government and the Making of Subjects.* Durham, NC: Duke University Press.

Albuquerque, Durval Muniz de

1999   *A Invenção do Nordeste e Outras Artes.* São Paulo: Cortez.

Almeida, Alfredo Wagner Berno de, Rosa Elizabeth Acevedo Marin, Ricardo Cid, and Emmanuel de Almeida Farias Júnior, organizers

2010   *Territórios Quilombolas e Conflitos.* Manaus: UEA Edições.

Alves, Giovanni

2000   "Do 'Novo Sindicalismo' à 'Concertação Social': Ascenção (e Crise) do Sindicalismo no Brasil (1978–1998)." *Revista de Sociologia e Política,* no. 15: 111–24.

Amado, Gilberto

1947   *A Chave de Salomão e Outros Estudos.* Rio de Janeiro: José Olympio.

Ansell, Aaron

2009   "'But the Winds Will Turn against You': An Analysis of Wealth Forms and Discursive Space of Development in Northeast Brazil." *American Ethnologist* 36, no. 1: 96–109.

2010   "Auctioning Patronage in Northeast Brazil: The Political Value of Money in a Ritual Market." *American Anthropologist* 112, no. 2: 283–94.

2011 "Double-Voicing in the Backlands: Negotiating Democratic and Clientelist Discourse in Northeast Brazil." Paper presented at the 2011 American Anthropological Association Meetings, Montreal, November 16–20.

Ansell, Aaron, and Kenneth Mitchell

2011 "Models of Clientelism and Policy Change: The Case of Conditional Cash Transfer Programmes in Mexico and Brazil." *Bulletin of Latin American Research* 30, no. 3: 298–312.

Arbix, Glauco, and Scott B. Martin

2011 "New Dimensions in Public Policy and State-Society Relations." In *The Brazilian State. Debate and Agenda*, edited by Maurício Font and Laura Randall, 59–83. Lanham, MD: Lexington.

Arruti, José Maurício Andion

1997 "A Emergência dos 'Remanescentes': Notas para o Diálogo entre Indígenas e Quilombolas." *MANA* 3, no. 2: 7–38.

2002 "'Etnias Federais': O Processo de Identificação de 'Remanescentes' Indígenas e Quilombolas no Baixo São Francisco." Ph.D. diss., Museu Nacional, Universidade Federal do Rio de Janeiro.

Auyero, Javier

2001 *Poor People's Politics: Peronist Survival Networks and the Legacy of Evita*. Durham, NC: Duke University Press.

Auyero, Javier, Pablo Lapegna, and Fernanda Page Poma

2009 "Patronage Politics and Contentious Collective Action: A Recursive Relationship." *Latin American Politics and Society* 51, no. 3: 1–31.

Balsadi, Otavio Valentim

2004 "O Programa de Aquizição de Alimentos da Agricultura Familiar em 2003." *Cadernos do Centro de Estudos Avançados Multidisciplinares (CEAM)* 4, no. 14: 51–73.

Balsadi, Otavio Valentim, Mauro Eduardo Del Grossi, et al.

2004 "O Programa Cartão Alimentação (PCA) em Números: Balanço de sua Implementação e Contribuições para as Políticas Sociais." *Cadernos do Centro de Estudos Avançados Multidisciplinares (CEAM)* 4, no. 14: 81–99.

Bandeira, William Jorge

1994 "A Nova Dinâmica do Setor Rural Piauiense." *CartaCEPRO* 15, no. 1: 46–55.

Barreira, César

2006 "Fraudes e Corrupções Eleitorais, entre Dádivas e Contravenções." In *Política no Brasil: Visões dos Antropólogos*, edited by Iryls Barreira e Moacir Palmeira, 151–65. Rio de Janeiro: Relume Dumará.

Barreto, Paula Adalberto de

1986   "A Romaria e a Doença." Paper presented at the meeting of the Latin American Studies Association, Boston, MA.

Barros, Alexandre Rands, and André Matos Magalhães

2009   "Northeast Brazil under the Lula Government." In *Brazil under Lula: Economy, Politics, and Society under the Worker-President*, edited by Joseph L. Love and Werner Baer, 283–305. New York: Palgrave Macmillan.

Barth, Fredrik

1969   "Introduction." In *Ethnic Groups and Boundaries: The Social Organization of Cultural Difference*, edited by Fredrik Barth, 9–39. Oslo: Universitetsforlaget.

Bastos, Elide Rugai

1984   *As Ligas Camponesas*. Petrópolis: Vozes.

Bauman, Richard

1984   *Verbal Art as Performance*. Prospect Heights, IL: Waveland.

Belik, Walter

2003   "Perspectivas para Segurança Alimentar e Nutricional no Brasil." *Saude e Sociedade* 12, no. 1: 12–20.

2011   "Mobilization of Enterprises and the Fight against Hunger." In *The Fome Zero (Zero Hunger) Program: The Brazilian Experience*, edited by José Graziano da Silva, Mauro Eduardo Del Grossi, and Caio Galvo de França. Pp. 113–43. Brasília: Ministry of Agrarian Development.

Bellah, Robert Neelly

1985   *The Habits of the Heart: Individualism and Commitment in American Life*. Berkeley: University of California Press.

Betto, Frei

2003   *Programa Fome Zero: Como Participar*. Rio de Janeiro: Cecip.

2004   "Zero Hunger." Zero Hunger Mobilization Group. Brasília: Government Press.

Bloch, Ernst

1986   *The Principle of Hope*. Cambridge, MA: MIT Press.

Bloch, Maurice, and Jonathan Perry

1989   "Introduction: Money and the Morality of Exchange." In *Money and the Morality of Exchange*, edited by Jonathan Perry and Maurice Bloch, 1–33. Cambridge: Cambridge University Press.

Bornstein, Erica

2005   *The Spirit of Development: Protestant NGOs, Morality, and Economics in Zimbabwe*. Stanford, CA: Stanford University Press.

Bourdieu, Pierre

1977   *Outline of a Theory of Practice*. Cambridge: Cambridge University Press.

Brandão, Tanya Maria Pires

1999   *O Escravo na Formação Social do Piauí: Perspectiva Histórica do Século XVIII*. Teresina: Universidade Federal do Piauí.

Branford, Sue, and Bernardo Kucinski

2003   *Lula and the Workers' Party in Brazil*. New York: New Press.

Burdick, John

1993   *Looking for God in Brazil: A Progressive Catholic Church in Urban Brazil's Religious Arena*. Berkeley: University of California Press.

Burgwal, Gerrit

1995   *Struggle of the Poor: Neighborhood Organization and Clientelist Practice in a Quito Squatter Settlement*. Amsterdam: Centre for Latin American Research and Documentation.

Burity, Valéria, Thaís Franceschini, Flávio Valente, Elisabetta Recine, Marília Leão, and Maria de Fátima Carvalho

2010   *Direito Humano à Alimentação Adequada no Contexto da Segurança Alimentar e Nutricional*. Brasília: ABRANDH.

Bursztyn, Marcelo

1984   *O Poder dos Donos: O Planejamento e Clientelismo no Nordeste*. Petrópolis: Vozes.

Caldeira, Teresa

1984   *A Política dos Outros: O Cotidiano dos Moradores da Periferia e o que Pensam do Poder e dos Poderosos*. São Paulo: Brasiliense.

2001   *City of Walls: Crime, Segregation and Citizenship in São Paulo*. Berkeley: University of California Press.

Campanhola, Clayton, and José Graziano da Silva

2000   "Desenvolvimento Local e a Democratização dos Espaços Rurais." *Cadernos de Ciência & Tecnologia* 17, no. 1: 11–40.

Campos, Alda Maria Siqueira

1998   *Literatura de Cordel e Difusão de Inovações*. Recife: Massangana.

Candido, Antonio

2001 [1948]   *Os Parceiros do Rio Bonito: Estudo sobre o Caipira Paulista e a Transformação dos Seus Meios de Vida*. São Paulo: Duas Cidades.

Cardoso, Ruth

2004   "Sustentabilidade, o Desafio das Políticas Sociais no Século 21." *São Paulo em Perspectiva* 18, no. 2: 42–48.

Carvalho, José Murilo de

1997 "Mandonismo, Coronelismo, Clientelismo: Uma Discussão Conceitual." *Dados* 40, no. 2: 229–50.

Castro, Josué de

2003 [1952] *The Geography of Hunger*. New York: Little, Brown.

Cehelsky, Marta

1979 *Land Reform in Brazil: The Management of Social Change*. Boulder, CO: Westview Press.

CESACF

2003 "Diagnóstico Alimentar e Nutricional, Programa Fome Zero—Estudo Piloto." Teresina: Governo do Estado do Piauí.

Chakrabarty, Dipesh

2007 "'In the Name of Politics': Democracy and the Power of the Multitude in India." *Public Culture* 19, no. 1: 35–57.

Chambers, Robert

1997 *Whose Reality Counts? Putting the First Last*. London: Intermediate Technology.

Chaui, Marilena

1987 "PT 'Leve e Suave.'" In *E Agora, PT? Caráter e Identidade*, edited by Emir Sadir, 43–100. São Paulo: Brasiliense.

Chaves, Christine de Alencar

2003 *Festas da Política: Uma Etnografia da Modernidade no Sertão (Buritis—MG)*. Rio de Janeiro: Relume Dumará.

Chilcote, Ronald

1990 *Power and the Ruling Classes in Northeast Brazil: Juazeiro and Petrolina in Transition*. Cambridge: Cambridge University Press.

Coelho, Alexandre Bragança

2004 "A Cultura do Algodão e a Questão da Integração entre Preços Internos e Externos." *Revista de Economia e Sociologia Rural* 42, no. 1: 153–69.

Collins, John F.

2008a "Public Health, Patronage and National Culture: The Resuscitation and Commodification of Community Origins in Neoliberal Brazil." *Critique of Anthropology* 28, no. 2: 237–55.

2008b "'But What if I Should Need to Defecate in Your Neighborhood, Madame?' Empire, Redemption, and the 'Tradition of the Oppressed' in a Brazilian World Heritage Site." *Cultural Anthropology* 23, no. 2: 279–328.

Comerford, John Cunha

1999   *Fazendo a Luta: Sociabilidade, Falas e Rituais na Construção de Organizações Camponesas.* Rio de Janeiro: Rulume Dumará.

Cooke, Bill, and Uma Kothari, eds.

2001   *Participation: The New Tyranny?* London: Zed Books.

Coordenadoria de Segurança Alimentar e Erradicação da Fome/Programa Fome Zero (Coordenadoria)

2003a   *Relatório — Visita ao Município de Passarinho 1/18/2003.* Teresina, PI: Government Printing Press.

2003b   *Relatório — Visita ao Município de Passarinho 1/21/2003.* Teresina, PI: Government Printing Press.

2004   *Síntese das Ações Realizadas pelo Programa Fome Zero em 2003.* Teresina, PI: Government Printing Press.

Costa, Alberto, Conrad Kottak, and Rosane Prado

1997   "The Sociopolitical Context of Participatory Development in Northeastern Brazil." *Human Organization.* 56, no. 2: 138–46.

Cruvinel, Tereza

2003   "Panorama Política." *O Globo.*

DaMatta, Roberto

1991 [1979]   *Carnivals, Rogues, and Heroes: An Interpretation of the Brazilian Dilemma.* Notre Dame: University of Notre Dame Press.

Daniel, Valentine E.

1984   *Fluid Signs: Being a Person the Tamil Way.* Berkeley: University of California Press.

Dent, Alexander Sebastian

2009   *River of Tears: Country Music, Memory, and Modernity in Brazil.* Durham, NC: Duke University Press.

Draper, Jack A., III

2010   *Forró and Redemptive Regionalism from the Brazilian Northeast: Popular Music in a Culture of Migration.* New York: Peter Land.

Eisenlohr, Patrick

2004   "Temporalities of Community: Ancestral Language, Pilgrimage, and Diasporic Belonging in Mauritius." *Journal of Linguistic Anthropology* 14, no. 1: 81–98.

Eisenstadt, S. N., and Luis Roniger

1984   *Patrons, Clients and Friends: Interpersonal Relations and the Structure of Trust in Society.* Cambridge: Cambridge University Press.

Elyachar, Julia

2005   *Markets of Dispossession: NGOs, Economic Development, and the State in Cairo.* Durham, NC: Duke University Press.

Escobar, Christina

1994   "Clientelism and Social Protest: Peasant Politics in Northern Columbia." In *Democracy, Clientelism and Civil Society,* edited by Luis Roniger and Ayse Gune-Ayata, 65–87. Boulder, CO: Lynne Rienner.

Faoro, Raymundo

1979 [1959]   *Os Donos do Poder: Formação do Patronato Político Brasileiro.* Volume 2. Porto Alegre: Globo.

Ferguson, James

1990   *The Anti-politics Machine: Development, Depoliticization, and Bureaucratic Power in Lesotho.* Cambridge: Cambridge University Press.

Filho, Antonio Claret Campos

2007   "Transferência de Renda com Condicionalidades e Desenvolvimento de Capacidades: Uma Análise a Partir da Integração dos Programas Bolsa Família e Vida Nova no Município de Nova Lima." Ph.D. diss, Escola Nacional de Saúde Pública. http://www.planejamento.gov.br/secretarias/upload/Arquivos/seges/EPPGG/producaoAcademica/Tese_Claret.pdf.

Fleischer, David

2008   "Political Outlook in Brazil in the Wake of Municipal Elections, 2009–2010." Paper presented at Brazil Institute, Woodrow Wilson International Center for Scholars, Washington, DC, November 10.

2011   "Political Reform: A 'Never-Ending Story.'" In *The Brazilian State: Debate and Agenda,* edited by Maurício Font and Laura Randall, 129–45. Lanham, MD: Lexington.

Font, Maurício, and Laura Randall (with the assistance of Janaina Saad), eds.

2011   *The Brazilian State: Debate and Agenda.* Lanham, MD: Lexington.

Forman, Shepard

1975   *The Brazilian Peasantry.* New York: Columbia University Press.

Fortes, Antônio Cézar Cruz

2000   "Medições do Nível de Desenvolvimento—PIB, IDH e IDF." *Carta CEPRO* 22, no. 1: 23–37.

Foster, George M.

1963   "The Dyadic Contract in Tzintzuntzan II: Patron-Client Relationships." *American Anthropologist* 65: 1280–94.

Fox, Jonathan

1994   "The Difficult Transition from Clientelism to Citizenship:
        Lessons from Mexico." *World Politics* 46, no. 2: 151–84.

Freitas, Geovani Jacó de

2003   *Ecos da Violência: Narrativas e Relações de Poder no Nordeste
        Brasileiro*. Rio de Janeiro: Relume Dumará.

French, Jan Hoffman

2009   *Legalizing Identities: Becoming Black or Indian in Brazil's Northeast*.
        Chapel Hill: University of North Carolina Press.

French, John D.

1992   *The Brazilian Workers' ABC: Class Conflict and Alliances in Modern
        São Paulo*. Chapel Hill: University of North Carolina Press.

2004   *Drowning in Laws: Labor Laws and Brazilian Political Culture*.
        Chapel Hill: University of North Carolina Press.

2009   "Understanding the Politics of Latin America's Plural Lefts
        (Chávez/Lula): Social Democracy, Populism and Convergence on
        the Path to a Post-neoliberal World." *Third World Quarterly* 30,
        no. 2: 349–70.

2010   "The Professor and the Worker: Using Brazil to Better Understand
        Latin America's Plural Left." In *Rethinking Intellectuals in Latin
        America*, edited by Mabel Moraña and Bret Gustafson, 91–115.
        Norwalk, CT: Vervuert.

French, John, and Alexandre Fortes

2012   "Nurturing Hope, Deepening Democracy, and Combating Inequali-
        ties in Brazil: Lula, the Workers' Party, and Dilma Rousseff's 2010
        Election as President." *Labor: Studies in Working-Class History of
        the Americas* 8, no. 1: 7–28.

Freyre, Gilberto

1986 [1933] *The Masters and the Slaves: A Study in the Development of Brazilian
        Civilizations*. Berkeley: University of California Press.

Fry, Gerald, and Ken Kempner

1996   "A Subnational Perspective for Comparative Research: Education
        and Development in Northeast Brazil." *Comparative Education* 32,
        no. 3: 333–60.

Fry, Peter

2005   *A Persistência da Raça: Ensaios Antropológicos sobre o Brasil e a
        África Austral*. Rio de Janeiro: Civilização Brasileira.

Gasques, José Garcia

2002   "Políticas Especificas de Combate à Fome: Mudanças na Política
        Agrícola e o Papel da Agricultura." In *Combate à Fome e à Pobreza
        Rural*, edited by Maya Takagi, José Graziano da Silva, and Walter
        Belike, 161–79. São Paulo: Instituto Cidadania.

Gay, Robert

1998   "Rethinking Clientelism: Demands, Discourses and Practices in
        Contemporary Brazil." *European Review of Latin American and
        Caribbean Studies* 65: 7–24.

Goertzel, Ted

2011   *Brazil's Lula: The Most Popular President on Earth*. Boca Raton, FL:
        BrownWalker.

Gohn, M. G.

2004   "Empoderamento e Participação da Comunidade em Políticas
        Sociais." *Saúde e Sociedade* 13, no. 2: 21–31.

Goldfrank, Benjamin

2011   "The Left and Participatory Democracy." In *The Resurgence of
        the Latin American Left*, edited by Steven Levitsky and Kenneth
        Roberts, 162–84. Baltimore: John Hopkins University Press.

Gomes Júnior, N. N.

2007   "Segurança Alimentar e Nutricional como Princípio Orientador de
        Políticas Públicas no Marco das Necessidades Humanas Básicas."
        Ph.D. diss., Universidade de Brasília.

Graeber, David

2011   *Debt: The First 5,000 Years*. New York: Melville.

Graziano da Silva, José

2005   Interview by Aaron Ansell. Tape recording. July. Ministry of
        Social Development and the Fight against Hunger, Brasília.

Graziano da Silva, José, Walter Belik, et al.

2002   "O que o Brasil Pode Fazer para Combater a Fome." In *Combate à
        Fome e à Pobreza Rural*, edited by Maya Takagi, José Graziano da
        Silva, and Walter Belik, 131–53. São Paulo: Instituto Cidadania.

Greenfield, Sidney, and Antônio Mourão Cavalcante

2006   "Pilgrimage and Patronage in Brazil: A Paradigm for Social Rela-
        tions and Religion Diversity." *Luso-Brazilian Review* 43, no. 2:
        63–89.

Gross, Daniel

1971   "Ritual Conformity: A Religious Pilgrimage to Northeastern
        Brazil." *Ethnology*, 10, no. 2: 129–48.

Guanziroli, Carlos

2007   "PRONAF Dez Anos Depois: Resultados e Perspectivas para o
            Desenvolvimento Rural." *Revista de Economia e Sociologia Rural*
            45, no. 2: 301–32.

Guilherme do Valle, Carlos

2010   "Quilombolas de Acauã—Terra, História e Conflito Social no Rio
            Grande do Norte." In *Territórios Quilombolas e Conflitos*, organized
            by Alfredo Wagner Berno de Almeida, Rosa Elizabeth Acevedo
            Marin, Ricardo Cid, and Emmanuel de Almeida Farias Júnior,
            132–39. Manaus: UEA Edições.

Gunes-Ayata, Ayse

1994   "Clientelism: Premodern, Modern, Postmodern." In *Democracy,
            Clientelism and Civil Society*, edited by Luis Roniger and Ayse
            Gunes-Ayata, 19–28. Boulder, CO: Lynne Rienner.

Habermas, Jürgen

1975   *Legitimation Crisis*. Translated by Thomas McCarthy. Boston:
            Beacon.

Hall, Anthony

2006   "From Zero Hunger to Bolsa Família: Social Policies and Poverty
            Alleviation under Lula." *Journal of Latin American Studies* 38:
            689–709.

Hall, Michael

2009   "The Labor Policies of the Lula Government." In *Brazil under
            Lula: Economy, Politics, and Society under the Worker-President*,
            edited by Joseph L. Love and Werner Baer, 151–67. New York:
            Palgrave-Macmillan.

Hanchard, George Michael

1994   *Orpheus and Power: The Movimento Negro of Rio de Janeiro and
            São Paulo, Brazil, 1945–1988*. Princeton, NJ: Princeton University
            Press.

Harris, Marvin

1956   *Town and Country in Brazil*. New York: Columbia University Press.

Hartikainen, Elina

2013   *A Candomblé Politics of Respect: Forming an African Religious
            Public in Multicultural Brazil*. Ph.D. diss., University of Chicago.

Heredia, Beatriz M. A. de

1996   "Política, Família e Comunidade." In *Antropologia, Voto e
            Representação Política*, edited by Moacir Palmeira and Marcio
            Goldman, 57–72. Rio de Janeiro: Contra Capa.

Herzfeld, Michael

2005 [1997] *Cultural Intimacy: Social Poetics in the Nation-State.* New York: Routledge.

Hirschman, Albert

1963 *Journeys toward Progress.* New York: Twentieth Century Fund.

Hochstetler, Kathryn

2000 "Democratizing Pressures from Below? Social Movements in the New Brazilian Democracy." In *Democratic Brazil: Actors, Institutions, and Processes,* edited by Peter R. Kingstone and Timothy J. Power, 167–85. Pittsburgh: University of Pittsburgh Press.

Holanda, Sérgio Buarque de

1982 [1926] *Raizes do Brazil.* Rio de Janeiro: J. Olympio.

Holston, James

2008 *Insurgent Democracy: Disjunctions of Democracy and Modernity in Brazil.* Princeton, NJ: Princeton University Press.

Hunter, Wendy

2007 "Rewarding Lula: Executive Power, Social Policy, and the Brazilian Elections of 2006." *Latin American Politics and Society* 49, no. 1: 1–30.

2010 *The Transformation of the Workers' Party in Brazil, 1989–2009.* Cambridge: Cambridge University Press.

Ianni, Octávio

1984 *Origens Agrárias do Estado Brasileiro.* São Paulo: Brasiliense.

Instituto Brasileiro de Geografia e Estatística (IBGE)

2000 *Censo Demográfico.* Brasília: IBGE.

2003 *Censo: Produto Interno Bruto.* Brasília: IBGE.

Junge, Benjamin

2012 "NGOs as Shadow Pseudo-publics: Grassroots Community Leaders' Perceptions of Change and Continuity in Porto Alegre, Brazil." *American Ethnologist* 39, no. 2: 407–24.

Kearney, Michael

1996 *Reconceptualizing the Peasantry: Anthropology in Global Perspective.* New York: Westview.

Keck, Margaret

1992 *The Workers' Party and Democratization in Brazil.* New Haven, CT: Yale University Press.

Kinzo, Maria D'Alva Gil

1988 *Legal Opposition under Authoritarian Rule in Brazil: The Case of the MDB, 1966–79.* London: Macmillan Press.

L'Abbate, Solange

1988   "As Políticas de Alimentação e Nutrição no Brasil: Período de 1940 a 1964." *Revista de Nutrição PUCCAMP* 1, no. 2: 87–138.

Laclau, Ernesto

2005   *On Populist Reason.* London: Verso.

Landé, Carl H.

1977   "The Dyadic Basis of Clientelism." In *Friends, Followers and Factions: A Reader in Political Clientelism*, edited by Steifen W. Schmidt, James C. Scott, Carl Landé, and Laura Guasti, xiii–xxxvii. Berkeley: University of California Press.

Landim, Leilah

1998   "Notas Sobre a Campanha do Betinho: Ação Cidadã e Diversidades Brasileiras." In *Ações em Sociedade: Militância, Caridade, Assistência, etc.*, edited by Leilah Landim and Emerson Giumbelli. Rio de Janeiro: Nau.

Leal, Victor Nunes

1977 [1948]   *Coronelismo, Enxata e o Voto: O Município e o Regime Representativo no Brasil.* Rio de Janeiro: Revista Forense.

Leite, Elaine da Silveira

2011   "Financialization, Crisis, and a New Mania in Brazil." In *The Brazilian State: Debate and Agenda*, edited by Maurício Font and Laura Randall, 297–317. Lanham, MD: Lexington.

Lemarchand, Rene, and Keith Legg

1972   "Political Clientelism and Development: A Preliminary Analysis." *Comparative Politics* 4, no. 2: 149–78.

Leopoldi, Maria Antonieta P.

2009   "Reforming Social Security under Lula: Continuities with Cardoso's Policies." In *Brazil under Lula: Economy, Politics, and Society under the Worker-President*, edited by Joseph L. Love and Werner Baer, 221–43. New York: Palgrave Macmillan.

Lessa, Orígenes

1973   *Getúlio Vargas na Literatura de Cordel.* Rio de Janeiro: Documentário.

Levine, Robert M.

1980   "Perspectives on the Mid-Vargas Years, 1934–1937." *Journal of Interamerican Studies and World Affairs* 22, no. 1 (February): 57–80.

Lindert, Kathy, Anja Linder, Jason Hobbs, and Bénédicte de la Brière

2007   "The Nuts and Bolts of Brazil's Bolsa Família Program: Imple-
        menting Conditional Cash Transfers in a Decentralized Context."
        Social Protection Discussion Paper no. 0709. May. Washington,
        DC: World Bank.

Linger, Daniel Touro

1992   *Dangerous Encounters: Meanings of Violence in a Brazilian City.*
        Stanford, CA: Stanford University Press.

Lipsky, Michael

1980   *Street-Level Democracy: Dilemmas of the Individual in Public
        Service.* New York: Russell Sage Foundation.

Love, Joseph, and Werner Baer, eds.

2009   *Brazil under Lula: Economy, Politics, and Society under the Worker-
        President.* New York: Palgrave Macmillan.

Lowy, Michel

1996   *War of Gods: Religion and Politics in Latin America.* London: Verso.

Mainwaring, Scott

1995   "Brazil: Weak Parties, Feckless Democracy." In *Building Democratic
        Institutions: Party Systems in Latin America,* edited by Scott
        Mainwaring and Timothy R. Scully, 354–59. Stanford: Stanford
        University Press.
1999   *Rethinking Party Systems in the Third Wave of Democratization:
        The Case of Brazil.* Stanford, CA: Stanford University Press.

Maloney, Clarence, ed.

1976   *The Evil Eye.* New York: Columbia University Press.

Maluf, Renato S., Francisco Menezes, and Flávio L. Valente

1996   "Contribuição ao Tema da Segurança Alimentar no Brasil." *Revista
        do Núcleo de Estudos e Pesquisas em Alimentação NEPA/UNICAMP
        Cadernos de Debate* 4: 66–88.

Marques, Ana Claudia

1999   "Algumas Faces de Outros Eus: Honra e Patronagem na
        Antropologia do Mediterrâneo." *MANA* 5, no. 1: 131–47.
2002   *Intrigas e Questões: Vingança de Família e Tramas Sociais no Sertão
        de Pernambuco.* Rio de Janeiro: Relume Dumará.

Mauss, Marcel

1990 [1950] *The Gift: The Form and Reason for Exchange in Archaic Societies.*
        London: Routledge.

Maybury-Lewis, Biorn

1994   *The Politics of the Possible: The Brazilian Rural Workers' Trade Union Movement, 1964-1985*. Philadelphia: Temple University Press.

McLean, Paul

2007   *The Art of the Network: Strategic Interaction and Patronage in Renaissance Florence*. Durham, NC: Duke University Press.

Mendes, Mary Alves

1997   *Discursos Sobre o Agro Piauiense: Bibliografia Analítica da Questão Agrária no Piauí*. Teresina: Fundação CEPRO.

Ministério de Desenvolvimento Social e Combate à Fome (MDSCF)

2005   *Execução Fisco-Financeira—Fome Zero—2005*. Brasília: Government Printing Press.

Mintz, Sidney W., and Eric R. Wolf

1950   "An Analysis of Ritual Coparenthood (Compadrazgo)." *Southwestern Journal of Anthropology* 6, no. 4: 341-368.

Mitchell, Sean

2013   "Racialization and Racial Legislation: Rethinking Ethnoracial Mobilization and Identification in Brazil's Contemporary Quilombos." Unpublished manuscript.

Monteiro, Jorge Vianna

2009   "Policy Making in the First Term of the Lula Government." In *Brazil under Lula: Economy, Politics, and Society under the Worker-President*, edited by Joseph L. Love and Werner Baer, 47-67. New York: Palgrave Macmillan.

Moraes, Adolfo Martins de

2003   "Algumas Singularidades do Planejamento no Estado do Piauí." *CartaCEPRO*, 22, no. 1: 7-23.

Morais, Clodomir Santos de

1997   *História das Ligas Camponesas do Brasil*. Brasília: Lattermund.

Moreira Alves, Maria Helena

2001   "Interclass Alliances in the Opposition to the Military in Brazil: Consequences for the Transition Period." In *Power and Popular Protest: Latin American Social Movements*, edited by Susan Eckstein and Manuel Antonio Garetón Merino, 278-99. Berkeley: University of California Press.

Mosse, David

1999   "Colonial and Contemporary Ideologies of 'Community Management': The Case of Tank Irrigation Development in South India." *Modern Asian Studies* 33, no. 2: 303-38.

Mott, Luiz

1985   *Piauí Colonial: População, Economia e Sociedade.* Teresina: Projeto
Petrônio Portella.

Mouffe, Chantal

1993   *The Return of the Political.* London: Verso.

Muehlebach, Andrea

2011   "On Affective Labor in Post-Fordist Italy." *Cultural Anthropology*
26, no. 1: 59–82.

Munn, Nancy

1986   *The Fame of Gawa: A Symbolic Study of Value Transformation
in a Massim (Papua New Guinea) Society.* Durham, NC: Duke
University Press.

Nelson, Donald, and Timothy Finan

2009   "Praying for Drought: Persistent Vulnerability and the Politics of
Drought in Ceará, Northeast Brazil." *American Anthropologist* 111,
no. 3: 302–16.

Nicolau, Jairo

2002   *A História do Voto no Brasil.* Rio de Janeiro: Jorge Zahar.

Nylen, William

2000   "The Making of a Loyal Opposition: The Workers' Party (PT) and
the Consolidation of Democracy in Brazil." In *Democratic Brazil:
Actors, Institutions, and Processes,* edited by Peter Kingstone and
Timothy Power, 126–44. Pittsburgh: University of Pittsburgh
Press.

2003   *Participatory Democracy versus Elitist Democracy: Lessons from
Brazil.* New York: Palgrave Macmillan.

O'Donnell, Guillermo

1996   "Illusions and Conceptual Flaws." *Journal of Democracy* 7, no. 4:
160–68.

O'Dwyer, Eliane Cantarino

2007   "Terras de Quilombo: Identidade, Étnica e os Caminhos do
Reconhecimento." *TOMO* 11 (July–December): 43–58.

Oliveira, Francisco de

1977   *Elegia para uma Religião: SUDENE, Nordeste, Planejamento e
Conflito de Classes.* Rio de Janeiro: Paz e Terra.

Oliveira, Mauro Wagner de, Francisco Morel Freire, Geraldo Antônio Resende
Macêdo, and José Joaquim Ferreira

2007   "Nutrição Mineral e Adubação da Cana-de-Açúcar." *Informe
Agropecuário* 28, no. 239: 30–43.

Oliveira, Simplício Mário de

2004   "Síntese das Ações Realizadas pelo Programa Fome Zero em 2003."
            Coordenadoria Estadual de Segurança Alimentar e Erradicação da
            Fome. Teresina, Piauí: Governo do Estado do Piauí.

Palmeira, Moacir

1992   "Voto: Racionalidade ou Significado?" *Revista Brasileira de Ciências
            Sociais* 7, no. 20: 26–30.
1996   "Política, Facções e Voto." In *Antropologia, Voto e Representação
            Popular*, edited by M. Palmeira and M. Goldman. Rio de Janeiro.
            Contra Capa.

ParanáOnline

2005   "Marcha Não É Contra Lula, diz Líder do MST." April, 5, 2005.
            https://parana-online.com.br/editoria/pais/news/120695/?
            noticia=MARCHA+NAO+E+CONTRA+LULA+DIZ+LIDER+DO
            +MST, accessed October 5, 2013.

Pedroza Júnior, Dinilson, Thiago Alexandro N. Andrade, and Cristine Viera
do Bonfim

2011   "Instituições e Políticas Regionais: Uma Proposta para a Nova
            Sudene." *Revista de Economia Política* 31, no. 5: 813–31.

Pereira, Anthony W.

1997   *The End of the Peasantry: The Rural Labor Movement in Northeast
            Brazil, 1961–1988*. Pittsburgh: University of Pittsburgh Press.
2012   "Continuity Is Not Lack of Change." *Critical Sociology* 38, no. 6:
            777–86.

Pessar, Patricia R.

2004   *From Fanatics to Folk: Brazilian Millenarianism and Popular
            Culture*. Durham, NC: Duke University Press.

Pinheiro, Anelise Rizzolo de Oliveira

2009   "Análise Histórica do Processo de Formulação da Política Nacional
            de Segurança Alimentar e Nutricional (2003–2006): Atores,
            Ideias, e Instituições na Construção de Consenso Político." Ph.D.
            diss., Universidade de Brasília.

Pinzani, Alessandro e Rego, and Walquira Domingues Leão Rego

2013   *Vozes do Bolsa Família: Autonomia, Dinheiro, e Cidadania*.
            São Paulo: Editora UNESP.

Pontes, Reinaldo

2003   "A Evolução do Combate à Pobreza no Brasil e o Papel do 'Fome
            Zero.'" *Belém* 4, no. 1: 89–96.

Price, Richard

1999   "Reinventando a História dos Quilombos: Rasuras e
            Confabulações." *Afro-Ásia* 23: 1–25.

Putnam, Robert, with Robert Leonardi and Raffaella Y. Nanetti

1993   *Making Democracy Work: Civic Traditions in Modern Italy.*
Princeton, NJ: Princeton University Press.

Radcliff-Brown, A. R.

1965   "On Joking Relationships." In *Structure and Function in Primitive Society*, 90–104. New York: Free Press.

Ramos, Graciliano

1965   *Barren Lives.* Translated by Ralph Edward Dimmick. Austin: University of Texas Press.

Rebhun, L. A.

1994   "Swallowing Frogs: Anger and Illness in Northeast Brazil." *Medical Anthropology Quarterly* 8, no. 4: 360–82.

1999   *The Heart Is Unknown Country: Love in the Changing Economy of Northeast Brazil.* Stanford, CA: Stanford University Press.

Reis, Elisa

2000   "Modernization, Citizenship and Stratification: Historical Processes and Recent Changes in Brazil." *Daedalus* 129, no. 2: 171–94.

Ribeiro, Efrém

2003   "Wellington Dias Acredita que o Fome Zero Vai Marcar a História do Brasil." *Meio Norte*, March 30.

Rocha, Jonas

1988   "A Pequena Produção Rural no Estado do Piauí." *CartaCEPRO* 13, no. 1: 29–69.

Roett, Riordan

1999   *Brazil: Politics in a Patrimonial Society.* 3rd ed. New York: Praeger.

Rogers, Thomas D.

2010   *The Deepest Wounds: A Labor and Environmental History of Sugar in Northeast Brazil.* Chapel Hill: University of North Carolina Press.

Roniger, Luis

1990   *Hierarchy and Trust in Modern Mexico and Brazil.* New York: Praeger.

Sampaio, Plinio de Arruda

1986   "O PT na Encruzilhada." In *E Agora, PT? Caráter e Identidade*, 111–41. São Paulo: Brasiliense.

Samuels, David

2003   *Ambition, Federalism, and Legislative Politics in Brazil.* Cambridge: Cambridge University Press.

Sangren, Steven P.

1993   "Power and Transcendence in the Ma Tsu Pilgrimages of Taiwan."
            American Ethnologist 20, no. 3: 564–82.

Sansone, Lívio

2003   *Blackness without Ethnicity: Constructing Race in Brazil.* New York:
            Palgrave Macmillan.

Santos, Martha

2012   *Cleansing Blood with Honor: Masculinity, Violence and Power in the
            Backlands of Northeast Brazil.* Stanford: Stanford University Press.

Scheper-Hughes, Nancy

1992   *Death without Weeping: The Violence of Everyday Life in Brazil.*
            Berkeley: University of California Press.

Schmitter, Philippe

1971   *Interest, Conflict and Political Change in Brazil.* Stanford, CA:
            Stanford University Press.

Schwarz, Roberto

1992   *Misplaced Ideas: Essays on Brazilian Culture.* London: Verso.

Schwarzer, Helmut.

2000   *Impactos Socioeconômicos do Sistema de Aposentadorias Rurais no
            Brasil—Evidências Empíricas de um Estudo de Caso no Estado do
            Pará.* Rio de Janeiro: IPEA.

Scott, James C.

1976   *The Moral Economy of the Peasant: Rebellion and Subsistence in
            Southeast Asia.* New Haven, CT: Yale University Press.

Sheriff, Robin E.

2001   *Dreaming Equality: Color, Race, and Racism in Urban Brazil.* New
            Brunswick, NJ: Rutgers University Press.

Silverstein, Michael

1993   "Metapragmatic Discourse and Metapragmatic Function." In
            Reflexive Language: Reported Speech and Metapragmatics, edited
            by John A. Lucy, 33–58. Cambridge: Cambridge University Press.

Skidmore, Thomas E.

1993   *Black into White: Race and Nationality in Brazilian Thought.*
            Durham, NC: Duke University Press.

Slater, Candace

1982   *Stories on a String: The Brazilian Literatura de Cordel.* Berkeley:
            University of California Press.

Soares, Fábio Veras, Rafael Perez Ribas, and Rafael Guerrero Osário

2010   "Evaluating the Impact of Brazil's Bolsa Família: Cash Transfer
         Programs Comparative Perspective." *Latin American Research
         Review* 45, no. 2: 173–90.

Soares, Fabio Veras, Sergei Soares, et al.

2005   "Programas de Transferências de Renda no Brasil: Impactos sobre
         a Desigualdade e a Pobreza." *Instituto de Pesquisa Económica
         Aplicada*, 31. Brasília: IPEA.

Soares, Gláucio Dillon

1973   *Sociedade e Política no Brasil*. São Paulo: Difel.

Sobrinho, Barbosa Lima

1946   *O Devassamento do Piauí*. São Paulo: Companhia Editora
         Nacional.

Sorokin, Pitirim

1975   *Hunger as a Factor in Human Affairs*. Gainesville: University Press
         of Florida.

Sotelino, Fernando

2011   "The Financial Services Industry." In *The Brazilian State: Debate
         and Agenda*, edited by Maurício Font and Laura Randall, 247–79.
         Lanham, MD: Lexington.

Sousa Martins, Agenor de, Almir Bittencourt da Silva, Antonio Cezar Cruz Fortes,
Antônio José Castelo Branco Medeiros, Felipe Mendes de Oliveira, Joas Rocha,
José Fonseca Ferreira Neto, and Manuel Domingos Neto

2003   *Piauí: Evolução, Realidade, Desenvolvimento*. Teresina: Fundação
         CEPRO.

Stokes, Susan

1995   *Cultures in Conflict: Social Movements and the State in Peru*.
         Berkeley: University of California Press.

2005   "Perverse Accountability: A Formal Model of Machine Politics
         with Evidence from Argentina." *American Political Science Review*
         99, no. 3: 315–25.

Strickon, Arnold, and Sidney Greenfield

1972   "The Analysis of Patron-Client Relationship: An Introduction." In
         *Structure and Process in Latin America: Patronage, Clientage, and
         Power Systems*, edited by Arnold Strickon and Sidney Greenfield,
         12–18. Albuquerque: University of New Mexico Press.

Takagi, Maya

2006   "A Implantação da Política de Segurança Alimentar e Nutricional
         no Brasil: Seus Limites e Desafios." Ph.D. diss., Universidade
         Estadual de Campinas.

Takagi, Maya, Mauro Eduardo Del Grossi, et al.

2006   "O Programa Fome Zero Dois Anos Depois." Paper presented at the
            2006 Meeting of the Latin American Studies Association.

Tarlau, Rebecca

2013   "Coproducing Rural Public Schools in Brazil: Contestation,
            Clientelism and the MST in Politics and Society." Unpublished
            manuscript.

Tranjan, J. Ricardo

2011   "Civil Society Discourses and Practices in Porto Alegre." In *The
            Brazilian State: Debate and Agenda*, edited by Maurício A. Font
            and Laura Randall, 145–71. Lanham, MD: Lexington.

Turner, Victor

1967   *The Forest of Symbols: Aspects of Ndembu Ritual*. Ithaca, NY:
            Cornell University Press.
1973   "The Centre Out There: Pilgrim's Goal." *History of Religions* 12,
            no. 3: 191–230.

Turner, Victor, and Edith Turner

1978   *Image and Pilgrimage in Christian Culture*. New York: Columbia
            University Press.

Vasconcelos, Francisco de Assis Guedes de

2005   "Combate à Fome no Brasil: Uma Análise Histórica de Vargas a
            Lula." *Revista de Nutrição* 18, no. 4: 439–57.

Vidart, Maria

2011   "'That's How You Win Elections'": Electoral Transactions, Political
            Consultancy and the Personalization of Politics in Columbia's
            Democratic Reform." *Altérités* 8, no. 1: 117–40.

Villela, Jorge Mattar

2004   "O Dinheiro e Suas Diversas Faces nas Eleições Municipais em
            Pernambuco." *Mana* 11, no. 1: 267–96.
2012   "Confiança, Autonomia e Dependência na Política Eleitoral no
            Sertão de Pernambuco." In *Cultura, Percepção e Ambiente—
            Diálogos com Tim Ingold*, edited by Carlos Alberto Steil and Isabel
            Cristina de Moura Carvalho, 211–27. São Paulo: Terceiro Nome.

Viotti da Costa, Emilia

1985   *The Brazilian Empire: Myths and Histories*. Chicago: University of
            Chicago Press.

Von Mettenheim, Kurt

1995   *The Brazilian Voter: Mass Politics in Democratic Transition*.
            Pittsburgh: University of Pittsburgh Press.

Von Mettenheim, Kurt, and James Malloy, eds.

1998   *Deepening Democracy in Latin America*. Pittsburgh: University of
        Pittsburgh Press.

Wagley, Charles

1963   *An Introduction to Brazil*. New York: Columbia University Press.

Wang, Fang

1994   "The Political Economy of Authoritarian Clientelism in Taiwan."
        In *Democracy, Clientelism, and Civil Society*, edited by Luis Roniger
        and Aye Gune-Ayata, 181–207. Boulder, CO: Lynne Rienner.

Warren, Mike

1995   "The Self in Discursive Democracy." In *The Cambridge Companion
        to Habermas*, edited by Stephen K. White, 167–200. Cambridge:
        Cambridge University Press.

Weffort, Francisco

1988   "Why Democracy?" In *Democratizing Brazil*, edited by Stepan
        Alfred, 327–51. Oxford: Oxford University Press.

West, Harry

2008   "'Govern Yourselves!' Democracy and Carnage in Northern
        Mozambique." In *Democracy: Anthropological Approaches*, edited
        by Julia Paley, 97–123. Santa Fe, NM: School for Advanced
        Research Press.

Weyland, Kurt

1993   "The Rise and Fall of President Collor and Its Impact on Brazilian
        Democracy." *Journal of Interamerican Studies and World Affairs*
        35, no. 1: 1–37.

1996   *Democracy without Equity: Failures of Reform in Brazil*. Pittsburgh:
        University of Pittsburgh Press.

Wit, Joop W. de

1989   "Clientelism, Competition and Poverty: The Ineffectiveness
        of Local Organizations in a Madras Slum." In *Urban Social
        Movements in the Third World*, edited by F. J. Schuurman and
        T. van Naerssen, 63–90. London: Routledge.

Wolf, Eric

1966   "Kinship, Friendship, and Patron-Client Relations." In *The Social
        Anthropology of Complex Societies*, edited by Michael Banton,
        1–22. London: Tavistock.

Wolf, Eric, and Sidney Mintz

1957   "Haciendas and Plantations in Middle America and the Antilles."
        Social and Economic Studies 6: 386–412.

Woodard, James

    2005   "Coronelismo in Theory and Practice: Evidence, Analysis and Argument from São Paulo." *Luso-Brasilian Review* 42, no. 1: 99–117.

World Food Summit

    1996   "Rome Declaration on World Food Security." Available on http:// www.fao.org/docrep/003/w3613e/w3613e00.htm, accessed on October 5, 2013.

Yasbek, Maria Carmelita

    2004   "Fome Zero: Uma Política Social em Questão." *Saúde e Sociedade* 12, no. 1: 43–51.

Index

Envy, 52–53, 126–27; evil and, 63, 205 (n. 7)
Etiquette, 163–64, 207–8 (n. 1)
Evil eye, 52, 53, 203–4 (n. 1)

Factionalism, 111–12, 192; during election campaigns, 67–68, 70–71; and factional identity, 49; Management Committee overcoming of, 175, 177, 179, 180, 182, 184, 209 (n. 7)
Family microloans, 37
Faoro, Raymundo, 208 (n. 3)
Fictive kin system, 12
Fighting Rural Poverty Project, 44
Finan, Timothy, 204 (n. 3)
First Republic, 21–22, 164
Food and Agriculture Organization (FAO), 28, 139, 140, 142, 149
Food Card, 17, 34, 184, 191; allotment of, 179–80; Bolsa Família and, 36, 183, 201 (n. 9), 202 (n. 15); establishment and scope of, 33–34, 201–2 (n. 11); factional neutrality in distribution of, 175–76, 177, 179, 180, 182, 184; family eligibility for, 176–77, 208 (n. 5); marginalizing mayor in distribution of, 163, 167–70; selection mechanism created for, 36; suspension of, 182, 209 (n. 9)
Food-giving practices, 63–65
Food security movement, 28–31, 35, 168
Forms of address, 59–60, 73, 204 (n. 4)
Foster, George, 12
French, Jan, 140
Freyre, Gilberto, 10
Fugitive slave communities. See Quilombola villages
FUMAC (Municipal Community Aid Fund), 44, 164
Functionalism, 9

Gay, Robert, 13
Gift giving, 79–80, 134–35

God, 120–21, 125, 205 (n. 7)
Gomes Júnior, N. N., 35
Gossip, 3, 52, 53, 63, 124, 179
Goulart, João, 7, 23–24
Graeber, David, 11, 120
Graziano da Silva, José, 34, 93, 118–19, 202 (nn. 12, 14)

Harris, Marvin, 206 (n. 4)
Herbal remedy project, 156–57
Herzfeld, Michael, 10–11
Hierarchy: democracy and, 13; egalitarianism and, 16, 85, 187; patronage exchanges and, 9, 11, 22. See also Intimate hierarchy
Holanda, Sérgio Buarque de, 10, 20–21
Holston, James, 12, 14, 199–200 (n. 1)
Horizontal solidarity. See Solidarity, horizontal
Hospitals, 71, 205 (n. 1)
Hunger, 53, 84–85; concealment of, 62, 73–74, 177, 178–79; food security movement and, 28–31; in Passarinho, 44–45, 53–54; patronage and, 204 (n. 3); racial disparities in, 45–46; Scheper-Hughes on, 54–55; stigma of, 54, 61–62, 65, 179; symptoms and impact of, 45, 64; visibility of, 61–63
Hunter, Wendy, 25–26

Indigenous rights organizations, 140–41
Indignation, fostering, 17, 151, 153–54
Induced nostalgia, 114–36; as technique, 17, 116, 139, 148, 188. See also Nostalgia
Interhousehold sociability and cooperation, 15–16, 55, 77–78, 125
Intimate hierarchy, 67–90; in Brazilian history, 21–23; charity auctions and, 88–89; coercive stereotypes of, 9, 185; collective elements in, 13, 91, 135; as concept, 8–15; and democracy, 11, 14–15, 192, 193–94; and

egalitarianism, 11, 191; food security and fight against, 29–30; and horizontal solidarity, 11–12; and hunger, 204 (n. 3); as intimate alliance, 78, 153, 159; and local culture, 89–90; logic behind, 76; loyalty in, 9, 38, 81, 97, 135, 153, 191; and officeholder accountability, 193–94; officials' assault on, 32, 87, 89–90, 91, 149, 186, 187, 191–92; politicians' motivations in, 77; Productive Project and, 133–35; PT opposition to, 6–8, 68–69, 192; Quilombola Project and, 159; and reciprocity, 4–5, 9, 88, 207 (n. 1); scholarly condemnation of, 7–8, 11–12, 14–15, 48; short-term cash exchange contrasted to, 111; state officials' deployment of, 153, 190. *See also* Clientelismo; Coronelismo; Patronage exchanges

Irrigation, 110

Kinship, 12, 42, 188
Kirchner, Néstor, 6, 7

Land Law of 1850, 21
Land ownership, 21, 23–24, 39–40
Land reform, 27, 33, 119, 201 (n. 10)
Leal, Victor Nunes, 21–22, 68, 164
Level curve technique, 110
Liberalism, 20–21, 193; Holston definition of, 199–200 (n. 1)
Liberationist Christianity, 25, 86, 88, 130, 200 (n. 4)
Localism, 170–73
Lowy, Michael, 25
Lula da Silva, Luiz Inácio, 25, 70; cash transfer policies of, 32–33, 34; electoral victories of, 3, 19, 184; and fight against hunger, 30–31, 33, 201 (n. 7); ideology of, 7; left-wing neoliberalism of, 31–37; Misery Tour of, 92–94; parodying of, 105–7; rural development policy of, 36–37; United States and, 6–7; working-

class background of, 31, 106; and Zero Hunger Program, 33, 184

Management Committee, Zero Hunger, 174–80, 209 (n. 7); multifactional character of, 175, 177, 181, 182, 191; political season and collapse of, 181–84
Marginalizing the mayor, 162–85; in allocation of Food Cards, 170, 174–80; backfiring of, 173, 184–85; Suplicy and, 162–63; as technique, 8, 190–91
Marques, Ana Claudia, 60
Martin, Scott, 32
Marxism, 7, 26
Mayoral power, 70, 164–65, 167–69, 186, 208 (n. 3)
MDS (Ministry of Social Development), 36
Medical assistance, 83
Meio Norte, 166
MESA (Special Ministry of Food Security): and Food Cards, 34, 94, 175; and Quilombola Project, 139, 140; replacement of, 34, 202 (n. 12)
Middle class, 108, 109, 111, 166
Military dictatorship, Brazilian, 24, 25, 164; elections and limited democracy under, 3, 199 (n. 1), 200 (nn. 3, 5)
Mintz, Sidney, 12
Mitchell, Sean, 143–44
Morales, Evo, 6, 7
Movement for Ethics in Politics, 28
Movimento Negro (Black Movement), 137, 139, 140. *See also* Quilombola Movement
MST (Landless Workers' Movement), 27, 39, 119, 201 (n. 10)
Multiparty coalitions, 71, 181–82, 183
Mutirão, 56–59, 103–4, 130; idealization of, 115, 119. *See also* Collective labor
Mutual incompatibility premise, 11–12

National Development Bank, 35
Nelson, Donald, 204 (n. 3)
Neoliberalism, 27, 31–32, 56
New State, 23
Nostalgia: disjunctive, 116, 135–36; by officials, 16, 55, 93, 108, 110, 113; structural, 115; by villagers, 125, 129–30, 131. *See also* Induced nostalgia

O'Donnell, Guillermo, 8

Palmares, 140
Palmares Cultural Foundation, 140, 190, 207 (n. 4)
Palmeira, Moacir, 78
Passarinho: author's place in, 46–51; elections in, 71–73, 184–85; hunger, envy, and egalitarianism in, 52–66; marginalization of mayor in, 162–85; position of townspeople in, 108–12; Quilombola Project in, 142–45; social structure of, 41–46; as Zero Hunger pilot town, 4, 19, 37, 92, 94, 166, 172–73
Pastoral Land Commission, 88
Patronage. *See* Intimate hierarchy
Patronage exchanges, 55, 75, 169; cash in, 75, 83–84, 85–86, 111, 168–69; changes to, 85; coercion in, 9, 14, 69, 185; commodification of, 89; condemnations of, 6, 68–69, 91, 111; dignity in, 2, 10, 77; as encounter between unequals, 194; forms of address in, 73; hierarchical nature of, 9, 11, 22; humiliation in, 14, 205 (n. 2); moral distinctions in, 69–70, 84–85, 89–90; mutual vulnerability in, 2–3, 10, 11, 76, 77, 124; in Passarinho, 1–3, 47–48, 71, 72–78, 160–61; in Productive Project, 133–35; and reciprocity, 2, 16, 81, 164, 180; temporal dimension to, 78–85; vertical and horizontal complementarity in, 12–13; and vote-buying, 4

Peasant Leagues, 23, 27, 39
Peasants, 39–40, 41–42, 56, 110
Pereira, Anthony, 35
Perry, Jonathan, 78–82
Pessar, Patricia, 87–88
Petrolina, 50, 204 (n. 6)
Piauí: social and political characteristics, 37–40
Pilgrimages, 87–88, 100–101. *See also* Programmatic pilgrimage
PMDB (Brazilian Democratic Movement Party), 94, 165–66, 206 (n. 1); PT alliance with, 181–82, 183
Political allegiances, 86–87, 168; factionalism and, 49, 67–68, 70–71, 175, 180. *See also* Voting
Political season, 67–68, 181–84, 191
Pontes, Reinaldo, 29–30
Populist Democracy, 23–24
Portuguese colonization, 10, 146
Poverty, 3, 33, 38, 41, 65, 122, 190, 191; Brazi's reduction of rate of, 36, 191; difficulty in reporting of, 177–78; Lula on, 30–31, 32. *See also* Hunger
Price, David, 141
Productive Project: collective management aspect of, 124–25; concealment of wealth of, 126–29; difficulties of, 125–26; embezzlement of funds from, 157, 190; and intimate hierarchy, 133–35; local politicians' involvement in, 133–34, 188–89; and nostalgia for collective labor, 131–33; structure and phases of, 116–19; and Zero Hunger Program, 117, 118
Programmatic pilgrimage, 137–61; as rite of passage, 139, 147–48, 155; as technique, 8, 139, 148, 158, 189. *See also* Pilgrimages
PRONAF (Family Agriculture Support Program), 37
PT (Workers' Party), 19, 25–26, 110, 201 (n. 8); and capitalism, 25, 26, 27, 31; and corruption, 28, 35; and democracy, 26, 27, 31; and food

security movement, 28–31; founding of, 25; ideological turning point for, 27; left-wing neoliberalism of, 31–37; liberal ideology of, 7; patronage condemned by, 6–8, 68–69, 192; in Piauí, 37–38, 71–72, 87, 166–67, 181–82, 183, 184–85; pragmatism of, 25–26; and socialism, 25–26, 27; on state role in social policy, 37

Quilombola identity, 140–42, 144, 151, 207 (n. 3)
Quilombola Movement, 88, 157–58, 160–61, 189; left-wing message of, 87, 147; and Quilombola Project, 139, 140, 149
Quilombola Project, 147, 189; effects of, 158–59; impact on beneficiary villages, 156–58, 160–61, 190; of Passarinho, 142–45; and quilombola identity, 139–45; training center meeting on, 137, 145, 148–49, 151–56
Quilombola villages, 17, 146, 189, 190; collective property in, 149–50; qualification as, 151, 207 (n. 4); Quilombola Movement and, 160–61; women in, 157–58

Racial identity, 17, 44, 158–59, 189; fluidity of in Brazil, 141, 143–44; and quilombola identity, 141–42, 151, 190. *See also* Afro-Brazilians
Racism and discrimination, 44, 144–45, 147
Ramos, Graciliano, 205 (n. 2)
Ranching, 38–39
Rebhun, L. A., 203 (n. 1)
Reciprocity, 86, 135, 188; damaged, 115, 116; and exchange, 2, 16, 81, 164, 180; "open and balanced," 55; patronage and, 4–5, 9, 88, 207 (n. 1)
Remanescente, of quilombolas, 141–42, 207 (n. 3)
Roniger, Luis, 11

Rural culture, 15, 26, 92; stereotypes of, 110–12
Rural-urban distinction, 109, 206–7 (n. 4)
Rural Workers' Union, 87, 108, 149, 164, 168, 174, 177

Sampaio, Plinio de Arruda, 26
Scheper-Hughes, Nancy, 9, 65, 204 (n. 2); on hunger, 54–55
Schmitter, Philippe, 11–12
School Grant program, 167–68
Schwarz, Roberto, 20–21, 22, 187
Serafim, 138, 142, 152–53, 156–57, 161
Sertão, 1, 102, 187
Sheriff, Robin, 144
Single Registry, 168, 174, 182
Slavery, 10, 138; in Brazilian history, 21, 158; shared memory of, 146; slave resistance to, 148, 158. *See also* Quilombola villages
Social engineering, 6, 113, 139
Socialism, 24, 25–26, 27
Social policy, uses of, 187–88
Solidarity, horizontal, 145–48, 154; of Afro-Brazilians, 150, 158, 189; patronage and, 11–12; during slavery, 146
Stokes, Susan, 76
SUDENE (Superintendency for the Development of the Northeast), 42, 203 (n. 17)
Suffrage, 21, 24, 200 (n. 2)
Suplicy, Eduardo, 162–63, 165

Teresina, 40, 92, 94, 95, 166; programmatic pilgrimage to, 137, 138, 140, 145–46, 148
Time, 78–85
Turner, Victor, 100, 147

United States, 6, 24

Vaqueiro, 38–39
Vargas, Getúlio, 22–23

Vázquez, Tabaré, 6, 7
Villela, Jorge Mattar, 79, 83, 204
    (n. 4), 207 (n. 1)
Violence, 66, 67
Von Mettenheim, Kurt, 26–27
Vote-buying, 4, 69, 192
Voting: coronelismo and, 21, 68–69,
    200 (n. 2); factional allegiances in,
    49, 67–68, 70–71; and vote-buying,
    4, 69, 192
Voto de cabresto, 68–69
Vulnerable populations, 140, 207
    (n. 2)

Weyland, Kurt, 12
Wolf, Eric, 12
Women, 42, 64–65; gender role shifts
    for, 156–58, 189
World Bank, 44, 86, 117, 118

Zero Hunger Program: administra-
    tive problems of, 34, 202 (n. 12);
    ambiguity about implementation
    of, 109; and assistencialismo, 166;
    Bolsa Família transitioned to by, 3,
    17, 34, 114, 183, 201 (n. 9); campaign
    against patronage by, 4, 87, 89–90,
    185; cash grants of, 34, 36, 56, 99,
    108, 118, 205 (n. 6); and collective
    labor, 56–57; component programs
    of, 196; criticisms of, 105–7, 171, 173,
    202 (n. 12); democratizing function
    of, 20; explanation to beneficiaries
    of, 119–25; FAO plan as blueprint
    for, 28; funding of, 197, 202 (n. 13);
joint-venture administration of,
    97–98; lack of resources, 85–86;
    as Lula flagship policy, 3, 19; mu-
    nicipal development plans of, 171,
    208 (n. 4); nutritional diagnostic of,
    45–46; participatory features of, 20,
    108–10, 206–7 (n. 4); pilot towns
    selected for, 4, 19, 37, 92, 94, 166,
    172–73; policy modalities of, 33,
    201 (n. 9); Productive Project and,
    117, 118; propaganda campaign for,
    92–94, 102–4; and rural tradition,
    113, 115; as subculture within gov-
    ernment, 101. *See also* Food Card
Zero Hunger Program officials, 16,
    91–113; administrative pilgrimages,
    100–101; background of, 16, 95; and
    induced nostalgia, 114–36; inter-
    action with beneficiaries, 119–25,
    186; interaction with peasants,
    98–100, 186–87; interaction with
    state departments, 97–98; intimate
    hierarchy opposed by, 91, 112, 149,
    186, 187, 191–92; marginalization
    of mayor by, 170, 182, 185; nostalgic
    idealization by, 16, 55, 93, 108, 110,
    113; practical challenges of, 96; as
    prodigal liberators, 92, 95–97, 98,
    112; and programmatic pilgrimage,
    137–61; and Quilombola Project,
    149, 150, 154; rift with federal gov-
    ernment, 119; self-image of, 113;
    Sertanejo voice use by, 1, 102–7;
    social location of, 94–95; subjectiv-
    ity of, 91–92